The Economics of Law, Order, and Action

According to the standard position of the economic mainstream, the efficient production of so-called public goods, including law and defense, requires the use of territorial monopolies of coercive force. Two arguments are put forward for this position: a "positive" one, based on the claim that only such institutions can successfully supply society with crucial public goods, and a "negative" one, based on the claim that such institutions by themselves constitute inevitable "public bads".

This book challenges this assumption by utilizing the insights of the Austrian School of Economics, New Institutionalism, constitutional political economy, and other heterodox economic approaches, combined with economically informed ethical analysis. It puts forward a positive case for voluntary social organization that offers new insights into the intersection of economic logic, social philosophy, institutional analysis, and the theory of entrepreneurship. In other words, in an attempt to draw on the interdisciplinary spirit of classical political economy, this book aims at providing a comprehensive economic and ethical case for extending the applicability of voluntary, entrepreneurial cooperation to the realm of creating and sustaining legal and protective services together with attendant institutional frameworks.

Jakub Bożydar Wiśniewski is an affiliated scholar and a member of the board of trustees of the Ludwig von Mises Institute Poland and is an affiliated lecturer with the Polish-American Leadership Academy. He holds an MA in philosophy from the University of Cambridge and a PhD in political economy from King's College London.

Routledge Advances in Heterodox Economics
Edited by Mark Setterfield
The New School for Social Research, USA

Peter Kriesler
University of New South Wales

For a full list of titles in this series, please visit www.routledge.com/series/RAHE

Over the past two decades, the intellectual agendas of heterodox economists have taken a decidedly pluralist turn. Leading thinkers have begun to move beyond the established paradigms of Austrian, feminist, Institutional-evolutionary, Marxian, Post Keynesian, radical, social, and Sraffian economics – opening up new lines of analysis, criticism, and dialogue among dissenting schools of thought. This cross-fertilization of ideas is creating a new generation of scholarship in which novel combinations of heterodox ideas are being brought to bear on important contemporary and historical problems.

Routledge Advances in Heterodox Economics aims to promote this new scholarship by publishing innovative books in heterodox economic theory, policy, philosophy, intellectual history, institutional history, and pedagogy. Syntheses or critical engagement of two or more heterodox traditions are especially encouraged.

The Economics of Law, Order, and Action
The Logic of Public Goods

Jakub Bożydar Wiśniewski

Routledge
Taylor & Francis Group

LONDON AND NEW YORK

First published 2018 by Routledge

2 Park Square, Milton Park, Abingdon, Oxfordshire OX14 4RN

52 Vanderbilt Avenue, New York, NY 10017

Routledge is an imprint of the Taylor & Francis Group, an informa business

First issued in paperback 2020

British Library Cataloguing-in-Publication Data
A catalogue record for this book is available from the British Library

Library of Congress Cataloging-in-Publication Data
A catalog record for this book has been requested

ISBN: 978-0-8153-6787-1 (hbk)
ISBN: 978-0-367-59286-8 (pbk)

Typeset in Times New Roman
by Apex CoVantage, LLC

Contents

1 Introduction

1.1 Preliminary remarks

A recurring theme in the history of political philosophy is the suggestion that the existence of law and order requires the monopolization of violence in a given territory. Similarly, a common opinion in mainstream economics is that monopolized violence is the only reliable tool for the provision of "public goods", chiefly among them a well-functioning system of legal and defense services.

It might be argued that, widespread as they are, such suggestions and opinions contain at their core a rather conspicuous contradiction. After all, it would seem reasonable to assume that the monopolization of violence promotes the use of violence, whereas a lawful and orderly society is one from which violence has been largely eliminated. And similarly, it would seem reasonable to question the extent to which goods and services provided on the basis of monopolized violence – that is, in a paradigmatically non-consensual manner – can be seen as unambiguous public benefits.

Over the course of the history of social thought, this apparent contradiction has been especially emphasized and most eagerly explored by various schools of anarchism. Unsurprisingly, the typical conclusion reached by them is that the monopolization of violence, far from promoting genuine law and order, is actually antithetical to it. However, as convincing as their arguments might be taken to be, one of their potential shortcomings is that their acceptance requires certain prior moral commitments – for instance, a commitment to the ethics of universal and inalienable natural rights. Thus, while they constitute an important challenge to the mainstream treatment of the subject of law and order in the field of political philosophy, they may be seen as less applicable to the parallel investigations in the field of economics.

This is because sound economics adheres to the principle of value freedom, and all that it aims to establish is the logical feasibility (or lack thereof) of implementing specific organizational solutions. However, far from being uninteresting on account of its apparent ethical blandness, this is a highly value-relevant approach, because, by aspiring to show the impossibility of reaching certain goals, it also shows the futility of any ethical code that may motivate their pursuit. In other words, even if a philosophical anarchist succeeds in demonstrating the ethical unjustifiability of social organization grounded in monopolized violence, he may still fail to answer the public goods argument drawn from neoclassical economics, thus facing the uncomfortable conclusion that the ethical strength of his principles clashes with their logical infeasibility.

The present book is sympathetic to the ethical concerns of the anarchist tradition insofar as it is skeptical of the suggestion that monopolized violence can credibly serve as a foundation of law and order. At the same time, unlike the works of the majority of the classical representatives of this tradition, it makes explicit use of the tools furnished by the marginalist revolution in economics and emphatically recognizes the crucial role of private property and market entrepreneurship in creating advanced, well-functioning social orders. Thus, it is perhaps particularly well placed to evaluate critically the cogency of the neoclassical public goods arguments, especially as it employs for that purpose tools and arguments drawn from an alternative economic tradition originating in the marginalist revolution – that of the so-called Austrian School of Economics and its parent discipline of praxeology (i.e., the logical analysis of human action). Moreover, it subsequently uses these same tools to engage in a similarly critical evaluation of the "dark obverse" of the public goods argument – namely, the notion that territorial monopolies of force are "necessary evils", whose activities are hardly beneficial in absolute terms, but nonetheless cannot be replaced by any superior alternative.

In other words, the dual task of the present book is to highlight the shortcomings of the neoclassical and neoclassically influenced arguments in favor of the desirability or inevitability of territorial monopolies of force and to present a comprehensive theoretical framework for the voluntary, contractual provision of law and order.

It might be argued that a number of coinciding processes in the contemporary world make this topic particularly noteworthy. First of all, in an increasingly globalized and specialized economy, international businesses engage in increasingly more complex transactions across territories that constitute jurisdictions controlled by many different local monopolies of force. As a result, none of these monopolies can provide the businesses in question with a sufficient degree of legal and physical protection – both because none of them controls the whole territory within which they operate and because none of them is likely to keep pace with the complexity of their operations. Thus, they either have to rely on the services of specialized private arbitration agencies or devise their own internal regulatory frameworks and coordinate them with those similarly devised by their business partners. In other words, they have to provide themselves with the relevant "public goods" in a purely voluntary and contractual manner, and the present book supplies the logical framework for understanding this process.

Second, modern technological ingenuity allows for the implementation of organizational solutions that vastly increase the potential of entrepreneurial activities, including their potential for establishing effective governance structures. For instance, big data processing allows for effective detection and prevention of fraud, advanced trading platforms allow for conducting complex online transactions protected by powerful security protocols and verification algorithms, and distributed ledgers allow for convenient record management free from the danger of moral hazard. Again, such inventions, especially when linked with the global character of modern market entrepreneurship, vividly illustrate the emergence of contractual, polycentric legal orders and point to the desirability of subjecting this phenomenon to a broader theoretical analysis.

Third, the last decades have witnessed a rise in secessionist tendencies and sympathies for local self-determination. And although many of them are associated with nationalist leanings, which are often comfortable with the use of monopolized violence, many others embody a genuine desire to use political decentralization as a tool to create social orders that are more in line with the principles of voluntariness, contractuality, and unanimous consent. In other words, it might be plausibly argued that consensual secession and decentralization taken to their ultimate conclusion fully liberate the provision of law and order from the influence of monopolized violence, and many members of modern secessionist and decentralist movements seem to be motivated by this line of thinking.

And fourth, it is, perhaps, scarcely an exaggeration to suggest that the institution of the nation-state – the main contemporary locus of monopolized violence – has lost much of its prestige over the last few decades. Part of it may be due to the lasting memory of the destructive excesses of nation-states during World War II and its aftermath. Part of it may be due to the modern, technologically driven scrutiny with which we can observe the dark underbelly of political and bureaucratic operations. And part of it may be due to the emergence of various intellectual traditions – such as the public choice school – that use modern social scientific tools to analyze political motivations in a coldly realistic manner. Be that as it may, it seems fair to say that an interest in exploring alternative institutional arrangements is on the rise and that the present book may serve as a useful tool for guiding the relevant exploratory impulses.

Furthermore, the ongoing economic globalization, social complexification, entrepreneurial emancipation, and technological progress are only likely to accelerate all of the processes mentioned earlier, hence making the topic of the voluntary, contractual provision of law and order all the more significant. It is also likely that the unfolding of these processes will go hand in hand with the growing recognition that neoclassical economics – with its limited appreciation for entrepreneurial dynamism and its physicalistic presuppositions – is an inadequate tool for describing them in an accurate and illuminating manner. Thus, it is hard to think of a better topic as a crucial litmus test for the continuing relevance and explanatory power of the Austrian School and other "heterodox" traditions in economics that follow the interdisciplinary spirit of classical political economy.

In sum, a critical evaluation of the neoclassical and neoclassically influenced arguments surrounding the issue of public goods and their constructive reformulation in the light of an intellectual tradition that is particularly cognizant of the productive power of entrepreneurial dynamism and voluntary self-organization can be seen as a natural combination of the right subject matter and the right analytical approach used at the right time. It is my hope that the reader of the present work will walk away from it with a similar impression.

With this, let me now move to a detailed overview of the contents of the ensuing chapters, which will further clarify the aim and scope of my project.

1.2 Project overview

As mentioned in the previous section, the aim of the present book is to investigate the putative theoretical desirability and practical inevitability of the presence of a monopoly of force in any given system of political economy and argue against both, utilizing for that purpose the theoretical apparatus and analytical insights of praxeology, that is, the logical "science of human action" (Lachmann 1951), exemplified especially by economic thinking in the tradition of the Austrian School of Economics.[1]

In addition, on the methodological front I shall adopt the strategy of making my arguments maximally robust by assuming that the contingent elements of human character in any given system of political economy analyzed in the course of the present work are maximally favorable to the solutions offered by my intellectual opponents. This approach is based on the investigation of what has been termed "institutional robustness", that is, the ability of a given system of social organization to stand up to the test of "hard cases", that is, hypothetical scenarios under which the ideal assumptions concerning, for example, information and motivation possessed by the members of a given society are relaxed (Boettke and Leeson 2004; Leeson and Subrick 2006). Drawing on this notion and the attendant framework of testing various forms of political economy against scenarios involving less-than-optimal conditions, it might be argued that, for instance, classical liberalism is always more robust than socialism (or vice versa), even if an institutional setup based on the former (or latter) is introduced into a community populated by individuals who are selfish and ignorant, while that based on the latter (or former) is turned into a community controlled by benevolent and wise planners.[2]

The main contribution of the present book is to show that the combined analytical power of the two methodological approaches mentioned earlier is uniquely suited to presenting a comprehensive socioeconomic alternative to the view that sees the territorial monopoly of force as the foundation of institutional order in any working society.

Although the approaches in question have already been used to formulate similar arguments, the present book aims at bringing such arguments together, highlighting their interrelations, considering them from a broader range of perspectives, and tracing out their implications for a range of subjects and disciplines. To that effect, I will mainly analyze two major, but very different, justifications for the existence of territorial monopolies of force: a "positive" one, based on the claim that only such institutions can successfully supply society with crucial public goods, and a "negative" one, based on the claim that such institutions by themselves constitute inevitable "public bads". By proceeding in this way, I will try to demonstrate that the methodological tradition utilized in the present work is uniquely capable of exploring the question of the monopoly of force in its full complexity, dealing with multiple relevant areas of economic and social analysis:

economics and ethics, incentives and preferences, information and motivation, and hard and soft institutions. In addition, I believe that bringing all those areas together under the aegis of praxeological investigation allows the present book to put forward a positive case for voluntary social organization that offers new insights into the intersection of institutional analysis and the theory of entrepreneurship, thus suggesting that these disciplines can be much more ambitious in their intellectual scope than they are usually taken to be.

In sum, in an attempt to draw on the interdisciplinary spirit of classical political economy, the present work aims at providing a comprehensive economic and ethical case for extending the applicability of voluntary, entrepreneurial cooperation to the realm of creating and sustaining legal and protective services together with attendant institutional frameworks.

Now before delineating and then criticizing the main reasons adduced in the relevant literature in the aim of demonstrating the desirability or inevitability of the presence of a monopoly of force in any given system of political economy, let me define more precisely what I mean by the key concept in question. I shall do this by referring to and building upon some of the pertinent classical and contemporary definitions.

Max Weber famously wrote about the entity that "upholds the claim to the monopoly of the legitimate use of physical force in the enforcement of its order . . . [within] a given territorial area" (Weber 1978, p. 54). This definition generally corresponds to my understanding of the notion under discussion, but I consider it incomplete insofar as it does not specify the implications of the characteristic it mentions with respect to the concept of legitimacy. In other words, the relevant question here is: What makes the actions undertaken by a territorial monopoly of force "legitimate"? According to Weber himself, legitimacy stems from "a belief by virtue of which persons exercising authority are lent prestige" (Weber 1964, p. 382), a belief grounded in tradition, the charisma of the rulers, or trust in the rationality of their organizational decisions (Weber 1991).

This account of legitimacy, however, seems to me to make Weber's original description of a monopoly of force overly and unjustifiably restrictive. For one thing, it does not answer the question of how many inhabitants of a given territory must entertain the relevant beliefs towards their ostensible rulers. The very suggestion that there must be at least some of them who are not themselves members and employees of the local monopoly of force makes Weber's description too narrow to be applicable to, say, repressive tyrannies and slave systems, which, by virtue of their organizational character, have hardly any social legitimacy.

Thus, the account of legitimacy I find more persuasive is based on a paraphrase of a statement made by Thrasymachus in *The Republic*, who claimed with regard to justice that it is "nothing else than the interest of the stronger" (Plato 1953, p. 177). While I disagree with this opinion as applied to the concept of justice, it sounds much more plausible in connection with the concept of legitimacy – to contend that legitimacy is nothing else than the interest of the stronger (or, to be more precise, the strongest) is to recognize that although in a given territory many entities utilize the means of physical coercion, only the most powerful of them can meaningfully declare itself as "legitimate" (and may find it highly expedient to do so).

This is due to the fact that in any given society the verdict as to what is and what is not legally legitimate is passed by its judicial system, and, by definition, only the most powerful coercion-wielding entity can bring such a system under its monopolistic control (Stinchcombe 1968, p. 150; Tilly 1985, p. 171). Thus, if we generalize the earlier point, it follows that "the claim to the monopoly of the legitimate use of physical force" can be meaningfully and effectively made only by an entity that has the ability to utilize coercive means to exclude potential competition from any area of economic activity (in this case, the provision of legal services). It is this ability to pose a universal anti-competitive threat of initiatory violence that I consider to be the first necessary and defining characteristic of a monopoly of force.

This, however, still leaves the definition incomplete, because on the basis of this single characteristic it would be impossible to make a distinction between a monopoly of force and a firm that was granted an exclusive government privilege to produce a specific good or service (Rothbard 2004, ch. 10). Such a firm, albeit capable of generating its business revenue in an unfairly easy way as compared to what would be required of it under the conditions of free market competition, would nonetheless still generate it via what Franz Oppenheimer called the "economic means", that is, "one's own labor and the equivalent exchange of one's own labor for the labor of others . . . for the satisfaction of needs" (Oppenheimer 1922, p. 25). A monopoly of force, on the other hand, in addition to being the only entity within a given territory that can issue a credible threat of coercively eliminating potential competition from any area of economic activity, obtains its revenue through the same means by which it achieves its monopolistic status – namely, by the use of initiatory violence – or, to employ Oppenheimer's terminology again, by the use of the "political means", that is, "the unrequited appropriation of the labor of others" (Oppenheimer 1922, p. 25).

Thus, the second defining characteristic of a monopoly of force is encapsulated in Oppenheimer's preferred definition of the entity in question, which he described as "that summation of privileges and dominating positions which are brought into being by extra-economic power" (Oppenheimer 1922, p. 25). In other words, the position occupied by a monopoly of force allows it to engage in the practice of forcible extraction of funds from the inhabitants of a given territory for the purpose of financing its operations.

One of the most lucid contemporary definitions of the discussed entity, which includes both of the previously mentioned characteristics, was offered by Hans-Hermann Hoppe, who described it as "an agency that exercises a compulsory territorial monopoly of protection and the power to tax" (Hoppe 2003, p. 357). What I regard as the only shortcoming of this definition is that even though it lists the most important features of a monopoly of force, it does not sufficiently generalize their effects. Admittedly, the agency under discussion exercises a territorial monopoly of protection, but it also exercises a potential territorial monopoly of everything else (because it possesses sufficient coercive power to exclude potential competition from any area of economic activity over which it wishes to retain exclusive control). Similarly, it can finance its activities by utilizing its power to tax, but it can also accomplish the same purpose by resorting to other forms of "institutionalized fiat appropriation" (Hülsmann 2004), such as inflationary redistribution of the purchasing power of politically controlled fiat money or an increase in public debt (which can be thought of as delayed taxation or delayed inflationary redistribution).

Finally, it is worthwhile to mention in this context the third relevant characteristic, namely, the effective ability and willingness of a monopoly of force to compel the majority of the inhabitants of a given territory to purchase selected services and commodities that it produces (e.g., insurance) or to participate in certain programs organized by it, funded out of forcible contributions (e.g., public education). However, because fulfilling this criterion is not necessary for any given monopoly of force to retain its specific nature, I shall not consider it as an indispensable component of a satisfactory definition of the concept in question.

Having described in sufficient detail the relevant characteristics of the central notion of my investigations, let me now proceed to outlining the chapter structure of the present text.

The desirability of a given institutional setup can stem from considerations of economic efficiency or moral worth. The value of the former is, of course, based on an (implicit) moral assumption too – namely, on the assumption that a social state of greater satisfaction of wants (greater social well-being) is morally preferable to a social state of lower satisfaction of wants (lower social well-being) – but its acceptance is so widespread and its content so uncontroversial, especially among economists, that for the purpose of structural and argumentative tidiness, I shall treat efficiency as a separate evaluative category.

In the context of this category, although nowadays it is rarely contested that the free market (i.e., free exchange of privately owned goods and services between the totality of consumers, producers, and entrepreneurs) exhibits allocative and welfare properties that are clearly superior to those of the system of politically organized, centralized control of economic resources, some significant exceptions to this rule are often allowed. Perhaps the most important and widely recognized among them concerns the ostensible inability of the purely free market system to supply any given society with the requisite amount of the so-called public goods. The presence of such goods, whose alleged unique characteristics are usually taken for granted within the dominant neoclassical paradigm (see, e.g., Brennan and Buchanan 1985; Cornes and Sandler 1986; Sandler 1992; Mueller 1996; Willis 2002, pp. 161–3; Leach 2003; Arnold 2004, pp. 720–3; Ayers and Collinge 2004, pp. 555–9), is assumed to be a necessary condition for the existence of a well-functioning and stable market economy, a condition that cannot be met by the economy in question without coercive political aid (i.e., the aid afforded by a territorial monopoly of force).

According to the teachings of neoclassical economics, the previously mentioned unique characteristics of public goods are jointness of consumption (also called non-rivalrous consumption) and non-excludability (which results in the existence of positive externalities), the former meaning that the consumption of a unit of a given good by a particular person does not in any way diminish the ability of others to consume that same unit, and the latter meaning that a given good produces spillover effects, which enable the non-payers, or free riders, to benefit from the good without in any way contributing to its production. It is claimed that these two characteristics give rise to the corresponding two types of market failure – in the case of non-rival goods some people are excluded from consumption even though they would not generate any additional costs for the producer, whereas in the case of non-excludable goods the social gains, including the gains of the free riders, outweigh the private gains of the producer, which undermines the incentive to produce in the first place.

In Chapter 2 of the present text, I argue that the analytical tools provided by the Austrian School of Economics (ASE) allow one to question the logical cogency of the main assumptions contained in the neoclassical public goods literature. More specifically, I indicate that the relevant insights of ASE can raise serious doubts about the economic meaningfulness and operationalizability of the neoclassical public goods characteristics. Furthermore, I contend that even if for the sake of argument one were to accept the validity of the previously mentioned assumptions, the standard neoclassical conclusions regarding the desirability of establishing a monopoly of force and its efficiency regarding the provision of certain categories of goods would not follow. I then conclude by suggesting that the goods in question can in fact be reclassified as private goods and thus effectively supplied by the framework of free exchange of property unconstrained by the control of coercive political entities.

In Chapter 3, I extend and further develop the earlier argumentation by describing the workings of a socioeconomic system where defense, often taken to be the most paradigmatic example of a pure public good (Head and Shoup 1969, p. 567; Bush and Mayer 1974, p. 410; Buchanan and Flowers 1975, p. 27; Samuelson and Temin 1976, p. 159; Cowen 1992), is produced efficiently in a contractual order composed of competing private suppliers. In Chapter 4, I apply the same reasoning to the closely related issue of the provision of legal services, also often regarded as a quintessential example of a pure public good. In particular, I argue that in contrast to its "monocentric" counterpart, only the institutional framework of competitive legal polycentrism can establish effective and robust governance structures without simultaneously empowering them to overstep their contractually designated tasks and competences.

Having addressed the arguments that locate the desirability of a monopoly of force in its supposed unique ability to produce the equally unique yet crucial category of public goods, in Chapter 5 I move on to concentrate on the contentions of those who believe that the institution under consideration does not necessarily perform any socially beneficial function, but its existence is nonetheless a practical inevitability (Cowen 1992; Cowen and Sutter 1999, 2005; Holcombe 2004). The authors in question claim that competition between private protection and arbitration agencies is more likely than not to lead to the formation of networks capable of excluding new entrants and eventually colluding to establish monopolistic, coercive cartels. My main argument against this contention is that it underestimates the degree to which the effectiveness of any given incentive structure is conditioned by the underlying framework of ideas and preferences, whose shape is in turn to a large extent a function of successful intellectual entrepreneurship. If a given population realizes that embracing a certain set of logically cogent arguments and acting on the conclusions that follow from them may well usher in very considerable civilizational progress, it seems hardly inevitable that a relatively small group of well-organized malefactors will always be able to prevent it from implementing such promising ideas. And there appears to be no logically necessary reason to consider a competitive market for law and security as an exception in this regard.

Finally, in Chapter 6 I turn to investigating the arguments associated with the strictly moral desirability of a monopoly of force, that is, to the claims of those who see an important tradeoff between the economic efficiency of a given system of social organization and its ability to distribute the fruits of this efficiency in what they regard as a fair way (Rawls 1971; Dworkin 2000; Cohen 2009). After all, even if the competitive, purely contractual polycentric alternative described in the preceding chapters is more effective in absolute terms when it comes to producing every kind of social good, including the alleged public goods, could the desirability of its implementation not be questioned if it fails to provide these goods to those who need them the most, that is, to those who can least afford them?

At this point, one might suggest that addressing these explicitly moral considerations should not be postponed until the last chapter. However, I believe that, given the structure of the present text, there is a perfectly good reason for doing precisely that. All of the arguments elaborated in the preceding chapters are concerned with economic efficiency – namely, with the question of what ends are praxeologically achievable given the fact of the ineradicable scarcity of means. Coupled with the rather uncontroversial premise that there is no moral worth in pursuing what can be reasonably established to be impossible or incoherent, these arguments become moral arguments in their own right in virtue of ruling many moral counterarguments out as logically unsound. My aim in this chapter is precisely to indicate that the redistributive and egalitarian indictments of the private law and order society fall into the category of such counterarguments, and that therefore the economic opportunity costs of replacing whatever charitable efforts such a society is willing to engage in by political efforts to forcibly redirect the flow of its freely produced and exchanged resources are also, in an important sense, moral opportunity costs whose bearing is praxeologically unjustified. In other words, the chapter under discussion elaborates on the contention that "economics places parameters around people's utopias" (Boettke 1998, p. 215) and emphasizes that its truth applies to moral utopias in particular.

What I see as a distinctive research opportunity offered by pursuing the topics and questions outlined earlier lies in probing the reciprocal relationship between different institutional settings and the results of spontaneous (bottom-up) social cooperation that the settings in question both make possible and are made possible by. According to the predominant opinion within the field of so-called constitutional economics (Buchanan and Tullock 1962; Buchanan 1975, 1977), there is an essential connection between the shape of the "rules of the game", that is, the legal and regulatory framework within which economic activity takes place, and the efficiency of the "play of the game" (i.e., the economic activity in question). However, this connection is usually taken to be unidirectional – in other words, whereas the shape of the "rules of the game" affects the shape of the "play of the game", the latter does not affect the former. This is why, as the major constitutional economists suggest, a territorial monopoly of force is uniquely suited to create the former, which should thus be accorded the status of a public good.

What I would like to propose here is that the connection under consideration is actually bidirectional and reciprocal, and that market entrepreneurship should be thought of not only as the driving force of efficient economic activity, but also as the driving force creating efficient institutional frameworks for economic activity, thus making the latter an essentially private good (or a privately produced public good). In other words, my aim is to explain why building legal and regulatory setups for the smooth operation of entrepreneurial processes can and should be seen precisely as part of these processes, which, regardless of what goods and services they are intended to produce, are always most effective in the spontaneously emergent environment characterized by competitiveness, polycentricity, and self-enforcing contractuality.

Furthermore, I would like to suggest that it is only when creating institutional frameworks for economic activity is treated as something qualitatively different from all other forms of cooperative human action, and thus requiring monopolistic exclusivity and top-down coercive control, that the resulting institutional structure is capable of eroding and even destroying the natural entrepreneurial energies and qualities of any given society by making the relevant "rules of the game" either intersubjectively meaningless (due to their monopolistic character) or contrary to the goal of playing the "entrepreneurial game" (by, for instance, creating the conditions for the emergence of the so-called "regime uncertainty" [Higgs 1997]).

To sum up, exploring the reciprocal relationship between different institutional settings (as well as the results of spontaneous social cooperation that takes place within them) through the lens of Austrian economics and market process theory allows for arriving at (and evaluating the viability of) novel conclusions on the intersection of constitutional economics, the theory of public goods, and the theory of entrepreneurship. These conclusions suggest that various levels of social and institutional organization overlap and influence each other in a way that blurs the traditional distinction between public and private goods and that discovering and enforcing the rules of cooperative behavior, on the one hand, and utilizing them for the purpose of securing mutual gains from trade, on the other, are complementary parts of the same, self-sustaining process of entrepreneurial search for unanimously acceptable solutions to the fundamental problem of scarcity.

Moreover, adopting the perspective in question allows for exploring the relationship between positive economic theory and normative ethical considerations from a novel angle. If, as suggested in the preceding paragraphs, there does not seem to be a reason to treat the business of creating institutional frameworks for economic activity as something qualitatively different from all other forms of cooperative human action, there also does not seem to be a reason for believing that it is warranted to, in a sense, exempt the production of the ethically understood "public goods" (such as, for instance, the so-called "social safety net") from the assessment of its economic opportunity costs, which is what the claim that there is a tradeoff between efficiency and equity essentially amounts to. In other words, pursuing the discussed perspective to its logical conclusions reveals that economic opportunity costs are moral opportunity costs and vice versa, which reinforces the anti-Millian contention that "there is no separation between production and distribution", that "distribution is only the other side of the coin of production on the market" (Rothbard 2004, p. 623), and that social order cannot come into being if the process of its emergence is externally interfered with (Buchanan 1982), even if only on the "constitutional" level.

In yet other words, if primarily "social work-oriented" activities are to be efficient according to their own specific, non-monetary criteria, they have to become part of the market process rather than treat the outcomes of the market[3] process as givens to be taken and redistributed, let alone taken and redistributed coercively – otherwise, they are bound to remain self-undermining. Thus, positive political economy, while remaining positive, turns out to inevitably (and usefully) circumscribe the scope of rational normative theorizing on the question of social welfare, in an indirect way pointing out plausible directions for the development of the latter.

In conclusion, the aim of the present work is to provide and defend an unequivocal answer to some of the central questions of economics and political philosophy, utilizing the tools afforded by a consciously "heterodox", but also a methodologically integrated and philosophically meticulous (Gordon 1996) approach to the study of human action in its positive and normative aspects, thus hopefully making a praxeological contribution to the field of social ethics and comparative economic systems in particular and to the broader tradition of "mainline economics"[4] (Boettke 2012) in general.

With this said, let me proceed to the next chapter, in which I utilize the tools of the Austrian School to produce a substantive critique of the neoclassical theory of public goods.

Notes

1 For a comprehensive yet accessible overview of the Austrian School's main scholarly discoveries and their significance, see Littlechild (1978); Spadaro (1978); and Taylor (1980).
2 I believe that the agenda of investigating institutional robustness can be fruitfully developed by distinguishing between different forms and possible subcategories of the informational and motivational deficiencies present in hard cases. The continuum of motivation, for instance, can stretch from utter selfishness on one extreme and utter selflessness on another, but it can also concern itself with such pairs of contrasting elements

as peacefulness and aggression or diligence and indolence. Likewise, lack of relevant information might be read as the inability of a hypothetical state central planning board to absorb what F. A. Hayek termed "tacit information" or "the specific circumstances of time and place" (Hayek 1945, 1948), or as the inability of such an institution to convert the totality of available information (even if it is full and stable) into a single scale of exchange value expressible in terms of cardinal numbers and reflective of socially meaningful utility appraisals (Salerno 1990, 1993; Rothbard 1991; Herbener 1996). Such an extension seems to me to allow for exploring a number of additional and important dimensions along which any given system of political economy can be shown to fail or prosper (under specific assumptions concerning these dimensions).

3 It has to be remembered that the market, in the broadest sense of the term (i.e., the sum total of all voluntary human interactions) is a market not only for (physical) barter and monetary exchanges, but also for exchanges involving a practically endless variety of non-material goods, services, and values, such as, for instance, the gratitude of the needy and philanthropic satisfaction.

4 "Mainline economics" can be defined as the tradition of studying economic phenomena that starts from the observation that "the 'invisible hand postulate' reconciles self-interest with the general interest not by collapsing one into the other or by assuming super-human cognitive capabilities among the actors, but through the reconciliation process of exchange within specific institutional environments. . . . The 'invisible hand' solution does not emerge because the mainline economist postulates a perfectly rational individual interacting with other perfectly rational individuals within a perfectly structured market. . . . Instead, [he recognizes that] man is a very imperfect being operating within a very imperfect world. Sound economic reasoning, by focusing on exchange, and the institutions within which exchange takes place, explains how complex social order emerges through the aid of prices and the entrepreneurial market process" (Boettke 2012, p. xvii).

Bibliography

Arnold, R. A. (2004), *Economics* (Mason, OH: South-Western).

Ayers, R. M. and Collinge, R. A. (2004), *Economics: Explore and Apply* (Upper Saddle River, NJ: Prentice Hall).

Boettke, P. J. (1998), 'Controversy: Is Economics a Moral Science? A Response to Ricardo F. Crespo', *Journal of Markets & Morality*, 1 (2), 212–19.

Boettke, P. J. and Leeson, P. T. (2004), 'Liberalism, Socialism, and Robust Political Economy', *Journal of Markets & Morality*, 7 (1), 99–111.

Boettke, P. J. (2012), *Living Economics: Yesterday, Today and Tomorrow* (Oakland, CA: The Independent Institute).

Brennan, G. and Buchanan, J. M. (1985), *The Reason of Rules: Constitutional Political Economy* (Cambridge, UK: Cambridge University Press).

Buchanan, J. M. and Tullock, G. (1962), *The Calculus of Consent: Logical Foundations of Constitutional Democracy* (Ann Arbor: University of Michigan Press).

Buchanan, J. M. (1975), *The Limits of Liberty: Between Anarchy and Leviathan* (Chicago: University of Chicago Press).

Buchanan, J. M. and Flowers, M. R. (1975), *The Public Finances: An Introductory Textbook* (4th ed., Homewood, IL: Richard D. Irwin).

Buchanan, J. M. (1977), *Freedom in Constitutional Contract* (College Station: Texas A&M University Press).

Buchanan, J. M. (1982), 'Order Defined in the Process of its Emergence', *Literature of Liberty*, 5, 7–58.

Bush, W. and Mayer, L. (1974), 'Some Implications of Anarchy for the Distribution of Property', *Journal of Economic Theory*, 8, 401–12.

Cohen, G. A. (2009), *Why Not Socialism?* (Princeton, NJ: Princeton University Press).

Cornes, R. and Sandler, T. (1986), *The Theory of Externalities, Public Goods and Club Goods* (Cambridge: Cambridge University Press).

Cowen, T. (1992), 'Law as a Public Good: The Economics of Anarchy', *Economics and Philosophy*, 8, 249–67.

Cowen, T. and Sutter, D. (1999), 'The Costs of Cooperation', *Review of Austrian Economics*, 12 (2), 161–73.

Cowen, T. and Sutter, D. (2005), 'Conflict, Cooperation and Competition in Anarchy', *Review of Austrian Economics*, 18 (1), 109–15.

Dworkin, R. (2000), *Sovereign Virtue: The Theory and Practice of Equality* (Cambridge, MA: Harvard University Press).

Gordon, D. (1996), *The Philosophical Origins of Austrian Economics* (Auburn, AL: Ludwig von Mises Institute).

Hayek, F. A. (1945), 'The Use of Knowledge in Society', *American Economic Review*, 35, 519–30.

Hayek, F. A. (1948), *Individualism and Economic Order* (Chicago: University of Chicago Press).

Head, J. G. and Shoup, C. S. (1969), 'Public Goods, Private Goods, and Ambiguous Goods', *Economic Journal*, 79, 567–72.

Herbener, J. (1996), 'Calculation and the Question of Arithmetic', *Review of Austrian Economics*, 9 (1), 151–62.

Higgs, R. (1997), 'Regime Uncertainty', *Independent Review*, 1 (4), 561–590.

Holcombe, R. G. (2004), 'Government: Unnecessary but Inevitable', *Independent Review*, 8 (3), 325–42.

Hoppe, H.-H. (ed.) (2003), *The Myth of National Defense: Essays on the Theory and History of Security Production* (Auburn, AL: Ludwig von Mises Institute).

Hülsmann, J. G. (2004), 'The a Priori Foundations of Property Economics', *Quarterly Journal of Austrian Economics*, 7 (4), 41–68.

Lachmann, L. M. (1951), 'The Science of Human Action', *Economica*, 18 (72), 412–27.

Leach, J. (2003), *A Course in Public Economics* (Cambridge: Cambridge University Press).

Leeson, P. T. and Subrick, J. R. (2006), 'Robust Political Economy', *Review of Austrian Economics*, 19 (2–3), 107–111.

Littlechild, S. C. (1978), *Fallacy of the Mixed Economy: An Austrian Critique of Conventional Mainstream Economics and of British Economic Policy* (London: Institute of Economic Affairs).

Mueller, D. C. (1996), *Constitutional Democracy* (Oxford: Oxford University Press).

Oppenheimer, F. (1922) [1914], *The State* (New York: B.W. Huebsch).

Plato (1953), *The Republic*, B. Jowett (trans.) (Oxford: Clarendon).

Rawls, J. (1971), *A Theory of Justice* (Cambridge, MA: Belknap).

Rothbard, M. (1991), 'The End of Socialism and the Calculation Debate Revisited', *Review of Austrian Economics*, 5 (2), 51–76.

Rothbard, M. (2004) [1962], *Man, Economy, and State: A Treatise on Economic Principles with Power and Market* (Scholar's ed., Auburn, AL: Ludwig von Mises Institute).

Salerno, J. T. (1990), 'Postscript: Why a Socialist Economy Is "Impossible"', in L. Mises, *Economic Calculation in the Socialist Commonwealth* (Auburn, AL: Ludwig von Mises Institute).

Salerno, J. T. (1993), 'Mises and Hayek Dehomogenized', *Review of Austrian Economics*, 6 (2), 113–46.

Samuelson, P. A. and Temin, P. (1976), *Economics* (10th ed., New York: McGraw-Hill).

Sandler, T. (1992), *Collective Action: Theory and Applications* (Ann Arbor: University of Michigan Press).

Spadaro, L. M. (ed.) (1978), *New Directions in Austrian Economics* (Kansas City: Sheed Andrews and McMeel).

Stinchcombe, A. L. (1968), *Constructing Social Theories* (New York: Harcourt, Brace & World).

Taylor, T. C. (1980), *An Introduction to Austrian Economics* (Auburn, AL: Ludwig von Mises Institute).

Tilly, C. (1985), 'War Making and State Making as Organized Crime', in P. Evans, D. Rueschemeyer and T. Skocpol (eds.), *Bringing the State Back* (Cambridge: Cambridge University Press).

Weber, M. (1964), *The Theory of Social and Economic Organization*, T. Parsons (ed.) (New York: Free Press).

Weber, M. (1978) [1921], *Economy and Society*, Vol. 1, G. Roth and C. Wittich (eds.) (Berkeley and Los Angeles: University of California Press).

Weber, M. (1991) [1918], 'Politics as a Vocation', in H. H. Gerth and C. Wright Mills (eds.), *From Max Weber: Essays in Sociology* (London: Routledge).

Willis, J. (2002), *Explorations in Microeconomics* (Redding, CA: North West Publishing).

2 An Austrian critique of the theory of public goods

2.1 Introduction

Perhaps the most common argument describing a putatively beneficial function performed by a monopoly of force refers to its alleged ability to supply society with certain crucial, otherwise unattainable classes of goods. There are many names to designate such goods and many ways to categorize them, but for my purposes I shall regard them as falling into two relatively broad classes: club and common goods, which together constitute the category of public goods.

Various theorists writing on the subject in question identify the said goods according to various characteristics. Malkin and Wildavsky (1991) provide an illuminating insight into the degree to which there is no final agreement on the matter. Although in general the literature on public goods is "terminologically over-endowed" (Hummel 1990, p. 90), which engenders a great deal of semantic confusion, I believe that it is fair to say that since the publication of Samuelson's classic articles on the subject (Samuelson 1954, 1955), one strand of terminological convention has come to dominate the picture. According to this convention, club goods are defined as possessing the characteristic of joint (or non-rival) consumption (Buchanan 1965; Olson 1971; Berglas 1976; McNutt 1999), whereas common goods are defined as possessing the characteristic of non-excludability (or the existence of related externalities) (Musgrave and Musgrave 1980; Kim and Walker 1984; Ostrom 1990).

The former means that the consumption of a unit of a given good by a particular person does not in any way diminish the ability of others to consume that same unit, whereas the latter means that a given good produces spillover effects, which enable non-payers (most notably the so-called "free riders") to benefit from the good without in any way contributing to its production. Some standard examples of the former type of goods – that is, pure club goods (non-rival but excludable) – would be TV signals and computer software. Some examples of the latter type – that is, pure common goods (rival but non-excludable) – would be air and fish in the ocean. Finally, some paradigmatic examples of the goods combining the previous features, oftentimes called pure public (Leach 2003, pp. 171–86) or collective (Demsetz 1970) goods, include lighthouses and national defense.

It is often claimed that these two characteristics give rise to the corresponding two types of market failure – in the case of club goods, some people are excluded from consumption even though they would not generate any additional costs for the producer, whereas in the case of common goods the social gains, including the gains of free riders, outweigh the private gains of the producer, which undermines the incentive to produce in the first place. Thus, a monopoly of force is expected to intervene and coerce every able member of society to contribute financially in order to secure a sufficient supply of the goods in question. Absent such a monopoly, the argument goes, the results are bound to be suboptimal. This line of argumentation, first developed in the late 1950s (Bator 1958), came to dominate the "market failure" literature of the succeeding decades (Baumol 1961, p. 268; Arrow 1969; Head 1972; Stiglitz 1989) and continues to be an integral element of economics textbooks (see, e.g., Willis 2002, pp. 161–3; Arnold 2004, pp. 720–3; Ayers and Collinge 2004, pp. 555–9), as well as a focal point of the literature devoted to the so-called "global economic problems" (Sandler 1997; Sandmo 2000).

By applying both the methodological tools developed by the Austrian School of Economics and the tools used to investigate the institutional robustness of various systems of political economy (Boettke and Leeson 2004; Leeson and Subrick 2006), I shall argue, first, that the earlier characteristics of club and common goods are based on a number of false assumptions or unacceptable oversimplifications, and second, that even if they were correct as stated, they would not establish the desirability of the existence of a monopoly of force. After developing a general critique and reconstruction of each part of the neoclassical theory of club and common goods, I shall apply the results to the issue of the provision of law and defense, which I think lends itself particularly well to being a promising case study in this context, because it is often seen as a paradigmatic example of a pure public good (Head and Shoup 1969, p. 567; Bush and Mayer 1974, p. 410; Buchanan and Flowers 1975, p. 27; Samuelson and Temin 1976, p. 159; Cowen 1992) or even a typical club good, which prompted some of those authors who believe that a sufficient amount of non-rival goods can be provided by voluntary means to analogize a monopoly of force to a private club or firm (Buchanan 1965, 1975; Blankart 1994, p. 273; Mueller 1996, pp. 81, 301).

Having made the previous introductory remarks, let us now consider some aspects of the theory under consideration in more detail.

2.2 Non-rivalness, subjectivity, and capital: the theory[1]

Let us start from an attempt at a reductio ad absurdum: if a viewer in a movie theater behaves appropriately (i.e., does not talk, eat loudly, etc.), he might be reasonably thought of as not imposing any costs on other viewers, or, in other words, as not in any way diminishing the value of their consumption. Hence, if only half of the tickets for a movie have been sold, the outcome is suboptimal as long as the remaining empty seats are not filled with additional viewers admitted free of charge. In view of this, movie theaters should be treated as club goods and thus either nationalized or at least subsidized or heavily regulated by a monopoly of force in order to ensure that no zero-cost consumers are excluded from their use (Hoppe 1989a, pp. 41–2).

It seems plausible to expect that the overwhelming majority of club goods theorists would reject such a conclusion. Because this reaction appears intuitively right, there must be something wrong with the underlying theory. I believe that there are several things wrong with it, and I think that the Austrian appreciation of the elements of value subjectivity and intertemporal coordination in economic processes highlights them particularly well.

As noted by James Buchanan in his summary of the theory of costs, "cost is subjective, it exists in the mind of the decision-maker and nowhere else. . . . [It] cannot be measured by someone other than the decision-maker because there is no way that subjective experience can be directly observed" (Buchanan 1969, p. 43). It might seem that no monetary (or perhaps "tangible") costs are involved in letting non-payers into the theater to fill up the hall, but this is actually a misperception, because an external observer is in no position to pass such judgments.

In reality, various individual costs are presumably present in the considered situation. First of all, there might be psychological costs for the viewers associated with decreased comfort brought about by the unexpected admittance of additional people into the hall (here we have to remember that the perception of crowding is also subjective). Second, there might be costs associated with the perception of being cheated by being treated on a par with non-paying free riders. These latter costs are initially purely psychological and borne exclusively by the paying viewers, but if one takes into account the passage of time (Lachmann 1986; Kirzner 1992), one should discover that as outraged customers begin to ostracize the theater and actively discourage their acquaintances from using it, what used to be subjective in the sense of being immaterial and financially impalpable turns into very objective, tangible monetary losses for the theater owner.

The general inference to be drawn from these considerations is that non-rival consumption can perhaps be seen as a useful analytical construct, but not as a tool for policy guidance. This is because whether a given good is non-rival can be established only by means of the intellectual division of labor performed by the totality of consumers engaged in voluntary transactions. In other words, the existence of non-rivalness can be borne out by the market process, but neither any of its individual participants nor any outside observer can be (or indeed needs to be) aware of whether the transacted goods have this characteristic or not.

However, it is possible to imagine a variety of club goods theorists who would be quite happy to embrace wholesale behaviorism or physicalism and rely on such doctrines as the basis for insisting that there remains a fundamental difference between the goods whose consumption is physically (and therefore objectively) rivalrous and the goods whose putative rivalness can be inferred only by accepting what they take to be dubious psychological-subjectivist assumptions. Furthermore, let us suppose that such theorists would be willing to bite the bullet and accept the aforementioned reductio ad absurdum by agreeing that movie theaters should indeed be subjected to the control of a monopoly of force. Such indeed would be a consistent decision to be drawn from the conclusion that consumption of movies is physically non-rivalrous.

But having bitten the bullet, they now have to answer the following two crucial questions: How much of the ostensible club good should be produced and how do we keep its production within the limits imposed by sound cost accounting? Being maximally sympathetic to an imaginary group of planners willing to grapple with these problems, and thus granting maximal robustness to the institutional framework they have to erect in order to implement their ideas, I am assuming they are fully aware that even though movies themselves are physically non-rival, the same cannot be said about the goods constituting the underlying capital structure. After all, the theater building has to be maintained continually, the screening equipment has to be conserved and eventually replaced, the management has to compile and update the movie repertoire, etc. It is thus crucial not to confuse the short-term costs of letting an extra person into the hall with the long-term costs of maintenance and management of the relevant capital assets (Brownstein 1980, pp. 101–2).

Now let us recall that the goal of our planners is to ensure efficient allocation of resources, by which they mean not excluding any zero-cost consumer from enjoying physically non-rival goods. However, because other essential costs are lurking in the background, some means of covering them have to be obtained if production is to be sustained.

The first method that can be resorted to in this context is the quasi-market procedure propounded by Taylor and Lange (Taylor 1929; Lange 1936), based on the attempt to mimic a perfectly competitive market environment, with the monopoly of force assuming the role of a Walrasian auctioneer, who alters the price of a given good in response to consumer reactions. Initially the price is set arbitrarily, but with the subsequent appearance of surpluses or shortages it is adjusted accordingly, downwards or upwards, until the equilibrium price is determined, supply meets demands, and efficient allocation is obtained. Furthermore, this price is then supposed to be imputable to the goods constituting the underlying capital structure, which allows for establishing their monetary value and subjecting them to financial profit-and-loss calculation.

Carrying this procedure out effectively might involve a host of separate problems, associated, for example, with potentially insufficient incentives of the theater managers (who, unlike private entrepreneurs, cannot benefit from the mobilizing power of the profit motive) or with covering the costs of integrating this particular managerial cell with the broader, vertical structure of the monopolist regulator. However, in the spirit of our methodology, let us assume that the planners can somehow solve these issues effortlessly.

But even given this, significant difficulties remain with the approach under consideration. Let us start analyzing them by quoting Hayek, who objects to the claim that "the valuation of the factors of production is implied in, or follows necessarily from, the valuation of consumers' goods" by noting that "implication is a logical relationship which can be meaningfully asserted only of propositions simultaneously present to one and the same mind" (Hayek 1948, p. 90). Because in the situation in question none of the consumers (moviegoers) is in a position to challenge the coercive monopolist by becoming a theater owner or a shareholder, no competitive appraisal of the relevant capital goods can take place, and thus no intersubjectively meaningful cardinal value (price) can be attached to them (Herbener 1996; Reynolds 1998). The appraisal in question can occur only if every individual, having evaluated a certain final good in his consumer's role (and confronted his evaluation with that of the totality of other consumers), can then proceed to become a producer or an entrepreneur and engage in competitive bidding against the rest of the producers and entrepreneurs for the ownership of the capital goods used in production of the aforementioned final good (Mises 1990, 1996, ch. 16). But as long as a "functional" gulf exists between the monopolist of force, who is the sole owner of a given stock of capital goods, and the consumers who are forcibly prevented from assuming any other role in a given area of economy, the production of any supposed club good is bound not to be efficient, but wasteful and unsustainable in the long run.

Equally important, it is necessary to realize that the putative equilibrium price of a final good, determined under conditions of initial ignorance with regard to the monetary value of the relevant factors of production, need not be optimal. In fact, it is very likely to lead to irremediable inefficiency. The entrepreneurial task of, say, the owner of a lemon orchard, is not to sell the entire supply of lemons at such a price that no customer is left empty-handed, but to sell enough lemons at a price sufficiently high to (at least) cover all the expenses associated with maintaining the orchard. In other words, he needs to know the monetary value of his capital assets in advance of determining the price of the final goods he wishes to sell, and only by utilizing his knowledge of the difference between the two can he sustain his enterprise, let alone make it profitable.

However, in the absence of signals associated with "counter-demands" for a given factor of production expressed by other entrepreneurs, based on their anticipations of the future market value of alternative final goods that could be produced with the use of the factor in question, its economic worth necessarily remains unknown, leaving no chance for establishing whether it is used efficiently (Böhm-Bawerk 1894/5). In other words, in the absence of competitive intellectual division of labor capable of establishing a uniform, monetary scale of exchange values expressible in cardinal terms, to which all goods and services can be reduced and which allows for determining the extent to which any given entrepreneur acts in line with consumer sovereignty, the notions of profit and loss, surplus and shortage, and revenue and cost (understood not as objective physical cost, but as social opportunity cost) are bound to be logically meaningless (Machaj 2007), and thus entrepreneurially useless. The crucial observation to be made in this context is that the market process of competitive appraisal operates simultaneously at two mutually informative levels – that of final consumption goods and that of factors of production of various orders – and that it cannot run smoothly with only one of these levels intact. If one relies on only one of them with the hope that the other is somehow "implied" in the former, then his actions will be necessarily (and fatally) uninformed.

Thus, we can see that the Taylor–Lange quasi-market procedure is crucially defective and that even the aforementioned narrower, "physical" variety of non-rivalness of certain consumption goods is subordinate to the ineradicable rivalness of the underlying capital goods. In other words, the said procedure does not offer the monopoly of force any promising way of managing effectively the production of what it considers to be club goods.[2]

Another method that a monopoly of force might resort to would be to dispense with trying to appraise the productive assets in its possession by using the dubious imputation strategy and instead impose a tax on society in order to finance the capital structure needed to produce the supposed club goods. This solution, however, seems even less promising than the previous one, because, unlike the latter, it does not even maintain the connection between the price of final goods and consumer demand demonstrated in concrete, voluntary actions. In other words, the compulsory payment that it proposes – being detached from the market price system – is likely to be completely arbitrary. And even if the payment in question were to be based on the prices prevailing among the private providers of any given club good, its imposition is bound to generate inefficiencies by distorting valuation information in other areas of the market, because a tax levied on other goods and/or their producers' income "will lead to inefficiently small rates of production of these . . . goods" (Demsetz 1964, p. 21).

Could such a trade-off be worthwhile? It appears difficult to conclude that it could, because it implies that society could be better off with a smaller amount of "private" goods (for which demand is voluntarily displayed) and with a larger amount of "public" (club) goods (for which there is no voluntary demand, and which are therefore funded coercively). Such a conclusion runs afoul of the principle of demonstrated preference (Rothbard 1956), which says that every free market transaction is a positive-sum game, where all involved parties demonstrate by their uncoerced actions that they prefer the post-transaction state to the pre-transaction state. Given the subjectivist approach to economics, it is thus hard to claim that the existence of monopolistically and coercively produced club goods is preferable on efficiency grounds to their non-existence coupled with the corresponding existence of a higher amount of competitively and voluntarily produced "private" goods. In sum, the tax-based strategy seems to be as untenable (if not more so) as the Taylor–Lange method.

Finally, because capital assets used in the production of club goods are not open to purchase by individual entrepreneurs, none of them can utilize his personal, "tacit" knowledge of the specific circumstances of time and place (Hayek 1945) in order to cater to the needs, tastes, and preferences of any given group of consumers with maximum efficiency. In the case of cinemas this would involve, for instance, diversification and constant updating of the movie repertoires.

Of course, a monopoly of force might try to engage in similar activities in an efficient manner by, for example, decentralizing its decision-making structure and encouraging local cinema managers to utilize their tacit knowledge as far as possible. However, if such managers are to remain managers of publicly owned capital goods rather than their private proprietors, they cannot become completely independent in their decisions – the vertical structure of the public sector requires that the relevant time- and place-specific information be gathered at the bottom and then either sent to the higher authorities for approval of the action plan that involves their utilization or at least periodically reported to those authorities. In both cases such a vertical relationship creates significant transaction costs, perhaps most notably time costs – in the best-case scenario the local managers are thereby slowed down in their decision-making processes, whereas in the worst-case scenario their efforts are rendered completely futile, because the information they collect may routinely become obsolete and useless before the authorities manage to put a stamp of approval on the business plan that draws on them.

Moreover, because in such cases the authorities can access the relevant information only in the form of indirect description rather than in the form of firsthand experience of specific circumstances of time and place, they are usually in no position to assess the accuracy of the local managers' reports and thus the usefulness of any given set of data to the success of the action plan under consideration. If, however, we were to assume that the remedy to this problem would be to give the managers full discretionary powers over the creation and execution of their plans, they would cease to be employees of the public monopoly and become private entrepreneurs instead (Rothbard 1991, pp. 57–60).

Having made these theoretical points, let us now see how they apply to the operation of the sector which, as I indicated earlier, is typically seen as particularly suited for being controlled by a monopoly of force, namely, law and defense.

2.3 Non-rivalness, subjectivity, and capital: the application[3]

There is no quick and easy answer to the question of whether law and defense constitute club goods, because they cannot be treated as any sort of homogeneous lump – instead, they come in various forms and categories (Hoppe 1989a, p. 35). What follows is that the relevant economic characteristics of some of them can be more readily identified than those of the others. I shall analyze what I take to be examples of goods belonging to both ends of this spectrum.

The issue seems relatively straightforward in this regard when it comes to a generic service that might be called "the availability of competent people" – in this case, for example, policemen and judges. One more policeman or one more judge present in region A means one less policeman or one less judge present in region B. One more representative of either of these professions occupied at any given time by person A means one less of such professionals capable of servicing person B at the same moment. Thus, the availability of services offered by people working in these sectors is fully rivalrous. This is because rather than being some monolithic wholes, the sectors in question consist of "specific resources committed in certain definite and concrete ways" (Rothbard 2004, p. 1032). Consequently, it is incorrect to claim that without ceding their management to a monopoly of force any zero-cost consumers will be inefficiently excluded from their use, because there are no such consumers.

The situation could seem to be somewhat different with respect to what might be termed "mid-range" protective services – for instance, the presence of surveillance cameras in a given area. It appears that no additional costs are generated by the fact that a camera observes an extra person. At the same time, the ex ante benefit of deterring criminals and the ex post benefit of their easier identification and apprehension seem to remain intact. Does that mean that surveillance cameras constitute an example of a club good?

My answer is negative – I contend that the earlier impression of non-rivalness is illusory for two main reasons. First, the previous brief remarks disregard the influence of the dimension of time and the corresponding phenomenon of crowding. As certain areas become more frequented due to their reputation for being safe, the human traffic in them gets much denser and thus more difficult to monitor effectively. And although it seems reasonable to conclude that such a change is likely to make certain sorts of crimes (e.g., shop robbery, car theft) less frequent, it might facilitate undertaking other kinds of criminal activity (e.g., assault, pickpocketing). In any event, it is not implausible to argue that increases in human traffic in area A should lead to an increase in the number of cameras in the same region – and hence to an increase in the relevant costs – which highlights the rivalrous character of the amenity in question.

Second, and perhaps more importantly, even prior to the occurrence of crowding, surveillance can perhaps be treated as temporarily non-rival, but the capital structure needed for its operation cannot. This is a general point that I already gestured toward in the previous section, and I think of it as universally applicable to the field under consideration. If we look at the right type of cost – that is, not the cost of letting an extra person enjoy any given amenity, but the cost of creating that amenity in the first place – we have to conclude that every good whose building materials are not available in superabundance is, in an important sense, rivalrous.

It is particularly worthwhile to notice that the earlier observation applies also to what might be termed "long-range" protective assets – for example, anti-ballistic missiles and nuclear weapons (thought of as deterrents) – as well as to their legal counterparts,[4] such as the institutions responsible for promoting and reinforcing the concept of the rule of law (Hayek 1960, 1973). Admittedly, in this context it is impossible to envisage the phenomenon of crowding to have any relevant effect on the degree to which the previous elements can successfully perform their intended functions. And yet, neither their creation nor their operation can be maintained without costs. Moreover, if these goals are not only to be achieved, but also to be achieved effectively, then it is crucial not only to realize that the procedures that have to be undertaken to this end are costly, but also to determine which of them (and there is an endless number to choose from) is least costly or at least inexpensive enough to be sustainable.

To be successful in this task, one needs to have a meaningful price system to rely on, a price system reflecting the relative scarcities of goods and the social demand for them. Such a system, however, as mentioned in the previous section, can emerge only in a freely competitive environment of private property rights and the voluntary exchange of property titles. Competition should be seen in this context as the process whereby subjective appraisals are turned into intersubjective exchange ratios, or, in other words, as the process whereby prices are rationalized. Thus, it is perfectly legitimate to view competition as, to echo Hayek's (2002) words, a "discovery procedure", a process as rivalrous as it is cooperative, in which "each and every type of productive service is objectively appraised in monetary terms according to its ultimate contribution to the production of consumer goods" (Salerno 1990, p. 36).

As should have already become clear from the earlier remarks, the management of production by a monopoly of force is antithetical to the existence of any meaningful price system, because it is also antithetical to the existence of free competition. This applies to every area of service, including law and defense. What should perhaps be mentioned in this connection is that trying to wed these two modes of production by allowing a competitive private sector to arrive at market prices and then instructing the public officials to copy them for the purpose of developing efficient public policy is problematic as well, because covering the costs of the eventual implementation of that policy would require taxing the market participants, which would necessarily degrade valuation information in the taxed industries and thus distort the price mechanism.

Lastly, it should be noted that even if it were granted for the sake of argument that law and defense are non-rival, it would not follow that they could be assumed to be universally regarded as goods. This, in turn, implies that their coercively funded, monopolistic production could actually be regarded by certain individuals as a "bad". There exist anarchists who oppose every form of initiatory violence and thus regard levying forced contributions as an unacceptable encroachment on legitimate property rights (Rothbard 1981). There exist pacifists who consider the existence of vast military arsenals, even if ostensibly accumulated for defensive purposes only, as necessarily increasing the risk of armed conflict.[5] There exist those who see the monopolistic production of the putative club goods as creating worse free-rider problems than their decentralized, private production does (de Jasay 1989). None of these groups can be declared to benefit from judicial or protective dirigisme. To claim otherwise is to disregard the teachings of subjectivist economics and subscribe to an unfounded psychological assumption that an individual's costs and benefits can be measured by or shifted to a third party. Alternatively, it might indicate contravening the principle of *Wertfreiheit* (Rothbard 1973a; Block 1975) and asserting that individuals can be coerced for their own good, which moves the asserter from the realm of positive political economy into the realm of normative ethics.

In conclusion, law and defense do not differ from other scarce goods in terms of rivalness. Moreover, they are similar to all other scarce goods in that if their production is detached from the market price system, their relative worth vis-à-vis other goods, as well as their most cost-efficient production method, cannot be determined. Finally, the subjective nature of benefits and losses makes it impossible to presume that to the extent that consumption of these goods can be considered as temporarily non-rival, being able to so consume them is unanimously accepted as advantageous.

Now, it is an entirely different question whether in the cases where the market price system reveals this information to the producers of protective and judicial services, they are able to generate sufficient revenue to cover all the necessary expenses, or whether free-rider problems are bound to make their enterprises unsustainable in the long run. This is the issue I shall focus on in the following section.

2.4 Non-excludability, externalities, and entrepreneurship: the theory[6]

In the preceding paragraphs I dealt with the contention that the existence of a monopoly of force in any given territory is desirable for the purpose of providing the so-called club goods. More specifically, I attempted to show that not only is their allegedly costless consumption a myth, but also that without the free exchange of private property titles in these goods (as well as the capital goods needed for their production), no intersubjective determination of the actual costs of their consumption and production can be made. Finally, I illustrated this conclusion with the example that is perhaps the most frequently invoked one in the context of discussing ostensibly non-rival goods – namely, that of law and defense.

The next step is to ask whether the aforementioned goods, which turn out to be in a crucial sense rival (or, to use a term synonymous in this context, private), can be effectively produced by means of voluntary actions of private individuals. If not, then we have to confront an uncomfortable dilemma: either such goods will be produced in a wasteful and haphazard fashion by a monopoly of force or they will not be produced at all. Given such a choice, it is quite probable that many – especially the recipients of such coercively created goods who are not themselves coerced to contribute to their production or are coerced only to the degree capable of being psychologically compensated – will opt for the former alternative. To paraphrase the issue concisely, it needs to be asked whether the aforementioned goods exhibit the feature of non-excludability.

As I mentioned in the introduction, non-excludable (common-pool) goods are alleged to generate positive externalities – that is, they are said to be capable of benefitting free riders, who cannot be excluded from using what they refuse to pay for. Thus, the crucial question in this context is: Is the existence of free riders sufficient for discouraging private individuals from engaging in the production of such goods?

However, before exploring this particular issue, let us focus for a while on the following preliminary objection – one might suggest that I am far too quick in describing the production of common goods by a monopoly of force as "wasteful and haphazard". If my conclusions from the previous sections are correct, the argument might go, then perhaps it is indeed advisable to dispose of the notion of non-rivalness and the attendant justifications for leaving the production of the putative club goods in the hands of a monopoly of force. But at the same time, it might be claimed that as soon as the market price system and the underlying intersubjective value determination mechanism are in place, the monopoly of force can estimate the monetary value of the otherwise unproducible common goods by noting the difference in prices of various non-common goods in the period before and after the appearance of the relevant positive externality. Think, for instance, of the difference in the value of a piece of real estate before and after the establishment of an infrastructural network in its vicinity (Smerk 1965, p. 241).

Could the monopoly of force engage in the efficient production of common goods on the basis of the earlier procedure? As I see it, there seems to be a number of serious problems plaguing this proposal. First of all, because the market data – including most notably the tastes and preferences of consumers – are in constant flux (Shackle 1958, 1968; O'Driscoll and Rizzo 1996; Klein 2008a, pp. 172–5), the managers employed in gathering them would have to engage in the process of endless and constant surveillance of ever-changing prices and even the pre-transaction opinions of prospective buyers and sellers. Moreover, they would have to be able to identify and winnow out every conceivable factor other than the appearance of a specific positive externality that could influence the price of any given surveyed non-common good at the same time as the externality in question (the inability to perform such a winnowing-out procedure would almost certainly make them fall prey to the *post hoc ergo propter hoc* fallacy). This is obviously not an insurmountable task for the private sector, where "prices afford a highly effective system of signals that obviate the need for the transmission of detailed, factual information to decisionmakers" (Kirzner 1988, p. 4), but it appears a daunting challenge for a centralized, public agency. However, in view of our methodological assumption of maximal robustness with regard to the activities of any given monopoly of force, let us put this particular objection aside. There are yet other, more difficult objections that have to be countenanced by the proponent of the standard, neoclassical theory of common goods in the present context.

For instance, it has to be realized that even if the employees of the monopoly of force were able to keep up to date with all the relevant prices and were capable of eliminating every intervening irrelevant factor from their analysis, their estimation of the would-be price of any given common good would, entrepreneurially speaking, already belong to the past. And although very important for the entrepreneurs, "the prices of the immediate past are for them only the starting point of deliberations leading to forecasts of future prices" (Mises 1996, p. 336). The question to be asked in this connection, then, is: Could a manager employed by a centralized, coercive agency appraise future prices just as efficiently as a private entrepreneur? It appears to me that the answer is yes, he could, provided that he were as independent and unconstrained in his decision making as a private entrepreneur; that is, if he were free to "establish corporations and other firms, enlarge or reduce their size, dissolve them or merge them with other enterprises; . . . buy and sell the shares and bonds of already existing and of new corporations; . . . grant, withdraw, and recover credits" (Mises 1996, p. 704), as well as bear the full financial consequences of engaging in any of these activities. This, however, he is incapable of doing by definition, because he is not the owner of the assets he manages, but only their temporary caretaker. As a result, it is difficult to conceive of the possibility that his forecasts (as opposed to his forecasting skills) could be even marginally as accurate as that of a full-blooded businessman.

Hence, we can see the unworkability of the procedure of, say, levying a more or less arbitrary tax on the public in order to finance the production of a given common good and then returning the surplus to the taxpayer as soon as the monetary value of the common good in question is determined on the basis of the increase in value of the goods and assets affected by the relevant, newly emergent positive externality. The crucial point here is that a given amount of money paid in taxes today is not equivalent in value to the same amount of money returned to the taxpayer in the future,[7] and because, as follows from the earlier remarks, a manager employed by a monopoly of force is in no position to appraise the future value of tax money on the basis of its present value, it can easily be claimed that the whole tax-produce-and-return procedure would result in suboptimal social outcomes. In fact, in addition to the manager's inability to determine what constitutes a "due" compensation to the taxpayer, what also raises doubts about the workability of the procedure in question is the fact that imposing a tax on the members of any given society is bound to change the value rankings of its members. Thus, their valuations of the goods and assets affected by the appearance of a given positive externality are going to be conditioned by the preceding tax imposition, and hence are useless as a benchmark for determining the "tax-neutral" value of the common good that generates the externality in question.

Furthermore, a point should be made about the unsuitability of the use of econometric equations in the context at hand. The crucial assumption underlying the nature of the events they purport to analyze is the possibility to abstract from them in order to produce a series of random occurrences (i.e., all openings of new segments of road infrastructure, all creations of public parks, etc.) and then study them in terms of 'class probability', where

> we know, or assume to know, with regard to the problem concerned, everything about the behavior of a whole class of events or phenomena; but about the actual singular events or phenomena we know nothing but that they are elements of this class.
>
> (Mises 1996, p. 107)

Only provided such an assumption would it be possible to measure the extent to which the introduction of any given common good is supposed to raise the value of the surrounding assets. It is the case, however, that the events in question are in their nature unique and discrete, thus being at most amenable to study in terms of 'case probability', where "we know, with regard to a particular event, some of the factors which determine its outcome; but there are other determining factors about which we know nothing" (Mises 1996, p. 110). Not belonging to any homogeneous collectives, the probability of occurrence of whose particular members tends asymptotically towards fixed limits, where such limits are not affected by any place selection (Mises 1957; Hoppe 2007), such events are not amenable to analysis in terms of the probability calculus.

Next, it should be borne in mind that any coercive interference with the social system of voluntary transactions (including interferences aimed at the production of common goods) is bound to generate a number of what might be regarded as negative externalities – for example, erosion of respect for property rights (Malkin and Wildavsky 1991), diminution of entrepreneurial incentives (Hoppe 1989b, ch. 4), and distortionary effects on profit-and-loss calculation (Salerno 1993, p. 131). The disutility thereby created is, of course, a subjective quantity, unamenable to cardinal measurement, but because the processes leading to its creation by definition prevent some mutually beneficial interpersonal interactions, it can nonetheless be objectively identified as a disutility. On the other hand, because the putative utility derived from the existence of positive externalities is also subjective, and because, *ex hypothesi*, people are supposed to be unwilling to pay for the production of common goods, it cannot really be said from the third-person point of view whether the existence of any supposed common good benefits society on the whole.

It is worthwhile to mention in this connection that many privately produced goods can be said to generate externalities, both positive and negative (Block 1983, pp. 1–2). For instance, some people might enjoy the sight and smell of roses cultivated in private (but publicly visible) gardens, whereas some might abhor them. Without the possibility of making interpersonal comparisons of utility, it is unfeasible to determine whether roses are a common good, common "bad", or neither. The same goes for, say, the melodies played by street musicians, the facades of residential buildings, the smell of deodorants used by our fellow passengers on the bus, the knowledge of any given place that its residents are willing to share with the tourists for free, and so on, practically ad infinitum. Be that as it may, it is undeniable that such services, commodities, and manifestations of human activity exist in abundance without any incentivization or supervision from a monopoly of force, so in this context there appears to be no reason to suppose that it would be any different with what neoclassical economics describes as common goods.

Moreover, if, pace Rothbard (1956), we confine our analysis of economic efficiency to the study of actual transfers of property titles as revealing the underlying preference rankings of the involved parties (while dismissing the attendant third-party verbal declarations, complaints, approvals, etc., as amenable to psychological investigations only), then the very notion of positive externality turns out to be purely psychologistic (or, to put it more generally, economically unoperationalizable), whereas the notion of negative externality appears reducible to the effects of violating one's property rights. What follows is that the only potentially efficiency-enhancing role that a monopoly of force could play when it comes to securing the existence of the optimum amount of common goods would be protecting legitimate property titles, but we have seen in the previous sections that there are considerable economic problems with this proposal too.

It should be noted that the earlier remarks apply equally well to another, slightly different version of the theory of common goods, the one according to which the defining feature of a common good is that the benefits it produces are 'diffused', that is, impossible to impute to individual beneficiaries. The following statement encapsulates the view in question: "If it were agreed that the benefits from highway improvements are . . . diffused among inhabitants of a state . . . [then] highways should be supported from the general fund" (Netzer 1952, p. 109).

I suppose it should be apparent by now that this approach is as divorced from demonstrated preferences of consumers as the original one and thus equally questionable as a measuring rod for the efficiency of economically operationalizable results. First, if no individual beneficiaries of a given, supposedly common good can be identified, it seems worthwhile to ask whether there are any serious grounds for thinking that any such beneficiaries exist at all. After all, non-action on the part of any given agent can be given a number of mutually exclusive psychological interpretations of how he feels vis-à-vis the putative good in question (Fielding 1979). He might be interpreted as genuinely enjoying its consumption by means of (by definition undetectable) free riding. But he might equally well be interpreted as being indifferent toward it or even as passively hating its presence. And even if he were to say that he regards the good under consideration as very valuable and that he would willingly pay in taxes for its production and maintenance were it not for the existence of other free riders, who routinely damage its quality, we cannot therefore conclude that the utility he would derive from coercing other free riders to contribute would exceed the disutility the latter would derive from being coerced. As I have already signaled earlier, this follows from the fact that utility is a subjective, psychological magnitude, which cannot be measured against any physical, spatially extended yardstick and a fortiori compared interpersonally with any degree of economic precision (Robbins 1935, pp. 138–40; Rothbard 1956; Herbener 1997).

Second, if the notion of diffused benefits is to be treated seriously, what is to stop us from treating literally every good we can think of as a common good? If such benefits are undetectable by the persons concerned, is there a principled reason to deny the claim that they are present in every human activity? Consequently, is there any non-arbitrary stopping point for the monopoly of force tasked with the provision of common goods? What seems to me to testify to the strength of this reductio ad absurdum is the fact that presumably very few people would be willing to advocate a centralized, "public" production of, say, evening suits and computer software on the grounds that it cannot be disproved that these goods generate unrealized benefits for people other than their buyers and the immediate surroundings of the latter.[8]

Third and finally, it could be argued that the notion of diffused benefits was invented in order to bring utility theory and welfare economics in line with the mathematical modeling methods espoused by the neoclassicists.[9] If graphs such as cost curves and revenue curves are to be analyzable by means of differential calculus, they have to be plotted as smoothly continuous, which results in depicting economic action as consisting of a series of infinitely small steps. This, in turn, is entirely consistent with the claim that economic benefits, even if infinitely small and thus unnoticeable, can nonetheless be regarded as "real" (Block 1983, p. 22). However, this attempt at imparting mathematical elegance to economics comes at the price of falsifying the image of human action, which "can occur only in discrete, non-infinitely-small steps, steps large enough to be perceivable by a human consciousness" (Rothbard 1960, p. 167). In other words, as long as any given event remains unnoticed by the person concerned, it does not enter her realm of decision making and hence cannot be regarded as in any meaningful sense beneficial to her.

It might be argued in response that neoclassical economists are justified in using continuous functions to represent various aspects of human action because in a repeated game setting actions and their results do become increasingly small, the consequence being that a function will become more continuous (though perhaps not "fully" continuous) as long as the action is repeatable. However, there are several problems with this suggestion. First, repeated game settings can be justifiably thought of as artificial environments, thus having little relevance for analyzing the operation of human action in the realm of everyday, real-world scenarios. Second, there seems to be something inherently dubious in talking about repeatability of action in the sense of fitting its particular instances into homogeneous classes of events, because every instance of human action is a paradigmatic example of a unique event, caused to happen by a unique, time-bound, and agent-relative set of beliefs, desires, judgments, and preferences. Finally, if we analogize repeated game settings to institutional frameworks whose formation leads to the emergence of highly conditioned patterns of behavior, the existence of such frameworks can be plausibly regarded not as an economic good, but rather as a "*general condition* of human action and human welfare" (Rothbard 2004, p. 5). Consequently, it cannot be thought of as imparting any benefit to a given person, but rather as being a condition of that person's benefiting from the consumption of scarce goods. In the context under discussion, the same can be said about unnoticeable positive externalities.

All of the these considerations seem to me to make a strong case for the superiority of the approach confined to the study of preferences demonstrated in concrete actions (which expunges the notion of positive externality from the realm of economics and reduces the notion of negative externality to the effects of property rights violations) over the neoclassical approach, which cannot help making recourse to elements of heavy psychological speculation in order to support the claim that a non-perceivable or unconscious benefit is a coherent concept.

It might be argued, however, that the previously mentioned method of determining increases in social utility on the basis of recording voluntarily undertaken transactions is plagued by a number of conceptual difficulties. First, if no objective interpersonal comparisons of utility can be made, then even if it can be claimed that every voluntary transaction is utility enhancing, it does not necessarily follow that no coerced transaction can be even more utility enhancing. In other words, although it is true that every voluntary transaction increases the utility of all transacting parties (hence being a positive-sum game and a Pareto-superior solution) and that every coerced transaction increases the utility of the coercer and decreases the utility of the coerced (hence being a non–positive-sum game and a Pareto-inferior solution), it cannot be denied that if in the latter case the coercer is a "utility monster" (Nozick 1974, p. 41), an enormous amount of utility he derives from the act of coercion might be sufficient to outweigh the disutility incurred by the coerced. To generalize this point, even though within the analytical framework under consideration we can regard every voluntary transaction as efficient, by the same token we cannot regard every coerced transaction as *in*efficient – we can at most suspend our judgment concerning the efficiency of the latter (Caplan 1999). This, in turn, leaves us with a somewhat disconcerting conclusion that we cannot consider, say, Soviet war communism as a disastrously ineffective economic system.

I believe that the earlier criticism rests on a misunderstanding of what Pareto-inferiority really means. Pareto-inferior scenarios are not those in which both parties to a given transaction lose, but precisely those in which one party gains and the other loses, and this can happen only as a result of one party coercing the other to do something against the latter's will. A scenario in which both parties to a transaction lose in the ex ante sense is praxeologically impossible, because "acting man is eager to substitute a more satisfactory state of affairs for a less satisfactory. His mind imagines conditions which suit him better, and his action aims at bringing about this desired state" (Mises 1996, p. 13). Clearly, if every example of a Pareto-inferior outcome were to belong to the realm of logical impossibility, it would follow either that Pareto-superiority is an empty concept or that we live in a Panglossian world in which the optimality of outcomes is a ubiquitous and necessary phenomenon. Thus, it appears to me that the only useful and informative way of understanding the concept of Pareto-inferiority is the one in which we apply it to social interactions whose results, given the impossibility of performing interpersonal comparisons of utility, are indeterminate (as opposed to positive, characteristic of Pareto-superior interactions).

In view of these clarifications, we can see that within the subjectivist, demonstrated-preference-based framework of thinking about welfare economics, Soviet war communism can be considered disastrously ineffective in the sense that under such a regime all (or most) social interactions are coerced and thus no (or very few) increases in social utility can be said to take place. Under a free enterprise system, on the other hand, every social interaction can be said to increase social utility, because under such a system every social interaction is a voluntary exchange of legitimate property titles. Consequently, within the framework in question it is perfectly justifiable to regard free enterprise arrangements as highly conducive to economic efficiency.

Another criticism of the approach adopted here says that because the coerced cannot, by definition, demonstrate by their actions that they prefer not being coerced (because they are rendered passive by coercion), in view of the methodological framework under consideration, it cannot be determined what happens to the utility of the coerced. In every non-voluntary transaction, the coercer is the only active party, that is, according to the critic, the only party capable of demonstrating through its actions whether it prefers the post-coercion state to the pre-coercion state. Furthermore, because the coercer clearly demonstrates that he prefers the post-coercion state to the pre-coercion state, we seem to reach a troubling and counterintuitive conclusion that every coercive transaction is

Pareto-superior, strictly parallel in this regard to every voluntary transaction (Kvasnicka 2008).

I can think of two points that might be made in response. First, it can be claimed that the coerced do demonstrate that they object to being subject to coercion. Their engagement in activities such as tax evasion, the use of tax havens, looking for loopholes in the tax law, joining black or grey markets, etc., seems to provide ample testimony to this assertion. However, an immediate counterargument here might be that as soon as we invoke the previously mentioned activities, which can assume the form either of ex ante precautions or ex post reactions, we start to compare two systematic processes stretched over time – systematic coercion and systematic attempts to avoid that coercion – rather than two kinds of inter-actions undertaken at specific time points. The problem with the welfare analy-sis of processes is that it involves making intertemporal comparisons of utility, together with the attendant unwarranted assumption that the preference rankings of the involved parties are constant over time. The subjectivist, demonstrated-preference-based welfare theory expounded in this chapter avoids making the said assumption precisely by focusing on specific time points at which specific volun-tary or coerced interactions take place.

Thus, in order to defend the claim that coercive interactions are necessarily Pareto-inferior, we need to show that the coerced suffer a utility loss precisely at the moment in which they are coerced. One way of doing this could consist in making the critic realize the following: as long as the owner of the property title X does not trade X for something else or give it away, he demonstrates that he prefers keeping it. Hence, by coercively appropriating X, the coercer can be objectively shown to frustrate the original owner's preferences. After all, if the original owner were willing to part with X on his own, there would be no need for coercion – the would-be coercer could obtain X by means of trade or as a gift. In other words, "that he [the original owner] is not demonstrating a preference for the transfer in the case of aggressive violence used against him is inferred from his initial property ownership and that aggressive violence is an implicit, non-consensual claim on his property" (Herbener 2008, p. 61). In sum, non-action with respect to one's property implicitly presupposes that one prefers to keep the property in question, even if one does not actively use it at a given moment.

One might claim that this argumentation applies only to the overt, explicit kinds of coercion such as assault or burglary, but not to the more implicit and imperceptible ones, such as taxation – after all, judging by the way in which most of the people submit their tax forms, it might be thought that they are doing so vol-untarily as far as the observation of preferences expressed in actions goes. Such a contention, however, disregards the fact that a credible threat of violence is a type of violence in its own right. To think of a vivid analogy:

> Suppose someone approaches you on the street, whips out a gun, and demands your wallet. He might not have molested you physically during this encounter, but he has extracted money from you on the basis of a direct, overt threat that he *would* shoot you if you disobeyed his commands. He has used

the threat of invasion to obtain your obedience to his commands, and this is equivalent to the invasion itself.

(Rothbard 1998, p. 78)

Hence, insofar as the threat of imprisonment and even more intense expropriation in the event of disobedience constantly hovers above the taxpayers, their seemingly uncoerced payments cannot be truly considered as such.

Let us now move to another possible objection, which is the following: even though undertaking a certain action demonstrates that the agent prefers a given outcome to the available alternatives, it does not imply that as a result of achieving this outcome his utility increases overall. Think about the example of a few firms forming a voluntary cartel on the market and raising the prices of their products. Even if after the emergence of the cartel consumers continue to patronize it, thus demonstrating their preference for buying a certain good at a "natural monopoly" price over not buying it at all, it appears difficult to maintain that they are better off after the formation of the cartel than they were before it took place.

What this objection seems to overlook is that the welfare theory under consideration says only that every voluntary transaction is Pareto-superior within given momentary conditions, which are brought about by the preceding interpersonal transactions (voluntary or otherwise). It does not say, however, that those preceding (or subsequent) transactions cannot impose some sort of psychological disutility on a given person and alter his preference ranking. It cannot be guaranteed that, psychologically speaking, one will find the conditions prevailing at time t more favorable than the conditions prevailing at time $t-1$. The crucial point is that as long as one is permitted to act freely at t and $t-1$, each of those actions is going to be Pareto-superior, even though, holding other things constant, it is possible that one's action at $t-1$ is going to be capable of bringing him greater subjectively perceived satisfaction than his action at t.

Next, let us consider an interesting criticism based on the claim that even assuming that any coercive regime is necessarily less conducive to the promotion of social utility than a fully voluntary regime (because the latter, unlike the former, consists exclusively of mutually beneficial and thus Pareto-superior transactions), the same assertion cannot be made with respect to comparisons between various regimes belonging to the continuum stretching from pure voluntarism to extreme coercivism.[10] For example, both a minarchist system and a social democratic system represent a mix of voluntary and coercive transactions (i.e., a mix of Pareto-inferior and Pareto-superior transactions). The same can be said about, on the one hand, a regime in which attempts at aggression against legitimate property holdings are successfully fended off, which results in preserving the existing pattern of ownership, and, on the other hand, a regime in which such attempts are successful, thus changing the said pattern.

Now even though it is clear which system in both of the pairs involves more (successfully carried out) initiatory violence, it would seem that the ordinal character of utility and the non-comparability of individual utility rankings (Mises 1980; Herbener 1997; Rothbard 2004, pp. 18–20) do not allow us to say on purely economic grounds that either of the regimes in question generates more or less welfare than the other. This is because all these social arrangements are strictly symmetrical insofar as they result in mixes of individual gains and losses, and discounting the value of the aggressors' preference scales vis-à-vis the value of the non-aggressors' preference scales appears to be an arbitrary, logically unjustifiable move. Hence, is the demonstrated-preference-based welfare theory limited to the comparative economic analysis of pure voluntarism versus coercivism of any kind?

Again, two points can be made in response. First, it may be suggested that social arrangements can be classified as better or worse with regard to utility maximization depending on the extent to which they approximate the ideal type of pure voluntarism – hence, according to this criterion, minarchism is better than social democracy, the system that successfully fends off the actions of aggressors is better than the one that does not, etc. However, this answer might appear to be somewhat evasive insofar as, given the characteristics of utility mentioned in the previous paragraph, such approximations could seem to be conceptually incoherent, or at least incomparable in any meaningful sense.

A more promising reply consists in claiming that if we accept the definition of society along the lines of that proposed by Mises, who describes it as "the total complex of the mutual relations created by . . . concerted actions" aimed at "cooperation and coadjuvancy with others for the attainment of definite singular ends", whose results are "division of labor and combination of labor" (Mises 1996, p. 143), we can define the relevant criterion of social welfare as the extent to which individuals within a given group are enabled to "evaluate and allocate the means at their disposal when pursuing their goals through social action, i.e., action that makes use of voluntary exchange and the social division of labor to realize its aims" (Salerno 1993, p. 130). This, in turn, allows us to "discount any gains, in terms of direct utility or exchangeable goods, that accrue to the [aggressive] interveners and their beneficiaries, while remaining safely within the bounds of strict *Wertfreiheit*" (Salerno 1993, p. 131), because the actions of the said interveners

> necessarily distort or annul [the free market's] intricate calculational nexus coordinating consumer preferences and entrepreneurial choices, *ipso facto* generat[ing] a less efficient allocation of resources, i.e., one that does not completely and exclusively reflect the anticipated preferences of the participants in the social division of labor.
>
> (Salerno 1993, p. 131)

In sum, on a definitional level we may effectively exclude aggressors from society and thus rank regimes vis-à-vis their conduciveness to the promotion of social utility based on the degree to which they are free of institutional coercion and unobstructive with respect to bringing about the conditions under which it is possible to fend off non-institutional coercion successfully.

Let us now move to the issue of whether feeling regret about acting on a given desire proves that in hindsight we identify it as irrational (which might be problematic for the welfare theory under consideration if we take irrationality of any given action to be an indication of its Pareto-inferiority). One could think that this is evidenced by the desirer saying something like "this is not what I really wanted" as he reflects on his past choice and subsequently undertakes some actions to rectify this state of affairs. Here, I believe we need to insert a crucial qualification. As I have already emphasized repeatedly, I am perfectly sympathetic to the claim that voluntary actions reveal the agent's preferences, but:

> All we can say is that an action, at a specific point of time, reveals part of a man's preference scale *at that time*. There is no warrant for assuming that it remains constant from one point of time to another.
>
> (Rothbard 1956, p. 6)

Thus, if the desirer says at *t1* "this is not what I really wanted" with reference to his choice made at *t0*, this statement is not strictly speaking correct. "This is not what I want right now, but this is what I wanted back then" would be a much more accurate description of his intertemporal preferential makeup. And if this description is to be taken as indicative of the agent's irrationality, we have to make the assumption that rationality requires constancy of preferences over time. I see no reason to make such an assumption. As purposive and reflective beings, we can and often do change our goals and aims, both in response to continually accumulated new empirical data and their logical scrutiny, as well as in response to purely internal changes of heart, taste and evaluation.[11] What matters for rationality is not constancy, but consistency, and the previously mistaken identification of irrationality results from confusing the two:

> *Constancy* and *consistency* are two entirely different things. Consistency means that a person maintains a transitive order of rank on his preference scale (if A is preferred to B and B is preferred to C, then A is preferred to C). . . . *Constancy* [means] that an individual maintains the same value scale over time. While the former might be called irrational, there is certainly nothing irrational about someone's value scales changing through time.
>
> (Rothbard 1956, p. 6)[12]

In sum, because rationality does not require constancy of preferences over time, feeling regret about one's past actions cannot be construed as an indication of their irrationality – and, by extension, of their Pareto-inferiority.

Finally, let us say a few words about the apparent asymmetry in the way in which the demonstrated-preference-based welfare theory treats the concepts of positive and negative externalities. As I have repeatedly indicated earlier, according to the framework that underlies the theory in question, a positive externality is an economically unoperationalizable term, because, by definition, there can be no demonstrated market demand for the goods alleged to exhibit such externalities. However, at the same time the framework under discussion admits that there exists a perfectly meaningful economic definition of negative externalities – that is, the effects of transactions between A and B which physically interfere with the property rights of C (Rothbard 1982; Cordato 1992, 2001). How can this conceptual asymmetry be explained?

To do so, it has to be noted that non-action with respect to someone else's assets that are alleged to create positive spillover effects can be given a number of equally plausible though mutually exclusive psychological interpretations (free-rider's enjoyment, indifference, dislike, etc.), but only one praxeological interpretation (a preference for non-payment over payment for the ostensible good under consideration). Likewise, non-action with respect to one's own assets can be psychologically interpreted in many different ways, but only one explanation makes praxeological sense in this context – namely, a preference for keeping the assets in question over trading them for something else, giving them away, or disposing of them in any other manner.

Hence, it becomes visible that an action (payment or other form of voluntary acceptance) is required on the part of the putative beneficiary of a positive externality to prove that he is in fact one, but no action is required on the part of someone whose property is uninvitedly interfered with to classify any such interference as a negative externality. This, as I see it, is because the benefits derived from keeping one's property assets can be traced back to the preceding action of acquiring them (via the regression theorem of social interactions) (Herbener 2008, pp. 63–4), but the benefits of being affected by positive externalities can be traced back to none of the preceding actions of the ostensible beneficiaries.

This point can be further illustrated by reflecting on an argument often encountered in debates on full-reserve banking versus fractional-reserve banking. Many advocates of fractional-reserve banking argue that cash balances held in demand deposit accounts are idle and because depositors are not actively using them, banks are free to exercise control over them and lend them out for investment purposes. The advocates of full-reserve banking, on the other hand, take the view that these supposedly idle reserves indicate a conscious decision on the part of depositors and that a bank that lends them out is making an erroneous assumption that the depositors' putative idleness stems from the fact that they do not currently need their deposits. However, holding money in a cash balance does, in fact, serve a concrete and important function, which is hedging against uncertainty through the accumulation of liquid assets (Hutt 1956; Hülsmann 1996, p. 12; Rothbard 2004, p. 265).[13] This is yet another illustration of the fact that non-action with respect to one's assets has to be interpreted in light of one's previous decisions and that it cannot be taken as an indication that, at least for the time being, the assets in question dropped out of one's preference scale.

Having thus defused a number of objections and dealt with a number of conceptual tangles related to the subjectivist, demonstrated-preference-based welfare theory adopted and defended in this chapter, as well as having explored in more detail some of the more general considerations dealing with entrepreneurial methods of solving the free-rider problem, let us now move on to investigating how these considerations would play themselves out in the context of entrepreneurial practice in the area of competitive law and defense provision.

Notes

1 This section incorporates material from Wisniewski (2013a).
2 Interestingly, and quite tellingly, the Austrian rebuttals to the Taylor–Lange quasi-market solution to the problem of economic calculation under socialism were not addressed in any systematic manner by the sympathizers of the latter. Instead, the neoclassical mainstream largely accepted the alleged viability of the solution in question, thereby declaring market socialists the winners of the original calculation debate (see, e.g., Arrow 1974, p. 5; Lavoie 1985). In addition, the post-Soviet collapse treatments of the topic of market socialism by the neoclassicists (e.g., Roemer 1994; Stiglitz 1994), although mentioning and acknowledging the significance of some aspects of the previously mentioned Austrian rebuttals, nevertheless contain assertions and conclusions that betray a continued lack of understanding of their general import, let alone their finer details (Hill 1997; Wohlgemuth 1997).
3 This section incorporates material from Wisniewski (2013a).
4 Counterparts in terms of the range at which they operate rather than the mode in which they operate.
5 Some of the public goods theorists seem to understand this point clearly. See, for instance, the following quotation: "In the case of a pure public good, voluntarism may be absent, since the good may harm some recipients (e.g., defense to a pacifist, fluoridation to someone who opposes its use)" (Cornes and Sandler 1986, p. 159). However, this supposed understanding does not stop them from maintaining that something that is harmful for some people may nonetheless be regarded as a "pure public good", a conclusion I find logically incoherent insofar as the existence of "pure public goods" is supposed to be beneficial to payers and non-payers alike, which, given that these two categories exhaust the set of potential recipients, logically implies that, in the context at hand, the set of harmed recipients is empty.
6 This section incorporates material from Wisniewski (2013b).
7 Even if we were to assume that the tastes and preferences of the public are constant over time, intertemporal variation in the value attached to any given good would result from the existence of positive time preference (Böhm-Bawerk 1890).
8 It might be claimed, for instance, that the masses benefit greatly from an increase in the availability of all sorts of knowledge due to the proliferation of computer software even though they do not realize the extent of these benefits, because computers have already become quite commonplace objects.
9 For a selection of academic textbooks describing the mathematical modeling methods that dominate the neoclassical tradition, see Hoy, Livernois, McKenna, Rees and Stengos (2001); Hands (2003); and Chiang and Wainwright (2005).
10 What would seem to be the strict opposite of pure voluntarism, namely, pure coercivism, is a praxeologically impossible construct, because there can be no system consisting exclusively of coercees – for an act of coercion to take place, there has to be a coercee and a coercer. Admittedly, we can imagine a system in which coercers and coercees periodically switch roles, thus leaving nobody uncoerced in a diachronic perspective, but it is by no means obvious that such an arrangement is not preferable to that in which the whole society suffers slavery under a single master. Hence, the furthermost negative extremity of the continuum in question cannot attain the same level of purity as its furthermost positive extremity.
11 A determinist would probably not want to distinguish between these two possible reasons for change in one's goals and aims, because he would like to claim that the latter (i.e., "internal" changes of heart) are always ultimately determined by the former (i.e., external, empirical factors). As I am not going to pursue the issues dealing with the metaphysics of free will here, let us leave this matter undecided.
12 On the distinction between constancy and consistency of preferences, see also Mises (1996), p. 103.
13 This response does not apply to those advocates of fractional-reserve banking (including many advocates of fractional-reserve free banking) who explicitly construe bank

demand deposit contracts as debt rather than bailment contracts and the deposited money as "call loans" rather than property held in trust.

Bibliography

Arnold, R. A. (2004), *Economics* (Mason, OH: South-Western).

Arrow, K. (1969), 'The Organization of Economic Activity: Issues Pertinent to the Choice of Market versus Nonmarket Allocation', in *The Analysis and Evaluation ofPublic Expenditure: The PPB System*, Vol. 1, U.S. Joint Economic Committee, 91st Congress, 1st Session (Washington, DC: U.S. Government Printing Office).

Arrow, K. (1974), 'Limited Knowledge and Economic Analysis', *AmericanEconomic Review*, 64 (1), 1–10.

Ayers, R. M. and Collinge, R. A. (2004), *Economics: Explore and Apply* (Upper Saddle River, NJ: Prentice Hall).

Bator, F. M. (1958), 'The Anatomy of Market Failure', *Quarterly Journal of Economics*, 72 (3), 351–79.

Baumol, W. J. (1961), 'Review of *Politics, Economics and Welfare*', in *Economic Theory and Operations Analysis* (Englewood Cliffs, NJ: Prentice-Hall).

Berglas, E. (1976), 'On the Theory of Clubs', *American Economic Review*, 66, 116–21.

Blankart, C. B. (1994), 'Club Governments versus Representative Governments', *Constitutional Political Economy*, 5 (3), 273–86.

Block, W. (1975), 'On Value Freedom in Economics', *American Economist*, 19, 38–41.

Block, W. (1983), 'Public Goods and Externalities: The Case of Roads', *Journal of Libertarian Studies*, 7 (1), 1–34.

Boettke, P. J. and Leeson, P. T. (2004), 'Liberalism, Socialism, and Robust Political Economy', *Journal of Markets & Morality*, 7 (1), 99–111.

Böhm-Bawerk, E. (1890), *Capital and Interest* (London: Macmillan).

Böhm-Bawerk, E. (1894/5), 'The Ultimate Standard of Value', *Annals of the American Academy of Political and Social Science*, 5, 149–208.

Brownstein, B. (1980), 'Pareto Optimality, External Benefits and Public Goods: A Subjectivist Approach', *Journal of Libertarian Studies*, 4 (1), 93–106.

Buchanan, J. M. (1965), 'An Economic Theory of Clubs', *Economica*, 32, 1–14.

Buchanan, J. M. (1969), *Cost and Choice* (Chicago: Markham Publishing Company).

Buchanan, J. M. (1975), *The Limits of Liberty: Between Anarchy and Leviathan* (Chicago: University of Chicago Press).

Buchanan, J. M. and Flowers, M. R. (1975), *The Public Finances: An Introductory Textbook* (4th ed., Homewood, IL: Richard D. Irwin).

Bush, W. and Mayer, L. (1974), 'Some Implications of Anarchy for the Distribution of Property', *Journal of Economic Theory*, 8, 401–12.

Caplan, B. (1999), 'The Austrian Search for Realistic Foundations', *Southern Economic Journal*, 65 (4), 823–38.

Chiang, A. C. and Wainwright, K. (2005), *Fundamental Methods of Mathematical Economics* (4th ed., New York: McGraw-Hill).

Cordato, R. E. (1992), *Welfare Economics and Externalities in an Open Ended Universe* (Boston: Kluwer Academic Publishers).

Cordato, R. E. (2001), 'The Polluter Pays Principle: A Proper Guide for Environmental Policy', in *Studies in Social Cost, Regulation, and the Environment* (Washington, DC: Institute for Research on the Economics of Taxation).

Cornes, R. and Sandler, T. (1986), *The Theory of Externalities, Public Goods and Club Goods* (Cambridge: Cambridge University Press).

Cowen, T. (1992), 'Law as a Public Good: The Economics of Anarchy', *Economics and Philosophy*, 8, 249–67.

De Jasay, A. (1989), *Social Contract, Free Ride: A Study of the Public Goods Problem* (New York: Oxford University Press).

Demsetz, H. (1964), 'The Exchange and Enforcement of Property Rights', *Journal of Law and Economics*, 7 (1), 11–26.

Demsetz, H. (1970), 'The Private Production of Public Goods', *Journal of Law and Economics*, 13, 293–306.

Fielding, K. T. (1979), 'Nonexcludability and Government Financing of Public Goods', *Journal of Libertarian Studies*, 3 (3), 293–8.

Hands, D. W. (2003), *Introductory Mathematical Economics* (2nd ed., Oxford: Oxford University Press).

Hayek, F. A. (1945), 'The Use of Knowledge in Society', *American Economic Review*, 35, 519–30.

Hayek, F. A. (1948), *Individualism and Economic Order* (Chicago: University of Chicago Press).

Hayek, F. A. (1960), *The Constitution of Liberty* (Chicago: University of Chicago Press).

Hayek, F. A. (1973), *Law, Legislation and Liberty* (Chicago: University of Chicago Press).

Hayek, F. A. (2002), 'Competition as a Discovery Procedure', *The Quarterly Journal of Austrian Economics*, 5 (3), 9–23.

Head, J. G. and Shoup, C. S. (1969), 'Public Goods, Private Goods, and Ambiguous Goods', *Economic Journal*, 79, 567–72.

Head, J. G. (1972), 'Public Goods: The Polar Case', in R. M. Bird and J. G. Head (eds.), *Modern Fiscal Issues: Essays in Honour of Carl. S. Shoup* (Toronto: University of Toronto Press), 7–16.

Herbener, J. (1996), 'Calculation and the Question of Arithmetic', *Review of Austrian Economics*, 9 (1), 151–62.

Herbener, J. (1997), 'The Pareto Rule and Welfare Economics', *Review of Austrian Economics*, 10 (1), 70–106.

Herbener, J. (2008), 'In Defense of Rothbardian Welfare Economics', *New Perspectives on Political Economy*, 4 (1), 53–78.

Hill, P. J. (1997), 'An Economist's Surprise', *Liberty*, 10 (3), 69–70.

Hoppe, H.-H. (1989a), 'Fallacies of the Public Goods Theory and the Production of Security', *Journal of Libertarian Studies*, 9 (1), 27–46.

Hoppe, H.-H. (1989b), *A Theory of Socialism and Capitalism* (Boston: Kluwer Academic Publishers).

Hoppe, H-H. (2007), 'The limits of numerical probability: Frank H. Knight and Ludwig von Mises and the frequency interpretation', *Quarterly Journal of Austrian Economics*, 10 (1), 3–21.

Hoy, M., Livernois, J., McKenna, C., Rees, R. and Stengos, T. (2001), *Mathematics for Economics* (Cambridge, MA: MIT Press).

Hülsmann, J. G. (1996), 'Free Banking and the Free Bankers', *Review of Austrian Economics*, 9 (1), 3–53.

Hummel, J. R. (1990), 'National Goods versus Public Goods: Defense, Disarmament, and Free Riders', *Review of Austrian Economics*, 4, 88–122.

Hutt, W. H. (1956), 'The Yield of Money Held', in M. Sennholz (ed.), *On Freedom and Free Enterprise: Essays in Honor of Ludwig von Mises* (Princeton, NJ: Van Nostrand), 196–216.

Kim, O. and Walker, M. (1984), 'The Free Rider Problem: Experimental Evidence', *Public Choice*, 43, 3–24.

Kirzner, I. M. (1988), 'The Economic Calculation Debate: Lessons for Austrians', *The Review of Austrian Economics*, 2, 1–18.

Kirzner, I. M. (1992), *The Meaning of Market Process* (London: Routledge).

Klein, P. G. (2008a), 'The Mundane Economics of the Austrian School', *Quarterly Journal of Austrian Economics*, 11 (3), 165–87.

Kvasnicka, M. (2008), 'Rothbard's Welfare Theory: A Critique', *New Perspectives on Political Economy*, 4 (1), 41–52.

Lachmann, L. M. (1986), *The Market as an Economic Process* (Oxford: Basil Blackwell).

Lange, O. (1936/7), 'On the Economic Theory of Socialism', *Review of Economic Studies*, 4, 53–71; *Review of Economic Studies*, 5, 132–42.

Lavoie, D. (1985), *Rivalry and Central Planning: The Socialist Calculation Debate Reconsidered* (Cambridge: Cambridge University Press).

Leach, J. (2003), *A Course in Public Economics* (Cambridge: Cambridge University Press).

Leeson, P. T. and Subrick, J. R. (2006), 'Robust Political Economy', *Review of Austrian Economics*, 19 (2–3), 107–11.

Machaj, M. (2007), 'Market Socialism and the Property Problem', *Quarterly Journal of Austrian Economics*, 10 (4), 257–80.

Malkin, J. and Wildavsky, A. (1991), 'Why the Traditional Distinction between Public and Private Goods Should Be Abandoned', *Journal of Theoretical Politics*, 4 (3), 255–78.

McNutt, P. (1999), 'Public Goods and Club Goods', in B. Bouckaert and G. De Geest (eds.), *Encyclopedia of Law and Economics* (Cheltenham, UK: Edward Elgar Publishers and Belgium: University of Ghent).

Mises, R. (1957), *Probability, Statistics and Truth* (New York: Dover Publications).

Mises, L. (1980) [1912], *Theory of Money and Credit* (Indianapolis: Liberty Classics).

Mises, L. (1990) [1920], *Economic Calculation in the Socialist Commonwealth* (Auburn, AL: Ludwig von Mises Institute).

Mises, L. (1996) [1949], *Human Action* (4th ed. revised, San Francisco: Fox and Wilkes).

Mueller, D. C. (1996), *Constitutional Democracy* (Oxford: Oxford University Press).

Musgrave, P. B. and Musgrave, R. A. (1980), *Public Finance in Theory and Practice* (London: McGraw-Hill).

Netzer, D. (1952), 'Toll Roads and the Crisis in Highway Finance', *National Tax Journal*, 5 (2), 107–19.

Nozick, R. (1974), *Anarchy, State, and Utopia* (New York: Basic Books).

O'Driscoll, G. P., Jr. and Rizzo, M. J. (1996) [1985], *The Economics of Time and Ignorance* (New York: Routledge).

Olson, M. (1971) [1965], *The Logic of Collective Action: Public Goods and the Theory of Groups* (Cambridge, MA: Harvard University Press).

Ostrom, E. (1990), *Governing the Commons: The Evolution of Institutions for Collective Action* (Cambridge: Cambridge University Press).

Reynolds, M. O. (1998), 'Impossibility of Socialist Economy, or, a Cat Cannot Swim the Atlantic Ocean', *The Quarterly Journal of Austrian Economics*, 1 (2), 29–43.

Robbins, L. (1935), *An Essay on the Nature and Significance of Economic Science* (2nd ed., London: Macmillan).

Roemer, J. E. (1994), *A Future for Socialism* (Cambridge: Harvard University Press).

Rothbard, M. (1956), 'Toward a Reconstruction of Utility and Welfare Economics', in M. Sennholz (ed.), *On Freedom and Free Enterprise: Essays in Honor of Ludwig von Mises* (Princeton, NJ: Van Nostrand), 224–62.

Rothbard, M. (1960), 'The Mantle of Science', in. H. Schoeck and J. W. Wiggins (eds.), *Scientism and Values* (Princeton, NJ: D. Van Nostrand), 159–80.

Rothbard, M. (1970) [1962], *Man, Economy, and State: A Treatise on Economic Principles* (Los Angeles: Nash Publishing).

Rothbard, M. (1973a), 'Value Implications of Economic Theory', *The American Economist*, 17, 35–39.

Rothbard, M. (1981), 'The Myth of Neutral Taxation', *Cato Journal*, 1, 519–64.

Rothbard, M. (1982), 'Law, Property Rights, and Air Pollution', *Cato Journal*, 2 (1), 55–100.

Rothbard, M. (1991), 'The End of Socialism and the Calculation Debate Revisited', *Review of Austrian Economics*, 5 (2), 51–76.

Rothbard, M. (1998) [1982], *The Ethics of Liberty* (New York, NY: New York University Press).

Rothbard, M. (2004), *Man, Economy, and State: A Treatise on Economic Principles with Power and Market* (Scholar's ed., Auburn, AL: Ludwig von Mises Institute).

Salerno, J. T. (1990), 'Postscript: Why a Socialist Economy Is "Impossible"', in L. Mises, *Economic Calculation in the Socialist Commonwealth* (Auburn, AL: Ludwig von Mises Institute).

Salerno, J. T. (1993), 'Mises and Hayek Dehomogenized', *Review of Austrian Economics*, 6 (2), 113–46.

Samuelson, P. A. (1954), 'The Pure Theory of Public Expenditure', *Review of Economics and Statistics*, 36, 387–9.

Samuelson, P. A. (1955), 'Diagrammatic Exposition of a Theory of Public Expenditure', *Review of Economics and Statistics*, 37, 350–6.

Samuelson, P. A. and Temin, P. (1976), *Economics* (10th ed., New York: McGraw-Hill).

Sandler, T. (1997), *Global Challenges: An Approach to Environmental, Political, and Economic Problems* (Cambridge: Cambridge University Press).

Sandmo, A. (2000), *The Public Economics of the Environment* (Oxford: Oxford University Press).

Shackle, G. L. S. (1958), *Time in Economics* (Amsterdam: North Holland Publishing Company).

Shackle, G. L. S. (1968), *Expectations, Investment, and Income* (2nd ed., Oxford: Oxford University Press).

Smerk, G. M. (1965), *Urban Transportation: The Federal Role* (Bloomington, IN: Indiana University Press).

Stiglitz, J. E. (1989), 'Markets, Market Failures, and Development', *American Economic Review*, 79 (2), 197–203.

Stiglitz, J. E. (1994), *Whither Socialism?* (Cambridge, MA: MIT Press).

Taylor, F. M. (1929), 'The Guidance of Production in a Socialist State', *American Economic Review*, 19 (1), 1–8.

Willis, J. (2002), *Explorations in Microeconomics* (Redding, CA: North West Publishing).

Wisniewski, J. B. (2013a), 'Nonrivalness, Subjectivity and Capital: An Overview of the Austrian Theory of Club Goods', *New Perspectives on Political Economy*, 9 (1–2), 24–37.

Wisniewski, J. B. (2013b), 'Non-Excludability, Externalities, and Entrepreneurship: An Overview of the Austrian Theory of Common Goods', *Journal of Prices & Markets*, 1 (1), 57–68.

Wohlgemuth, M. (1997), 'Has John Roemer Resurrected Market Socialism?', *Independent Review*, 2 (2), 201–24.

3 Defense as a private good in a competitive order[1]

3.1 Non-excludability, externalities, and entrepreneurship: the application

Let us begin this chapter by supposing that our critic agrees with all the theoretical points elaborated earlier and thus admits that there ultimately appear to be no cogent purely economic arguments in favor of the validity of the neoclassical theory of common goods, including its claim that the only effective way of producing law and defense is through a monopoly of force.

However, let us further suppose that our critic contends that adhering exclusively to economic arguments to the exclusion of broader issues of human psychology is not going to be conducive to the promotion of maximum efficiency in satisfying the wants of consumers. He might agree that if the members of a given community are unwilling to contribute voluntarily to the production of law and defense mechanisms as sizeable as those existing under a monopoly of force (i.e., those including, for example, anti-ballistic missiles and nuclear weapons), or even willing, but not to the extent sufficient for overcoming the free-rider problem, then, admittedly, they should be thought of as not regarding such mechanisms as goods (or at least goods more desirable than the existing alternatives). And yet, in the previous chapter I conceded that not every consumer choice is satisfactory ex post. Our preferences change and we tend to learn from our mistakes, or from what we consider as such.

Consequently, it is possible that the members of a society voluntarily unarmed in the way described earlier would reconsider the production of sufficient protective resources after, say, being hit by a hostile nuclear weapon. However, the crucial point is that is it likely that the weapon in question would obliterate them, thus leaving them no chance to rectify the tragic mistake of not devoting sufficient funds to anti-nuclear defense. Now, says the critic, even though I agree that their pre-attack choices were Pareto-superior, it seems highly counterintuitive to claim that the post-attack outcome is optimal in any genuinely robust sense of the term. And yet, because the critic is willing to admit that it is optimal in the economic sense (after all, it came about as a result of voluntary transactions – i.e., positive-sum games), it appears that economic optimality might be an insufficient indicator of the desirability of particular outcomes.

Hence, it seems that some additional, extra-economic arguments are needed to counter what looks like a psychologistic, but intuitively plausible, objection. Perhaps the best way to respond is to ask the objector about the alternative he proposes. If he were to suggest that only coerced levies collected by a monopoly of force can provide the means for producing the amount of protective resources sufficient to forestall the kind of disasters mentioned earlier, he could be easily charged with the nirvana fallacy, that is, the fallacy of propounding an ideal solution to a problem existing in a non-ideal setting (Demsetz 1969). After all, if the generality of the members of a given community are supposed to be lighthearted and short-sighted enough to allow the disaster to occur, why should the wielders of the monopoly of force present in that community be presumed to be any more trustworthy in these regards?

But perhaps there is a better answer than this rhetorical question that can be given here, an answer consistent with our methodological principle of charity, which entails granting the coercive, monocentric institutions in any given scenario maximal robustness (in this case maximal prudence and far-sightedness) in order to give our subsequent arguments for voluntarism and polycentrism extra strength. In the context under discussion, it might be argued that even if the generality of the members of the community in question lack the public-spiritedness present in the motivations of those who wield the local monopoly of force, this deficiency could be more than offset by the existence of profit incentives among the entrepreneurially minded inhabitants of the society, which would tap into the natural alertness of those people to find remunerative methods of excluding free riders, internalizing the relevant externalities, etc. (Kirzner 1973, 1997; Huerta de Soto 2010).

Furthermore, as was already indicated in the previous sections of this chapter, only unrestricted valuational and trade activities between the totality of consumers, producers, and entrepreneurs can produce an intersubjective, uniform scale of exchange value expressible in cardinal terms (i.e., the price system), which is a tool necessary to compare the potential monetary costs and benefits of any undertaking, thus allowing for efficient allocation of resources. In other words, no matter how selfless and diligent we assume the controllers of the monopoly of force to be, the organizational framework within which they operate by definition precludes them from being effective in carrying out their aims.

Moreover, even if we assume that the controllers of the monopoly of force are the most creative minds of the society, moving the production of law and defense into a competitive, polycentric environment would allow them to aggregate their creativity with that of the rest of entrepreneurially minded individuals, which would both increase the total sum of entrepreneurial creativity present in the productive sector and allow its fruits to be judged against the objective benchmark of consumer satisfaction. If, next to superior predictive skills and exceptional responsiveness to profit opportunities, we shall identify creativity as one of the defining characteristics of a successful entrepreneur (Schumpeter 1975, pp. 42–5), and the free market as the background against which this feature can develop and function most effectively, then the claim that voluntary, polycentric arrangements will not be able to deal with the free-rider problem appears implausible and quite presumptuous. As soon as we realize that excludability is not an inherent feature of any good or service (Malkin and Wildavsky 1991; Wildavsky 1994) but a function of entrepreneurial inventiveness, we should be able to see coercive preemption on the part of a monopoly of force with regard to any given productive activity as preventing the emergence of effective solutions rather than implementing the only viable solution. It seems very likely that in such contexts "there is nothing in principle to prevent excludability – there is only a lack of a past history of market operation in this area and the limited powers of imagination on the part of economists" (Block 1983, p. 14).

In fact, one could reverse the common goods argument for the desirability of a monopoly of force and contend that the phenomenon of free riding is not the reason for, but precisely the consequence of its existence. After all, it seems natural to suppose that if one is aware of one's free-rider status, this awareness might exert some mitigating influence on one's attempts to consume various ostensibly non-excludable goods and services without paying for them, because such activity might result in one's ostracization and exclusion from that part of society which plays by the rules. On the other hand, if any given good or service is "generally provided free and more or less indiscriminately to the citizens, it naturally follows that every individual – assured of the service – will try to shirk his taxes" (Rothbard 1956, p. 36). In other words, it might be argued that far from eliminating or even abating the free-rider problem, bringing a monopoly of force into the picture reinforces the problem in question by providing systematic, institutional incentives for the kind of parasitic activities that it allegedly tries to combat.

Another important point to be made in this context is that out of the interplay of the two entrepreneurial characteristics mentioned in the preceding paragraphs – namely, profit orientation and creativity – there emerges what might be half-jokingly called the theorem of the harmlessness of externalities. Just as the Coase theorem suggests that – absent excessive transaction costs[2] – any given marketable property title is going to end up in the hands of the person most able to derive monetary profits from its use (Coase 1960), it could be argued that this person is also going to be the one most skillful in eliminating profit-reducing externalities. In other words, if internalizing externalities is likely to increase significantly the profitability of a given enterprise, the businessman concerned is likely to find a way of doing this. If, on the other hand, the costs of such an operation can be expected to outweigh the anticipated profits, it is likely that the losses associated with the presence of free riders are small enough not to prevent the businessman from operating his enterprise prosperously.

Having made all of the preliminary remarks concerning the nature of entrepreneurship vis-à-vis the issues of exclusion of free riders and externality internalization in the generic context of business activity, let me now move to the more specific case of law and defense provision.

3.2 Short-range protection goods

How might private, voluntary, decentralized protective arrangements look? Again, as in the case of my analysis of these amenities in the context of their putative non-rivalness, let me start by emphasizing the fact that protective and legal services cannot be treated as a homogeneous lump and that their different categories should be thought of as facing different facets of the ostensible problem posed by non-excludability. I shall analyze these distinct categories in turn.

To be sure, there appears to be no relevant difficulty in the context of providing protective services designed so as to be restricted to specific households. A specific individual (or group of individuals) contracting with a private firm for protecting his life and property does not seem to generate any noticeable spillover effects.[3] At most, one might argue that when a given household is closely surrounded by other households (as in an apartment building or a row of terraced houses), some of the inhabitants of the latter could conceivably risk not buying the services of any protection agency in the hope that, if targeted by criminals, they could count on their neighbors sending their contracted protectors to their rescue. Such a claim might seem plausible insofar as it does not presuppose any angelic benevolence on the part of the free riders' neighbors, but only a mundane, self-interested concern for keeping one's surroundings free of dangerous incidents (both for reasons of personal comfort and residential prestige). In fact, it appears quite intuitive to expect that most people would call upon their protection agencies if they noticed that something unsavory is happening in their neighbor's house.

However, it is equally intuitive to expect that one is not going to undertake the risk of depending solely on one's neighbor's immediate interventions. Anticipatory free riding of the kind just described differs sharply from that of the kind usually discussed by common goods theorists. In the latter case the free rider can be properly characterized as hiding behind her neighbor's back. But in the former case it is the neighbor who stands behind the so-called free rider's back, while the free rider hopes that he is going to attack her possible oppressors from this backline position. Or, to rely on another, more institutionally oriented example, the latter case corresponds to the situation of a welfare recipient, who can be said to free-ride on the work of the employed, whereas the former case corresponds to the situation of a resident of a country with no welfare system who quits his job and enters self-imposed poverty in the hope that his actions are going to prompt the establishment of such a system. To be sure, the former is a widespread, theoretically explained (e.g., Mises 1951, pp. 475–8; Hoppe 1989b, ch. 4), and empirically recorded (e.g., Murray 1994; Niskanen 1996; Bradley and Rector 2010) phenomenon, but the analysis of and evidence for the latter is lacking. Hence, I believe there are sufficient reasons for dismissing the putative spillover effects of the kind mentioned earlier as non-existent.

3.3 Mid-range protection goods

Let us now turn to the possibly more challenging issue of effective private provision of what might be called mid-range protection goods and services – that is, street patrols and surveillance cameras in public use areas. Here, it could be claimed, the free-rider problem becomes much more pronounced, up to the point of actually threatening the profitability of supplying such amenities. After all, extending the ambit of protection to the area which one neither inhabits permanently nor uses to store one's property might be said to generate a kind of bonus – something highly convenient, but not always necessary. By the same token, however, this bonus becomes easily exploitable by free riders. It should also be added that in such contexts the most potentially pernicious group of free riders is likely to consist not of "outsiders", that is, individuals external to the community, who never thought of contributing to its defense and thus just happen to enjoy a free privilege as they pass through it, but of "insiders", that is, people who have a self-interest in keeping their community safe, but may nonetheless decide to risk shirking their unwritten social duties and consequently burden their neighbors with the entire cost of fulfilling them. No further comments are needed to realize that such an arrangement can plausibly result in a classic "tragedy of the commons" (Hardin 1968). Let us consider in turn a few proposals on how to prevent it from happening.

One way of internalizing the relevant externalities could consist in the use of restrictive covenants. As Block (1983, p. 13) puts it: "people could simply refuse to sell their homes (or rent their apartments) to those who would not agree, and also hold all future owners to agree, to a contract calling for payments to a defense company". However, it might be argued that this approach in a sense already presupposes the solution to the problem that it aims to address, thus only pushing it one level up. In other words, it could be said that this proposal assumes that a given community was created either by a single developer who entered a contract with a private protection agency and hence is in a position to oblige every newcomer in the community to honor this contract, or that it was started by a group of individuals who concurred in advance with regard to their attitude towards communal safety and obliged one another (as well as any prospective subsequent owners of their houses) to enter individual contracts with a given protection agency (or agencies). And yet, it is certainly conceivable that the original founders of a given community may fail to solve this kind of coordination problem, which might result in some of them trying to free-ride on the defense services bought by others. In such cases the idea of establishing restrictive covenants seems hardly realizable. In sum, although by no means without merit, the proposal in question could be reasonably criticized by a supporter of the monocentric-coercive solution as likely to be applicable in fewer cases than his own alternative. Let us then move to other pertinent suggestions complementary to the one just described.

It might be argued that the reason why protection services such as street patrols are seen as non-excludable in the first place is because they operate in non-excludable areas. If roads and pavements were private, the problem would disappear, because private property is exclusive.[4] However, the crucial question to ask in this context is: Would road owners be willing to contract with protection agencies? On the one hand, it would seem that it would be in the interest of every road owner to make his property as safe as possible, because otherwise he might lose customers to his competitors. But on the other hand, it seems possible that unlike the regular residents and users of the buildings on a given road, casual passersby (especially those not on foot) may be more willing to accept the risk of relying exclusively on self-defense than to pay regular contributions for the maintenance of professional protection services in the areas which they visit only occasionally. After all, it appears to me that most people would find it less problematic to have to occasionally walk (let alone drive) through a dodgy neighborhood or a dark park than to co-finance patrols in such areas on a permanent basis. Hence, paradoxical as it may seem at first glance, the road owners who would offer only minimal or no protection to their customers might possibly be able to undersell those whose offers are more comprehensive in this respect. Consequently, in order to supply themselves with the requisite level of professional protection, the permanent residents of any given area would have to shoulder the entire burden of financing appropriate services. This, in turn, may well make the free-rider problem return with a vengeance.

In fact, even in isolated communities with no thoroughfares, whose roads are likely to be used by their permanent residents only, an infrastructure provider who would not require its users to pay for its protection could attempt to undersell those of his competitors who would have such a requirement. Consequently, if his offer managed to initially attract at least a few potential free riders, the per capita cost of the alternative bundled offer (infrastructure plus protection) would immediately go up, possibly triggering a snowball effect whose result would be the conversion of ever more members of the community to the free-rider attitude.[5] Because exclusion appears prima facie much easier in the case of infrastructure services than in the case of protection services, the previously mentioned business strategy should not be considered untenable.

At this point, it is worthwhile to notice that there exists a "thinner" way in which the owners of roads might cooperate with protection agencies – not in the sense of requiring their customers to pay an additional premium for defense provision, but in the sense of legally allowing the employees of protection agencies to do either or both of the following: 1) randomly stop the users of a given road, check whether they are insured with any protection agency, and collect fines from those found to be free riders or 2) collect fines from those found to be free riders after being rescued from criminal situations on the road. However, as promising as these thinner exclusionary methods may seem, one could again argue that they would be effective only to the extent that those using them would not be undersold by their competitors who would promise their customers not to burden them with such inconveniences.

Perhaps the last thing to be mentioned in this context is that because private patrols would be a positive externality[6] for the road owners, the latter would be very unlikely to charge the patrollers for using their roads. By the same token, protection agencies might threaten to leave a given area if the local road owners do not start cooperating with them (i.e., require their clients to pay a defense premium). As we noted earlier, such a threat should not necessarily bother the owners of thoroughfares. It would probably be more effective with regard to pressuring the owners of roads in isolated, mostly residential communities. However, it appears that even in those cases road owners would ultimately retain a greater bargaining power than protection agencies. After all, by refusing to operate in a given area, a protection agency effectively removes itself from the local market for defense services, which need not prevent the local infrastructure provider from sustaining his business. This is because in a modern economy one can hardly live without modern transport infrastructure, but one can live without patrolled transport infrastructure. Thus, it seems likely that even in the previously mentioned cases the protection agency would be unable to "threaten" the road owner(s) into cooperation and would have to continue operating in its local area without being able to utilize the excludable character of road infrastructure to counter the pernicious influence of free riders.

In sum, the set of solutions based on road privatization, although arguably capable of alleviating or even eliminating the free-rider problem under certain favorable conditions, nevertheless does not seem to be specifically relevant to the worry in question. In other words, rather than solving it, the previously mentioned proposals seem to merely shift it to a different, not necessarily more comfortable level. In the case under discussion they only serve to make us realize that the mentality of road owners vis-à-vis free riding need not be in any appropriate sense different from that of individual inhabitants of any given community. Let us then move to discussing an altogether different set of solutions.

Obviously, it is not only in the interest of the 'honest' members of the community to deal effectively with free riders. It is equally in the interest of the protection agency serving the former, because too much free riding may ultimately cause even its existing customers to give up on paying for protection. Hence, let us for a moment shift our attention from the exclusionary actions and methods that could be undertaken by the members of the community (or by those who provide it with apparently more easily excludable communal services) to those that might be utilized by their protection agencies.

One of these methods might be for "the defense company . . . [to] announce that those who had not paid for [the] service would [not] be protected by its personnel" (Block 1983, p. 13). The information contained in this announcement might seem self-evident, but one should not underestimate the psychological effects that such reminders of the obvious might have on the attitude of free riders. After all, in such cases the stake is their health or even life. Thus, I think it is fair to say that these kinds of situations are qualitatively different from those involving other, perhaps more familiar examples of free riding, such as overgrazing a common meadow or waiting for one's neighbors to renovate the façade of one's apartment building. In the scenario under consideration, what the free rider stands to lose is the precondition of pursuing any further goals, including those which might possibly be attained by means of free riding.

Let us now list the alternatives facing him and his neighbors,[7] as well as their likely outcomes: 1) If from the very start neither he nor his neighbors pay for defense services, it indicates that none of them are interested in protection; the initial situation in which they are all free riders seems impossible, because one is unlikely to become a free rider unless he realizes the existence of some attractive externalities to exploit in the first place. 2) If he does not pay but his neighbors do, then his fate remains very precarious as long as this practice continues. After all, his neighbors, dismayed by the existing situation, might decide to change the nature of their protection contracts (e.g., restrict the protected area to their households or travel in the company of personal bodyguards instead of having them patrol the streets) or leave the community altogether. Our free rider has to weigh the benefit of (at least temporarily) living in a surrounding made safe by someone else against the danger of being suddenly left on one's own in a very dangerous territory. Because we are treading the waters of psychology here, there, of course, is no logically watertight proof that any given potential free rider is always going to conclude that such transitory gains are unworthy of pursuing given the attendant risks, but I believe this is what follows from the commonsense perspective of psychological probability.

A parallel argument can be deployed to illustrate the excludability of another supposedly common good: lighthouses. Free riding on the service provided by a lighthouse always puts a non-paying ship owner at the risk that at any moment he can be suddenly left in utter darkness, thus facing the prospect of either a deadly crash or desperate calling for help (Block and Barnett II 2009, p. 3), both alternatives being clearly more costly than contributing one's share to the upkeep of the lighthouse.[8]

In sum, the payoff matrix informally sketched earlier suggests that for every reasonably prudent, rationally self-interested person option 2) is worse than option 3), where he pays but his neighbors do not, because in the latter scenario it is his neighbors who stand to gain less from free riding than they stand to lose from being unexpectedly and completely deprived of protection, whereas his own safety is pretty much guaranteed. Furthermore, if, in view of the preceding arguments, we assume that a reasonably prudent, rationally self-interested person is much more likely to be a payer than a free rider, a community composed of such people, whose individual choices would be option 3), would collectively (and spontaneously) implement option 4), where everybody pays and hence the phenomenon of free riding is non-existent.

Furthermore, it is worthwhile to notice in this context that shirking payments to one's private protection agency is in every relevant respect similar in consequences to shirking payments to a monopoly of force – in the former case one risks being denied defense services and being left at the mercy of criminals, whereas in the latter case one risks being legally expropriated and imprisoned. In both cases there are possibilities to free-ride and the associated dangers. And yet, it is not the case that the monopolies of force that we all know to exist show any signs of imminent collapse under the burden of free riding. Why should it then be any different with private defense companies? In fact, because private defense companies could not, unlike the monopolies of force, externalize the costs of compensating for the actions of free riders onto their paying customers without discouraging the latter's support (Hoppe 1999, pp. 29, 42), they would naturally have a much greater incentive to identify free riders and desist from providing them with their services as quickly as possible.

Given today's advanced technology, this appears by no means an insurmountable task. For example, the clients of any given protection agency could be equipped with small, portable sensors. This way, whenever a patrol car would notice that someone is assaulted on the street, its crew could immediately determine whether the victim emits an appropriate signal and hence whether she qualifies to receive their help. At this point, the ex post method of actually refusing defense services to free riders in need, complementary to the ex ante method of announcing in advance that this is precisely how non-payers are going to be treated, comes into play. In fact, it seems plausible that the "shock value" of the former method would far exceed that of the latter – free riders would likely be much better disciplined by learning that one of their ilk was mugged in broad daylight just as a private police car happened to pass by than by simply being notified that this is the kind of danger they face as long as they refuse to contribute. Of course, any given defense company may occasionally come to the rescue of a free rider in order to show good will and add a charitable twist to its reputation, but obviously none of them can afford to do this too often, because, as was mentioned before, it is in their interest to leave non-payers in the state of permanent precariousness, thus providing them with a definite incentive to start contributing.

Moreover, it has to be noticed that the paying clients of any given protection agency have a strong incentive to help their defenders identify free riders, and subsequently ostracize them in order to (peacefully) force them to either leave the community or start paying their premiums (Ostrom 1990). Such ostracism could take the form of, for instance, refusing to enter in any business transactions with them, including the sale of food, clothing, electricity, and other basic amenities. It appears plausible to conclude that faced with the prospects of becoming virtual hermits and living in the state of primitive autarky, most free riders would join the ranks of honest payers. We should note here that to the extent the majority of people in any given territory genuinely desire having their communal space professionally protected, they are going to consider the payoff from not ostracizing free riders smaller than the payoff from refusing to do any business with them and thus non-violently persuading them to start paying protection premiums. Hence, in the context under consideration there should not be any collective action problems associated with organizing a unanimous and persistent boycott of the offending individuals (Benson 1993; Greif, Milgrom and Weingast 1994; Stringham 2003).

What is more, in a polycentric, competitive environment the payers are likely to be much more eager to engage in such actions than they would be under a monopoly of force, because in the former scenario it is clear that free riders are cheaters who attempt to benefit at the expense of others. On the other hand, their "counterparts" from the latter scenario (i.e., tax resisters) only strive to keep what they consider to be their rightful property, without by the same token trying to parasitize on the contributions of others, because they do not regard the services provided by such contributions as goods in the first place. Consequently, taxpayers often feel sympathy for them and, far from entertaining the thought of subjecting them to ostracism, they actually get inspired to emulate their actions (Adams 1998, p. 190; Ackerman and Duvall 2000, pp. 61, 75, 94–5).

One can sometimes encounter claims that it is not just protection that is supposedly non-excludable, but also the associated positive phenomena of deterrence and incarceration of criminals. Here is a typical comment to that effect:

> [A]n important part of the service provided by public police and systems of criminal justice generally is to deter potential violators from harming people. And this deterrence is an indivisible nonexcludable good to neighbors and visitors. . . . In addition to deterrence, there may be the benefits that follow from incarceration of the thief – namely, incapacitation – benefits that are also indivisible and nonexcludable.
>
> (Morris 1998, pp. 60–1)

It seems to me that such assertions can be countered on grounds of both praxeology and thymology, the former term meaning the logical analysis of the phenomenon of human action and the latter meaning the introspective study of "the content of human thoughts, judgments, desires and actions" (Mises 1985, p. 266).[9] The former discipline deduces and describes the logically necessary features of the application of scarce means to specific ends, whereas the latter focuses on historical understanding of the past value scales of specific individuals (or groups of individuals) and attempts to use the resulting data to predict heuristically those value scales' future shape.

As I have already repeatedly mentioned, if one refrains from paying for a given good or service and shows no other signs of being interested in it, no sound economic argument can be made for the claim that he in fact benefits from its provision and thus should be penalized as a free rider. Consequently, if one refuses to contribute voluntarily to the upkeep of a monopoly of force, whose actions can be deemed to generate benefits stemming from deterring and incarcerating criminals, then, praxeologically speaking, the coerced contributor is the last person to whom the said benefits could be imputed.

But next to the pure logic of action, the commonsensical understanding of the motives that impel people to safeguard their security suggests that there is nothing indivisible or non-excludable about the goods just mentioned. For instance, the fact that people possess and carry around private arms might be considered to provide precisely the same kind of deterrent effect as the one supplied by "public police". It seems scarcely plausible to assume that such individuals think along the lines of: Why should I buy a gun and thus scare away criminals from the area where I live if I can wait for my neighbor to do the same thing? On the contrary, they are often so eager to provide themselves with private, personal protection that the monopolies of force wishing to disarm them resort to introducing all sorts of regulations on the use of and access to guns.

Likewise, describing the benefits flowing from incarcerating criminals as non-excludable implausibly assumes that one's willingness to free-ride on the atmosphere of safety created by the contributions of others is stronger than one's fear that in the absence of appropriate penal institutions free-roaming criminals are likely enough to target him (which is an observation very similar in its structure and character to that made in the context of the provision of lighthouse services).

In sum, the praxeological insights concerning the notion of demonstrated preference, as well as the thymological considerations of what is psychologically plausible, seem as effective in countering the claim that deterrence and incarceration of criminals are common goods as they are in answering the contention that protection per se belongs to the same category.

3.4 Long-range protection goods

Let us now move to the possibly most challenging facet of the topic under discussion: the provision of what might be called long-range or large-scale protection goods and services, such as anti-ballistic missiles and deterrent nuclear weapons. Here, it would seem, the free-rider problem could assume potentially insurmountable proportions. And yet, I believe there are good reasons to regard this particular context as not qualitatively or even quantitatively more difficult to handle than the ones already tackled in this chapter. Let me discuss these reasons in turn.

For a start, let us recall briefly the set of standard arguments advanced by the authors working within the tradition of classical liberalism in favor of the polycentric, competitive, free enterprise system of economic organization: 1) the incentive argument (Smith 1976) (the profit motive promotes effectiveness, competition brings down prices and enhances quality); 2) the voluntariness argument (Say 2001) (voluntary transactions, as opposed to the coercive ones, never injure the productive forces aimed at satisfying the demand of customers); 3) the calculation argument (Mises 1990, 1996, part 3) (without private property rights in factors of production cost accounting and hence rational allocation of resources becomes impossible); 4) the knowledge argument (Hayek 1945, 1948) (only a decentralized system consisting of a multitude of independent decision-making units can make use of the relevant knowledge associated with specific circumstances of time and place); and 5) the capital accumulation argument (Böhm-Bawerk 1890) (when private property rights are secure, people have an incentive to save more, which allows for funding capital investments and more roundabout processes of production, resulting in higher productivity). A sole classical liberal, Gustave de Molinari (1977), consistently insisted that these arguments are just as applicable to the area of law and defense provision as they are to the production of any other good or service.

Thus, even if, in accordance with the adopted methodological principle of charity, we grant the supervisors of any given monopoly of force perfect motivations, perfect knowledge, and sufficiently low time preference (hence immunizing them against points 1, 4, and 5 from the list), the remaining points tip the balance of quality in favor of the voluntary, decentralized alternative. This has significant further consequences.

First, the system envisioned by classical liberals can be plausibly predicted to be, other things being equal, much more peaceful and economically prosperous than its monocentric, coercive counterpart. Its peacefulness can be inferred to stem from the fact that interpersonal interactions taking place within it employ primarily economic rather than political means (Oppenheimer 1922). This is because such a system minimizes the opportunities to externalize the costs of one's aggressive behavior onto others and perpetuates in its participants the awareness that peace is a necessary precondition of frugality, mutual trust, confidence in investing, eagerness for continued hard work, and other psychological traits characteristic of the members of well-off societies. Its prosperity, on the other hand, derives from the fact that the traits just mentioned can be successfully utilized in the institutional framework allowing for capital accumulation, cost accounting, unobstructed decision making, and quick transmission of relevant information.

Consequently, a territory whose inhabitants are animated by classical liberal principles is unlikely to pose a military threat to neighboring areas, but it is likely to be a very lucrative trade partner for them. To elaborate on the latter point, even though military conquest can gain one land and a slave labor force, such acquisitions are arguably much less valuable than opportunities to exchange goods, services, and ideas with representatives of highly developed civilizations. In sum, the characteristics of polycentric, competitive, free enterprise systems appear to make them very unlikely targets for war. Countries such as Switzerland and Liechtenstein, which may serve as plausible real-world approximations of the ideal type just described, seem to provide cogent historical and contemporary illustrations for these contentions.

One might object that not all wars, including the most expansive, total, and cruel ones, are motivated by the kind of economic rationality and cost–benefit calculations appealed to earlier. On the contrary, it could be argued that the most atrocious conflicts in human history were ideological in nature, spurred by forces such as nationalism, racism, and class envy. In view of this, could it not be convincingly suggested that an ideologically fundamentalist dictatorship rich with natural resources might attempt to launch an all-out suicide attack against an enclave of libertarian legal polycentrism?

It seems fair to agree that this is in fact a genuine possibility. However, it need not be thought of as particularly problematic, because for reasons enumerated in the preceding paragraphs the society in question is likely to be exceptionally efficient also in the area of self-defense (Tannehill and Tannehill 1970, pp. 129–31). The presence of a complex and extensive capital structure, entrepreneurial innovations, incentives to industriousness and diligence, means of rapidly coordinating decentralized decisions, and appraising their costs and benefits – all these features of competitive, free-enterprise–based communities can be plausibly argued to make their protective arsenal much more effective than the offensive arsenal of ideologically driven, militant collectivist dictatorships.

One might reply by suggesting that I am begging the question, insofar as I am assuming that entrepreneurs in the communities under discussion can accumulate sufficient monetary resources to build and maintain the sort of enormously costly devices that are usually financed out of coercive levies extracted from the vast majority of individuals employed in the private sector of a given economy. Is it reasonable to conclude that the clientele of such entrepreneurs can be equal in size to the group of non-voluntary contributors who provide for the expenses in question under monopolies of force? In other words, am I not presupposing rather than proving that the free-rider problem can be effectively solved under the conditions I envisage?

I believe that there is at least one good reason why this should not be thought of as an unargued presupposition. Just as in the case of smaller-scale or shorter-range protection goods and services, I think that the amenities constitutive of what is known today as "national defense" could be provided efficiently under polycentric, voluntary arrangements primarily thanks to the dual forces of positive and negative promotion.

By negative promotion I, of course, mean ostracism. How would it work in the context at hand? First, we need to realize that probably the most natural way of supplying the goods and services under consideration would consist in bundling them with their small-scale, more easily excludable counterparts (Long 1994), such as localized patrols and surveillance cameras. Furthermore, it is likely that in order to raise sufficient funds, the relevant companies would pool some of their earnings to finance the most costly elements of the overall defense structure and consequently profit from their operation (as well as be responsible for their maintenance) in proportion to their individual contributions. Alternatively, no pooling might take place, and cost-reducing cooperation between protection agencies might result from a simple overlap of profit opportunities on the defense market – if a given protection agency were to announce that it is going to bundle its more "local" services with the production of bombers, it would be an immediate profit signal for another agency of a similar sort that it is worthwhile to start building specially designed airports.

At this point one might immediately raise the objection that those protection agencies that would restrict their services to the local level could attempt to undersell those that would make their offer a bundle of short-range and long-range amenities. This is where the use of ostracism comes into play. It seems probable that companies of the former kind could find themselves a sufficiently sizeable niche to be able to operate profitably and survive in the longer term, but it is questionable whether that would be an optimal business policy for them to pursue, because insofar as the majority in a given society wishes to have a properly functioning national defense, such a niche would be heavily ostracized. In other words, the clients of "local-only" agencies would likely be cut off from all kinds of social and business relations with other members of their community, condemning themselves to living either in the state of primitive self-sufficiency or in a ghetto of inveterate non-contributors. Likewise, not wishing to join the ranks of such pariahs, individual buyers of protection services should have an incentive to ostracize the local-only agencies and hence successively push them out of the market. The same incentive would plausibly apply to the companies offering bundled protection goods inasmuch as that they would refuse to have any reciprocal, mutually beneficial agreements with their free-riding counterparts.

Of course, it should be added in this context that the method of ostracism is effective only insofar as those worthy of social disapprobation can be sufficiently easily identified. This, however, should not be thought of as much of a problem. If we assume that contributors to national defense would normally display some kind of sufficiently complex, non-counterfeitable signs (issued, presumably, by "full-blooded" protection agencies or their associations) on their houses or cars, indicating that they paid their share of the common costs, it follows that in such an environment it would be very easy to identify non-contributors. Moreover, low contribution rates within a given area would likely signal to others that the local "human capital" is not of a particularly high quality, which would result in bringing down the local property values and further discourage any outside entrepreneurs from interacting with the inhabitants of the area in question, expanding their businesses to it, etc. Hence, widespread free riding, instead of increasing the personal wealth of the members of a recalcitrant community, would probably lead to it becoming an impoverished ghetto, voluntarily cut off from all the benefits associated with the division of labor, capital accumulation, and the spirit of entrepreneurship.

Positive promotion, on the other hand, could consist of, for instance, the producers of various straightforwardly excludable goods voluntarily contributing to the production of supposedly non-excludable, long-range protection goods in order to build their market reputation as maximally consumer friendly, acquire an image of public-mindedness, etc. This, of course, would be more than likely to substantially increase their revenue, as well as create a recognizable and trustworthy brand, capable of overcoming the supposed "market failure" of asymmetric information between buyers and sellers (Akerlof 1970). A natural corollary of the development of such brands would be the emergence of informal 'grapevine' knowledge among satisfied customers and the tendency to pass it on to ever-wider circles of new potential clients (DiLorenzo 2011). Alerting the public to the fact that the producers in question participate in funding national defense would most probably be communicated through advertisements. The same means of disseminating reliable market information could also be used to denounce free riders and their patrons. Again, one might claim that such outlets could equally well generate fraudulent accusations, but the constant counterargument here is that any company that would engage in such a practice would by the same token become untrustworthy with respect to promoting its own products, hence magnifying the problem of asymmetric information and consequently damaging its own revenue.

Another method of positive promotion of one's company and its products that could be utilized by the agencies offering bundled protection goods could consist in offering various free extra services to their clients, services such as lessons in the use of personal weapons, which, upon completion, might entitle the successful trainees to lower personal and property insurance premiums. Finally, because the other side of the free-rider problem (attempting to benefit without contributing) is the so-called assurance problem (the uncertainty of whether free riding will not prevent accumulating sufficient funds to complete a given enterprise in the first place, hence making one's contribution to it a waste of money), one other important aspect of enticing customers to patronize only the companies contributing to national defense could be to offer guarantees to refund one's premiums if funds sufficient to create and maintain the necessary capital are not collected (Schmidtz 1991).

Let us conclude the present chapter by discussing the question of whether the social model just described would suffer from private protection agency infighting. To put it briefly, the issue is as follows – if various individuals contract for defense with different, profit-seeking companies, what should prevent the companies under consideration from overstepping their proper function and attempting to increase their revenue through initiatory violence directed against their competitors and the clients thereof (Rand 1967, p. 335)? If this is a plausible scenario, then would not its logical culmination be the dreaded Hobbesian war of everyone against everyone (Hobbes 1991, p. 88), a condition thoroughly unconducive not only to the existence of efficient national defense, but also to personal safety in even the most local sense?

There are, in fact, a number of reasons to resist this train of thought. First, it should be borne in mind that in a competitive market for defense provision, unlike under a monopoly of force, no provider could externalize the costs of its aggressive actions onto non-clients. To be more specific, there is, of course, no logical impossibility in any given provider trying to do so, but under a system characterized by a widespread opposition to such practices, their occurrence would be met with immediate ostracism – both "active" and "passive" – of their perpetrators. By "passive" ostracism I refer to the fact that, out of fear of being identified with violence mongers, the previous customers of aggressive agencies would have an immediate incentive to stop patronizing them, lest they become cut off from any business and personal dealings with the rest of society or even targeted by retaliatory actions of other protection agencies. By the same token, the clients of non-aggressors[10] would have an immediate incentive to desist from interacting with those who continue to support aggressors, be it financially or ideologically. Those of them who would not do so would not only perpetuate their own insecurity, but would also risk being classified as indirect supporters of the violence committed by rogue agencies.

By "active" ostracism, on the other hand, I mean non-aggressors ganging up against aggressors in order to nip any outbreak of initiatory violence in the bud. Insofar as the sudden appearance of a rogue agency is a genuine possibility, peaceful agencies would likely contractually oblige themselves vis-à-vis their patrons to act, either individually or jointly, to eliminate any emerging threat as quickly as possible.[11] Such concerted reactions would plausibly be particularly effective to the extent that the companies in question would find it expedient to pool their funds in order to build and maintain the most costly of the relevant capital goods.

Could those allegedly temporary retaliatory alliances possibly lead to the emergence of a coercive military oligopoly and finally to the re-emergence of a territorial monopoly of force? If our starting point is a polycentric, competitive, entrepreneurial order, I find this scenario unlikely. This is because in such an environment the companies temporarily ganging up against aggressors would be aware that their customers know that their competitive advantage lies in being able to offer the kinds of services and amenities that of necessity would be completely unavailable under a monopoly of force. This, in turn, follows from the fact that coercive-monopolistic conditions by definition prevent such efficiency-enhancing entrepreneurial practices as price differentiation, diversification of goods and services, thoroughgoing specialization, rapid utilization of knowledge of specific time and place, etc. (DiLorenzo 1986). Moreover, and perhaps more importantly, in the environment envisaged in this chapter the companies in question would know that their customers will patronize only those protection agencies than are truly and properly protective rather than aggressive, that is, sufficiently unlikely to ever engage in what Frédéric Bastiat described as "legal plunder" (Bastiat 1998), that is, the use of monopolized force to enact non-consensual redistribution of pre-existing property titles. Were any attempts at legal plundering to be undertaken, the bulk of the society under discussion would probably revolt against the would-be coercive monopolists and engage them in a protracted civil conflict, which, regardless of its eventual outcome, would ruin the financial prospects of the aggressors.

Consequently, for profit-maximizing companies, initiating such a conflict would be a lose-lose strategy. I shall elaborate on the crucial role played by ideas and preferences in shaping the underlying institutional framework and its impact on the development of such events in Chapter 5.

Going back to the subject of potential agency infighting, it also has to be noted that initiating acts of aggression would require the aggressor to impose additional costs on his clients over and above those normally incurred to protect them. In other words, it would require the agency in question to start charging higher premiums for as long as its aggressive behavior would continue, with their level likely corresponding to the intensity of its attacks and the extent to which it would need to replenish its arsenal. This, of course, would temporarily require defensive agencies to raise their premiums as well in order to mount an effective counterattack (or a purely defensive response aimed at eventually draining the aggressor of funds). However, this does not imply that the actions of defensive agencies can be considered as equally expensive as those of aggressive agencies, because the former raise the price of their services only in those cases in which such a step is necessary to allow them to perform their contractually designated function (namely protection), whereas the latter do so whenever they feel that predation is likely to bring them more revenue or more psychological satisfaction than performing the function just mentioned. In other words, defensive agencies can raise their premiums reactively, but, unlike their aggressive counterparts, never proactively.[12]

Consequently, the clients of rogue agencies would have an immediate incentive to desist from patronizing their hitherto protectors not only out of fear of being identified and ostracized as aggressors, but also because being a client of a rogue agency would simply be much more expensive than being a client of a legitimate one (i.e., one true to its contractual obligations).

It could be suggested in this context that:

> A very large firm could afford to use force and fraud to at least a limited extent, because the breadth of its market would prevent the news of its

aggressive actions from reaching enough of its customers and competitors to do it serious damage.

(Tannehill and Tannehill 1970, p. 49)

However, as the authors quoted here immediately point out, because in a free enterprise system unmet consumer demand is responded to by profit-seeking individuals as quickly as possible, and because it seems obvious that there would always exist a demand for such vital information, collecting them and divulging them to the public would constitute a steady source of profits for enterprising journalists, investigators, news agencies, etc.

Hence, just as the problem of "asymmetric information" between buyers and sellers can be addressed by such market solutions as the development of brands, certification companies, quality assurance services, and product guarantees (Klein 1997), the specific kind of information asymmetry just mentioned would most likely be beneficially exploited by news agencies and their highly specialized investigative employees:

Not only inventions and medical and scientific discoveries would be news, so would any aggression or fraud, especially when committed by large and well-known companies. It's very hard to hide things from hotly competing newspapermen looking for a "scoop," not to mention the representatives of radio, television, movies, magazines, and the wire services.

(Klein 1997, p. 49)

In addition, it should be remembered that aggressors are always dependent on wealth creators for their existence, because the former do not create their own means of survival, but only parasitize on those created by the latter. That is why looting is always more risky than producing when it comes to earning a living. Of course, this risk is vastly reduced if any given looter can secure the obedience of those whose resources he loots, be it through intimidation, intellectual or emotional persuasion, promise of participation in the process of looting, or any other means. However, to the extent that the starting point of our analysis is a society that derives its wealth through productive measures – division of labor, accumulation of capital, and entrepreneurship – thus clearly acting on the belief in their efficacy and moral worth, it should be thought of as singularly unsusceptible to the methods of subjection mentioned earlier (Friedman 1989, pp. 156–9; Hummel 2001). Hence, far from securing for itself a steady source of easily extractable income, a rogue agency bent on establishing its rule over the society in question would not only get bogged down in a drawn-out, financially ruinous conflict, but, even if it were eventually to win it, it would by the same token destroy the wealth creators the control over whom it craved.

Let me conclude this section by illustrating the contentions made earlier with an empirical example. Even though as of today practically the whole inhabited world is controlled by territorial monopolies of force, which are supposed to provide law and order to the communities they exercise their authority over, people continue to patronize private protection agencies, hire bodyguards, and otherwise increase their personal security by the use of market means. Their reason for doing this is their concern that they cannot rely on the protection and legal services provided by coercive governmental monopolies, because the latter are not constrained by the profit-and-loss test and thus need not care about the quality and cost efficiency of their operations (or, for reasons associated with their inability to perform meaningful cost and benefit calculations, cannot be said to possess any means of caring about those aspects of their operations even if they genuinely wanted to).

But if coercive governmental monopolies need not (or cannot) care about the quality and cost efficiency of their operations, and thus cannot be expected to effectively intervene if a given individual's personal security is threatened, then it must be concluded that with regard to the relationship between themselves and their clients, private protection agencies operate under the conditions of practical anarchy. Hence, as the critics of the idea of a private law society would have it, they should be continually aggressing against one another, as well as against their clients, eventually destroying what started out as a purely voluntary industry.

However, the very fact that the market for private protection not only exists,[13] but thrives (Benson 1998), proves beyond doubt that no such financially ruinous intra-industry conflicts take place. There is, after all, no reason why they should, because the existence of the market in question hinges on the fact that, unlike extra-market entities such as territorial monopolies of force, private protection agencies can survive only if they manage to maintain their professional reputation, and this they can do only if they consistently refrain from engaging in acts of initiatory aggression. In other words, the very fact that people turn to private means to safeguard their security indicates that there exists, at least as far as their subjective assessment of the matter is concerned, an "anarchic" vacuum of law and order whenever these two goods are supplied exclusively by territorial monopolies of force. Furthermore, and even more importantly, it indicates that neither the vacuum in question nor anything worse than it is re-created on the market for private defense, even though, according to the critics of its viability, it operates under conditions perfectly ripe for violent conflict.

In sum, these considerations aim at demonstrating that the social model described in this chapter would not suffer from the problem of private protection agency infighting, primarily because such infighting would always be more costly than peaceful cooperation. This, however, obviously does not preclude the all-too-real possibility that various kinds of disputes and verbal conflicts would arise among the agencies under discussion. How such disputes would be resolved without degenerating into violence is a separate issue, the one to be addressed in the next chapter.

Notes

1 This chapter incorporates material from Wisniewski (2014a).
2 Another limiting condition not mentioned by Coase is the existence of sentimental value that the original owner might attach to his property, which could make him unwilling to sell it to more skillful entrepreneurs.

3 Other than perhaps the effects stemming from the fact that his personal security benefits all those eager to interact with him, be it on a commercial or on a social level. However, as I already remarked earlier, in this sense everybody benefits from the existence of everybody else, and it would be extremely implausible to argue that this might make individuals in general unwilling to interact with others until the latter pay for their security expenses. In fact, this would logically lead to paralyzing all human interaction.

4 There are, of course, many common doubts about the viability of full-scale road and highway privatization, associated with, for example, the ostensible problem of effective fee collection, the danger of being "imprisoned" by hostile road owners, etc. I do not think that any of these doubts are ultimately justified, but is it beyond the scope of this text to investigate them and propose corresponding solutions. For perhaps the most comprehensive treatment of these issues, see Block (2009).

5 For a related argument, see Roy Childs' (1977, p. 31) criticisms of Robert Nozick's (1974) conception of the minimal state. According to Nozick, the minimal state differs from the ultraminimal state insofar as it not only forcibly excludes all competition in the area of law and defense provision, but also extends its services to those who explicitly refuse to be its clients, and to that extent relies on redistributive taxation. Hence, it essentially allows its non-clients to free-ride on the services that its clients pay for. This, Childs contends, is bound to lead to more and more people turning from the minimal state's clients into free riders, ultimately leading to the inevitable bankruptcy of the institution in question. Even though the Nozickian minimal state differs from the protection agencies in my examples insofar as it is not only susceptible to free riding, but actually encourages it, I think that the parallel between the two cases is still strong and visible.

6 Here and throughout the rest of this chapter, I am using the term "externality" in a purely psychological, not economic, sense.

7 To be more accurate, by 'neighbors' I mean 'at least some of his neighbors' – after all, the proportions between the payers and the non-paying free riders within any given community may vary. For the sake of simplification, in my scenario the latter group is identified with its single representative.

8 Coase (1974) suggests that in the period from the mid-16th to the late 19th centuries lighthouse services in Britain were provided on a voluntary market basis, which might lead one to think that the self-enforcing incentive mechanism just described was at work there. However, Van Zandt (1993) and Bertrand (2006) doubt whether the underlying arrangements could be properly described as voluntary. Block and Barnett II (2009) side with these authors against Coase, but remind their readers that, as in every case of governmental preemption, these observations need not indicate that genuine free market arrangements would not usher in effective provision of the services under consideration.

9 For an exhaustive discussion of the relationship between these two terms, see Mises (1985, ch. 12).

10 By non-aggression I, of course, do not mean pacifism or non-violence of the Tolstoyan or Gandhian variety, but simply non-initiation of physical force or threat thereof against others, which does not preclude physical retaliation against others if they are the original attackers.

11 Although it is certainly possible that in the competitive order envisioned in this chapter there would also be specifically neutral agencies, which would not react to the appearance of rogue agencies unless directly attacked by them.

12 Unless a defense agency decides to increase its arsenal in anticipation of a rogue agency's attack. However, to the extent that such anticipation proves correct, this decision can be properly regarded as reactive. If, on the contrary, it turns out to be incorrect, the agency that made it will damage its reputation and will consequently have to lower its premiums in order to regain some of its competitive advantage. If it becomes known

to make wrong predictions routinely, it will sooner or later go bankrupt and disappear from the market.

13 And has existed since at least medieval times (Foldvary 1994).

Bibliography

Ackerman, P. and Duvall, J. (2000), *A Force More Powerful: A Century of Nonviolent Conflict* (New York: Palgrave Macmillan).

Adams, C. (1998), *Those Dirty Rotten Taxes: The Tax Revolts That Built America* (New York: Free Press).

Akerlof, G. A. (1970), 'The Market for Lemons: Quality Uncertainty and the Market Mechanism', *Quarterly Journal of Economics*, 84 (3), 488–500.

Bastiat, F. (1998) [1850], *The Law* (Irvington-on-Hudson, NY: Foundation for Economic Education).

Benson, B. L. (1993), 'The Impetus for Recognizing Private Property and Adopting Ethical Behavior in a Market Economy: Natural Law, Government Law, or Evolving Self-Interest', *Review of Austrian Economics*, 6 (2), 43–80.

Benson, B. L. (1998), *To Serve and Protect: Privatization and Community in Criminal Justice* (New York: New York University Press).

Bertrand, E. (2006), 'The Coasean Analysis of Lighthouse Financing: Myths and Realities', *Cambridge Journal of Economics*, 30, 389–402.

Block, W. (1983), 'Public Goods and Externalities: The Case of Roads', *Journal of Libertarian Studies*, 7 (1), 1–34.

Block, W. (2009), *The Privatization of Roads and Highways: Human and Economic Factors* (Lewiston, NY: Edwin Mellen Press).

Block, W. and Barnett, W., II (2009), 'Coase and Bertrand on Lighthouses', *Public Choice*, 140 (1–2), 1–13.

Böhm-Bawerk, E. (1890), *Capital and Interest* (London: Macmillan).

Bradley, K. and Rector, R. (2010), 'Confronting the Unsustainable Growth of Welfare Entitlements: Principles of Reform and the Next Steps', *Backgrounder*, 2427, retrieved from www.heritage.org/research/reports/2010/06/confronting-the-unsustainable-growth-of-welfare-entitlements-principles-of-reform-and-the-next-steps.

Childs, R. A., Jr. (1977), 'The Invisible Hand Strikes Back', *Journal of Libertarian Studies*, 1 (1), 23–33.

Coase, R. H. (1960), 'The Problem of Social Cost', *Journal of Law and Economics*, 3, 1–44.

Coase, R. H. (1974), 'The Lighthouse in Economics', *Journal of Law and Economics*, 17 (2), 357–76.

Demsetz, H. (1969), 'Information and Efficiency: Another Viewpoint', *Journal of Law and Economics*, 12 (1), 1–22.

DiLorenzo, T. (1986), 'Competition and Political Entrepreneurship: Austrian Insights into Public Choice Theory', *Review of Austrian Economics*, 2 (1), 59–71.

DiLorenzo, T. (2011), 'A Note on the Canard of "Asymmetric Information" as a Source of Market Failure', *Quarterly Journal of Austrian Economics*, 14 (2), 249–55.

Foldvary, F. (1994), *Public Goods and Private Communities* (Edward Elgar Publishing).

Friedman, D. (1989) [1973], *The Machinery of Freedom: Guide to a Radical Capitalism* (2nd ed., La Salle, IL: Open Court).

Greif, A., Milgrom, P. and Weingast, B. R. (1994), 'Coordination, Commitment, and Enforcement: The Case of the Merchant Guild', *Journal of Political Economy*, 102 (4), 745–76.

Hardin, G. (1968), 'The Tragedy of the Commons', *Science*, 162 (3859), 1243–8.

Hayek, F. A. (1945), 'The Use of Knowledge in Society', *American Economic Review*, 35, 519–30.

Hayek, F. A. (1948), *Individualism and Economic Order* (Chicago: University of Chicago Press).

Hobbes, T. (1991) [1651], *Leviathan: Cambridge Texts in the History of Political Thought* (Cambridge: Cambridge University Press).

Hoppe, H.-H. (1989b), *A Theory of Socialism and Capitalism* (Boston: Kluwer Academic Publishers).

Hoppe, H.-H. (1999), 'The Private Production of Defense', *Journal of Libertarian Studies*, 14 (1), 27–52.

Huerta de Soto, J. (2010), *Socialism, Economic Calculation and Entrepreneurship* (Edward Elgar Publishing).

Hummel, J. R. (2001), 'The Will to Be Free: The Role of Ideology in National Defense', *Independent Review*, 5 (4), 523–37.

Kirzner, I. M. (1973), *Competition and Entrepreneurship* (Chicago: University of Chicago Press).

Kirzner, I. M. (1997), 'Entrepreneurial Discovery and the Competitive Market Process: An Austrian Approach', *Journal of Economic Literature*, 35, 60–85.

Klein, D. B. (ed.) (1997), *Reputation: Studies in the Voluntary Elicitation of Good Conduct* (Ann Arbor: University of Michigan Press).

Long, R. T. (1994), 'Funding Public Goods: Six Solutions', *Formulations*, 2 (1).

Malkin, J. and Wildavsky, A. (1991), 'Why the Traditional Distinction between Public and Private Goods Should Be Abandoned', *Journal of Theoretical Politics*, 4 (3), 255–78.

Mises, L. (1951) [1936], *Socialism: An Economic and Sociological Analysis* (New Haven: Yale University Press).

Mises, L. (1985) [1957], *Theory and History: An Interpretation of Social and Economic Evolution* (Washington, DC: Ludwig von Mises Institute).

Mises, L. (1990) [1920], *Economic Calculation in the Socialist Commonwealth* (Auburn, AL: Ludwig von Mises Institute).

Mises, L. (1996) [1949], *Human Action* (4th ed. revised, San Francisco: Fox and Wilkes).

Molinari, G. (1977) [1849], *The Production of Security* (New York: Center for Libertarian Studies).

Morris, C. (1998), *An Essay on the Modern State* (Cambridge: Cambridge University Press).

Murray, C. (1994), *Losing Ground: American Social Policy, 1950–1980* (10th Anniversary ed., New York: Basic Books).

Niskanen, W. A. (1996), 'Welfare and the Culture of Poverty', *Cato Journal*, 16 (1), 1–15.

Nozick, R. (1974), *Anarchy, State, and Utopia* (Basic Books: New York).

Oppenheimer, F. (1922) [1914], *The State* (New York: B.W. Huebsch).

Ostrom, E. (1990), *Governing the Commons: The Evolution of Institutions for Collective Action* (Cambridge: Cambridge University Press).

Rand, A. (1967), *Capitalism: The Unknown Ideal* (New York: Signet).

Rothbard, M. (1956), 'Toward a Reconstruction of Utility and Welfare Economics', in M. Sennholz (ed.), *On Freedom and Free Enterprise: Essays in Honor of Ludwig von Mises* (Princeton, NJ: Van Nostrand), 224–62.

Say, J. (2001) [1836], *A Treatise on Political Economy: Or the Production, Distribution, and Consumption of Wealth* (New Brunswick, NJ: Transaction Publishers).

Schmidtz, D. (1991), *The Limits of Government: An Essay on the Public Goods Argument* (Boulder, CO: Westview Press).

Schumpeter, J. (1975) [1942], *Capitalism, Socialism and Democracy* (New York: Harper).

Smith, A. (1976) [1776], *An Inquiry into the Nature and Causes of the Wealth of Nations* (Indianapolis: Liberty Classics).

Stringham, E. P. (2003), 'The Extralegal Development of Securities Trading in Seventeenth Century Amsterdam', *Quarterly Review of Economics and Finance*, 43 (2), 321–44.

Tannehill, M. and Tannehill, L. (1970), *The Market For Liberty* (Lansing, MI: Self-Published).

Van Zandt, D. E. (1993), 'The Lessons of the Lighthouse: "Government" or "Private" Provision of Goods', *Journal of Legal Studies*, 22 (1), 47–72.

Wildavsky, A. (1994), 'Reply to Cornes and Sandler', *Journal of Theoretical Politics*, 6, 387–8.

Wisniewski, J. B. (2014a), 'Defense as a Private Good in a Competitive Order', *Review of Social and Economic Issues*, 1 (1), 3–35.

4   Law as a private good in a competitive order

4.1 Introduction

Fielding (1978), following Locke (1967), contends that the primary benefit of having the opportunity to submit one's disputes to an independent, impartial arbiter consists in being able to avoid entering destructive aggression-overcompensation cycles, whereby setting up oneself as a judge in one's own case and punishing the offending individual according to one's own estimate of the harm sustained is more than likely to be perceived by the punished party as disproportionately severe, thus triggering retaliation, which in turn might seem excessive to the original punisher, hence provoking another retaliatory action, and so on ad infinitum. If, on the contrary, a punitive verdict is to be passed by an independent third party, neither of the participants to the dispute can legitimately complain that it is biased in favor of either of them.

In contrast to Locke, however, Fielding, as well as all other theorists of polycentric legal order, claim that a territorial monopoly of force is in no position to fulfill the role of a reliable, impartial arbitrator. This is because, insofar as instead of accepting the Lockean theory of social contract as a faithful representation of actual social relationships in the world, one decides to subscribe to the more historically accurate "conquest theory of the state" (Gumplowicz 1899; Oppenheimer 1922; Nock 1935; Jouvenel 1949; Tilly 1985), one immediately realizes that no private disputants ever signed an explicit arbitration contract with the monopoly of force under which they live.

At this point one might suggest that all of them did in fact sign an implicit contract with the said institution due to the fact that they all use various "club" and "common" goods provided by it, such as road infrastructure and national defense. However, because the necessity of using these "goods" was forcibly imposed on them by the institution in question (i.e., they could neither choose to patronize a different provider of the services under discussion nor refuse to be their users or beneficiaries altogether), it could be plausibly argued that the implicit contract they supposedly signed was a forced contract, thus deprived of any legitimacy and bindingness. Moreover, in view of the observations contained in Chapter 2, it is debatable whether the ostensible "club" and "common" goods can be regarded as goods at all, or, even if they can, whether they can be meaningfully distinguished from what is usually considered private goods, whose alleged positive externalities rarely make their owners think of their potential beneficiaries as parties to implicit contracts of any sort.

These remarks bring to the fore the following questions: Is it possible that any given group of people of the size corresponding to that of the population of an average present-day nation-state would freely decide to patronize a single provider of legal services? And also, is it possible that only one provider of legal services would appear on the market? These two questions would have to be answered affirmatively if one were to defend the claim that, economically speaking, the legal environment created by a territorial monopoly of force could be voluntarily re-created in a fully contractual, free community. It certainly does not seem that such a happening should be thought of as a logical impossibility. However, numerous empirical studies demonstrate that it most probably never occurred in recorded economic history (Kolko 1963; Thierer 1994; DiLorenzo 1996; Long 2008a). In other words, according to the authors just mentioned, there have never existed any "natural" monopolies – every company exercising an exclusive control over a given area of the market must have gained it through a grant of special privilege given to it by the only true monopoly, namely, the territorial monopoly of force. Furthermore, there are several conceptual difficulties with the way in which "natural monopolies" are defined in the neoclassical tradition (Block 1977, 2008; Armentano 1978; Hoppe 1989b, ch. 9).

However, regardless of the details of the definition of the concept in question that we decide to use, one thing is certain – monopolies are universally acknowledged to be detrimental from the point of view of consumers and potential producers.[1] Hence, if a single provider of certain goods or services were to be voluntarily patronized by the totality of the inhabitants of a given area, it would not deserve to be branded with this negative appellation. This is why I remarked earlier that even if one is to regard the non-coercive emergence of a monopoly as a logical impossibility, the same cannot be said with respect to the non-coercive emergence of a single provider of any given good or service. And yet, even though I do not consider such an event to be logically impossible, I certainly think of it as very highly improbable. Thus, I would complement Fielding's contention that a territorial monopoly of force is in no position to fulfill the role of a reliable, impartial arbitrator with the claim that a voluntarily patronized "quasi-monopolist" would be very unlikely to be given this function either.

To answer the question why I think this would be the case, we need to elaborate on the issue of the origins of law – that is, the issue of what does law derive from and how one gets to know its content. Two prima facie conflicting responses are usually given in this context, which correspond fittingly to two distinct kinds of rationalism described by Hayek (1967, pp. 82–95), namely, constructive rationalism and critical rationalism.

According to the constructive rationalist conception of law, which I regard as further subdivisible into hard and soft varieties, law is a product of deliberate human design, created in order to attain the goals of its authors in a possibly predictable and systematic fashion. What I designate as its hard variety traces all discoverable order in human society to deliberate human design and expresses contempt for institutions that are not consciously designed. . . . In order to facilitate central planning towards deliberately chosen goals, it would give political authorities a broad discretionary power to organize and direct all social and economic activities and to circumscribe human freedom.

(Miller 1976, p. 384)

A relatively moderate version of this kind of legal order would be the one whose creators wish to legislate into existence an institutional framework capable of effective provision of public goods as conceived in the neoclassical tradition. Its more extreme counterpart might aim at producing in a centralized, political manner all sorts of goods usually regarded as private, and to that effect its authors might contemplate forcibly wresting all the means of production from the hands of private owners living under their jurisdiction. Because I already pointed out the weaknesses of the moderate version of the institutional arrangement in question, it is needless to say that I take them to apply a fortiori to all of its more extreme forms.

On the other hand, the soft variety of the constructive rationalist conception of law conceives of it as consisting of "formal legal rules clearly expressed, prospectively promulgated, and equally applied" (Stringham and Zywicki 2011, p. 293). Perhaps the best exemplification of this conception is the continental civil law model, statute based and codified rather than interpreted by judges. Its classical liberal form confines the role of legislation to establishing transparent and universal rules concerning the acquisition, exchange, and protection of property. In other words, it proposes minimum conscious institutional design to ensure maximum liberty in acting on one's intentions and integrating them with a spontaneously emergent order of voluntary, mutually beneficial exchanges of legitimate property titles (Hayek 1944, 1960). In view of this, I regard the classical liberal supporters of the legislative rule of law model as belonging to the group of legal constructive rationalists, despite the emphasis they put on the importance and robustness of undesigned institutions and spontaneous arrangements in other, extra-legal areas of social life.

In distinct contrast to the ideas presented in the preceding few paragraphs, the critical rationalist conception of law conceives of the legal system of any given community not as created by the monopoly of force that imposes itself on the community in question, but as contained in the customs, conventions, and traditions stemming from free, gradually evolving, and solidifying interactions and associations among its members (Hume 1740, Book III, p. 541; Leoni 1972). This particular conception, I would argue, can also be subdivided into hard and soft varieties. According to the hard one, the legitimate function of territorial monopolies of force is not to design bodies of rules specifying the norms of social cooperation and requiring the inhabitants of specific geographic areas to conform to them in their everyday behavior, but to discover such rules that preexist in the organically, evolutionarily grown social tissue and pass judicial verdicts based on them:

The basic source of social order, however, is not a deliberate decision to adopt certain common rules, but the existence among the people of certain opinions of what is right and wrong . . . Except where the political unit is created by conquest, people submit to authority not to enable it to do what it likes, but because they trust somebody to act in conformity with certain common conceptions of what is just. There is not first a society which then gives itself rules, but it is common rules which weld dispersed bands into a society.

(Hayek 1979, p. 33)

At this point I should return to justifying my claim that I consider it highly unlikely that any given community would voluntarily decide to patronize a single provider of arbitration services. The logical justification of this contention is quite simple – just as people all over the world are very diverse with respect to, for example, their culinary, sartorial, and artistic preferences, and thus prone to patronizing different food, clothing, and art providers, they are also diverse with regard to their unwritten legal and moral customs, their beliefs concerning justice and fairness, etc., which, in the absence of coercive legal monocentrism, should result in them using the services of different specialized arbitration agencies or various informal means of dispute resolution.[2]

In other words, a voluntarily patronized "quasi-monopolist" could appear and function only in a society thoroughly uniform in its adherence to a given set of moral and legal conventions, which seems to me to be an entity as unlikely to exist as a society in which all members were to dine in a single restaurant. The vision of freely competing arbitrators aiming at discovering and applying the social conventions concerning law and justice is the alternative offered in this context by the proponents of what I would call the soft variety of the critical rationalist approach.

Of course, here one could wish to draw our attention to the fact that eating, dressing, and interacting with art are not in any standard sense associated with the business of conflict resolution, unlike acting within a given legal framework and requiring others to do so as well. Therefore, the critic might say, although there is certainly nothing objectionable in allowing people to patronize whichever food, clothing, or art providers they like, allowing them to use competing arbitration agencies is a sure recipe for endless, irresolvable disputes, which in the end would probably be settled by violence.

Such an objection, however, though seemingly straightforwardly relevant in this connection, in fact involves a deep misunderstanding of the procedure of law creation in a competitive order. Most importantly, it has to be borne in mind that in a competitive, free enterprise system every socially acceptable transaction would have to be based on a voluntary contract. In other words, the transacting parties would always have to specify in advance the terms of their cooperation, their mutual obligations, etc., and they would not be able to bind by their contract anybody except themselves (to do otherwise would amount to an act of initiatory violence).

Thus, every reputable protection agency would have to include in the contracts signed with its clients a clause specifying to what arbitration procedures it would submit itself in the event of a dispute between its clients and those of another protection agency (Osterfeld 1989, p. 56). This might involve either naming an arbiter who will represent the agency in question or making the obligation to negotiate the choice of a common arbiter with the representatives of the other side of the dispute. In the former case the arbiters designated by the two opposing sides would have to arrive at a common verdict, or, in the event of being unable to do so, designate a superarbiter whose verdict they would bind themselves to accept (if they were to be unable to agree on the choice of a superarbiter, they might resort to any alternative mutually acceptable selection procedure, e.g., random picking or delegating the choice to another specialized company). In the latter case the two opposing sides would have to consent to accept the verdict passed by a mutually agreed single arbiter.

Because the market, including the market for legal services, is an endless process of entrepreneurial discovery and adjustment to the needs and desires of the totality of consumers, it is impossible to say in advance which of the methods described here would become the standard or the more popular one. There seem to be advantages and disadvantages to both of them. On the one hand, it might be advisable to know beforehand who is going to be the legal representative of one's chosen protection agency. On the other hand, one could reasonably assume that no arbiter can have sufficient knowledge and expertise to be able to deal competently with every conceivable kind of dispute situation, so it might be better to choose arbiters ex post, after the nature of any given dispute is already known.

To reiterate what has already been said: it is impossible to predict what specific mix of these two (or other) methods would emerge out of free interactions of the totality of consumers, producers, and entrepreneurs in a competitive, fully contractual order (Stringham 1999, pp. 73–4) – it is likely that it would vary across communities, cultures, ethnic groups, etc. In any case, however, it appears safe to say that those protection agencies that would not include arbitration clauses in their contracts would be ostracized and shunned by prospective clients just as much as those, discussed in the previous chapter, that would refuse to contribute to the production of long-range, "non-excludable" protection goods or engage in acts of initiatory violence. This should happen for the simple reason that declaring in advance that under no conditions would one submit to any form of peaceful, mutually agreed arbitration automatically removes the declarer, as well as his clients, from the purview of law, understood as a generally accepted set of rules for non-violent conflict resolution. This, in turn, not only condemns them to living in the state of primitive autarky or in self-sufficient ghettos, but also exposes them and their possessions[3] to constant depredations by the rest of society, which under such conditions could not be proscribed as instances of theft or robbery, because the "outlaws" under consideration could not establish themselves as owners in the first place.

Such "rogue" protection agencies and their clients would most likely occupy that place in the overall social structure which is occupied by various unambiguously criminal organizations, protection rackets, mafia groups, etc., in the social structure of today. In the worst-case scenario their influence would equal that of the previously mentioned entities, minus that part of it which comes from their association with the territorial monopolies of force and from the economic inability of the non-criminals to protect themselves against them as effectively as they could if their entrepreneurial efforts towards that goal were not obstructed by the said monopolies.

4.2 Legal polycentrism and victimless crimes

Having read this rudimentary exposition of how a polycentric, fully contractual legal system, based on the soft variety of the critical rationalist approach would operate, the critic might suggest that there is a potentially irresolvable tension between two of its most constitutive elements, namely, polycentricity and contractuality. Taking a cue from Schumpeter (1975), who articulated the curious claim that "the success of the capitalist mode of production makes capitalism itself redundant (and) undermines the social institutions that protect it" (Heertje and Middendorp 2006, p. 7), he could argue that as soon as some of the competing arbitration agencies amass sufficient wealth from their successful practices and attract a sufficient number of authoritarian-minded clients to their side, they might start to prosecute "victimless crimes", such as gambling, prostitution, or trading and using drugs. This would indicate that an allegedly consent-based system turns against fully consensual activities, thus undermining its central foundation. Furthermore, the critic might claim, because the scenario in question involves otherwise very respectable legal institutions, which arbitrate the cases not involving the previously mentioned victimless crimes with the degree of logical rigor and factual precision that contributes significantly to the preservation of an impressively stable and generally accepted legal order, it might, all things considered, not be in the interest of the society to stop patronizing (or even start ostracizing) these agencies in an attempt to remove them from the market for legal services.

Hence, the conclusion here appears to be that a comparatively small minority of selectively authoritarian-minded people could successfully undermine the consensual character of the system under consideration and avoid all the market checks and balances that are supposed to prevent such a scenario from happening.

A concession has to be made at this point that such a development of events is certainly not logically impossible. After all, there seems to be ample evidence, coupled with the corresponding theoretical justifications, that it is ultimately social legitimacy that keeps every institutional arrangement in place and maintains its influence (Hume 1971; Higgs 1987; Mises 1996, pp. 188–91; Boetie 1997). Thus, if the majority of the population in question were to perceive the benefits stemming from the existence of a generally stable, uncorrupted, and logically robust legal system as greater than the losses associated with the emergence of elements of non-consensuality in it, such elements would be likely to survive and could even intensify over time. In fact, if the reputation of the offending arbitration agencies were to be solidified in an ideological form, and if they were to utilize this fact to form a close-knit cartel, the culmination of the process under consideration could be a re-establishment of a legal and protective monopoly of force. Although this "return to square one" could be seen as the worst-case scenario for the social system under discussion, it cannot be denied that the power of ideology makes it logically (and even psychologically) feasible.[4]

However, as feasible as it may be, I believe that it would also be very unlikely given the prior existence of the institutional arrangements described earlier. In order to demonstrate this, let me fall back on Caplan's (2000, 2007) analysis of the extent to which different systems of social interaction facilitate the pursuit of irrational policies, where irrationality shall be defined as entertaining beliefs that find no substantiation in either logical reasoning or long-standing empirical evidence. In essence, Caplan argues that irrationality can be treated as a consumption good like any other, similarly subject to the law of demand – thus, the smaller its opportunity costs, the more widespread its presence. Next, Caplan claims that political democracies are bound to be plagued by a particularly high level of irrationality in the sphere of public policy making, because they make electoral irrationality very cheap. There are two main reasons for that: first, political democracies allow for externalizing the costs of one's individual actions onto others via redistributive means; and second, they make each individual vote very unlikely to exert a determining influence on the outcome of any given election (when informed by this second premise, mass-scale actions based on irrational beliefs can obviously lead to a tragedy of the commons).

In distinct contrast, the so-called market democracy, where "every penny constitutes a vote [and] all decisions are dependent on the will of the people as consumers" (Mises 1978, p. 178), every individual choice is effective in the sense of resulting in a specific action (an individual customer does not have to consult his decisions with other customers and cannot be outvoted by them), and its costs cannot normally be shifted onto others. Consequently, in a market democracy irrationality is usually quite costly, much costlier than in a political democracy.

Now, because the polycentric legal system described in the preceding paragraphs is a clear example of market democracy, and insofar as prosecution of victimless crimes can be seen as irrational with respect to the goal of effective, contractual prevention and prosecution of "real" crimes, it appears that the previously mentioned "authoritarian-minded" arbitration agencies would be very unlikely to operate profitably, because it would be they themselves that would have to cover the costs of harassing gamblers, marijuana consumers, etc., which, if reflected in higher premiums, would plausibly discourage their previous clients from continuing to patronize them. Far from being a serious problem for the competitive, market-based system envisaged in this chapter, the phenomenon of mass support for the criminalization of all sorts of non-aggressors is typical precisely for political democracies, where voters can costlessly burden their fellow citizens with injunctions and prohibitions based on their subjective whims and dislikes. Thus, I believe we can safely conclude that the quasi-Schumpeterian objection considered here fails to undermine the viability of legal polycentrism.[5]

4.3 Legal monocentrism and the paradox of government[6]

In this section I shall argue that, in contrast to its monocentric counterpart, only the institutional framework of legal polycentrism can overcome the problem of the so-called "paradox of government" – that is, establish effective and robust governance structures without simultaneously empowering them to overstep their contractually designated tasks and competences. Furthermore, I shall critically evaluate the logical consistency of the solutions advanced in this context by the proponents of legal monocentrism, based on the claim that institutional constraints in the form of democratic elections or checks and balances can place working constitutional limitations on the power of a coercive monopolist of law and defense.[7]

The paradox of government may be described in the following terms: "The fundamental political dilemma of an economic system is this: A government strong enough to protect property rights and enforce contracts is also strong enough to confiscate the wealth of its citizens" (Weingast 1995, p. 1).

On the face of it, this issue might be thought of as raising the plain old incentive problem, associated with Lord Acton's warning about the relationship between power and corruption. However, I believe that it actually points towards a more fundamental, conceptual difficulty,[8] which stems from the fact that a monopolistic lawgiver and law interpreter cannot make a logically meaningful distinction between obeying the law (i.e., making verdicts compatible with the binding legal code) and only claiming to obey it, just as the user of a private language cannot make a logically meaningful distinction between obeying the rules of such a language and only claiming to obey them (Wittgenstein 1953; Kripke 1982; Nielsen 2008). This difficulty, which may be termed the legal rule-following paradox, necessarily follows from the peculiar position of the coercive monopolist of law, which allows its representatives to claim justifiably that any of their interpretations of any rule is consistent with the legal code that they themselves established beforehand, just as the user of a private language can justifiably claim that any use of words on his part is correct from the point of view of the rules governing the communication system that he himself devised in the first place.[9] Such an observation motivates the conclusion that

> the fact is that there is no such thing as a government of law and not people. The law is an amalgam of contradictory rules and counter-rules expressed in inherently vague language that can yield a legitimate legal argument for any desired conclusion. For this reason, as long as the law remains a state monopoly, it will always reflect the political ideology of those invested with decisionmaking power.
>
> (Hasnas 1995, p. 233)[10]

Hence, in order to salvage the meaningfulness of the coercive monopolist's legal verdicts, there arises a need to have an external arbiter, who will be able to evaluate impartially whether the institution in question does not renege on the principles that it established and promised to safeguard. In other words, when a legal monopoly of force devises a constitution aimed at constraining its own power (thus attempting to make itself more trustworthy), the crucial problem to address is that of constitutional enforceability.[11] Unfortunately, all too often this problem is brushed aside, assumed to be self-solving, or taken to be neutralized by the existence of relevant historical evidence. The following remarks can be seen as quite typical in this respect:

> We reject the Hobbesian presumption that the sovereign cannot be controlled by constitutional constraints. Historically, governments do seem to have been held in check by constitutional rules. . . . Our whole construction is based on the belief, or faith, that constitutions can work.
>
> (Brennan and Buchanan 2000, pp. 13–14)

Such a statement, it seems to me, is a fatal concession that the issue remains essentially unresolved, not only (or even not mainly) due to ignoring the question of incentive compatibility, but more importantly due to pushing one level up the aforementioned problem of legal politicization without taking the sting out of it.

Let us now survey some potential solutions to the earlier difficulty that might be offered by the supporters of legal monocentrism committed to the viability of the notion of the rule of law. First, they could suggest that democratic elections might serve as an institutional guarantee of constitutional enforceability (Holcombe 2011, p. 18). In this proposal, the voting public is supposed to be an external arbiter of whether the legal monopoly of force abides by the constitution in making any of its decisions, and whenever it does not, the dissatisfied society can decide not to reelect its failed representatives. Thus, the constitution does not have to be thought of as self-enforcing – instead, it can be seen as proximately enforced by the legal monopolist, but ultimately enforced by the sovereign people, who freely choose and dismiss their administrators and public servants.

There are several problems with this solution that have to be mentioned here. First, the familiar considerations of rational ignorance (Downs 1957; Matsusaka 1995) make it unlikely that an average member of the voting public will have a sufficient incentive to familiarize himself with the details of the binding constitutional principles and their relationship with the decisions actually made by the functionaries of the existing judicial system. This is because the likelihood of his particular vote having a decisive influence on the outcome of any given election is infinitesimally small, hence making the potential benefits of contributing successfully to the election of a constitution-abiding representation far outweighed by the costs associated with acquiring relevant information.

Second, as suggested by Caplan (2000, 2007), the practical insignificance of any single vote (as well as the fact that the costs of electoral decisions are spread over the whole society) makes the majority of voters not only rationally ignorant, but also rationally irrational – that is, willing to indulge in making choices based on even the most wildly implausible beliefs rather than simply vote at random. As noted earlier, under political democracy irrationality is comparatively cheap, unlike under market democracy. This, in turn, makes it difficult to have much faith in the arbitrational skills and constitutional expertise of the voting public.

Third, because, ceteris paribus, it is always easier for a minority to overcome the collective action problem (Olson 1971; Ostrom 1990), as within small groups benefits are more highly concentrated, interests are more uniform, and effective monitoring of free riders is more feasible, it is likely that as long as a given democratic system enjoys general legitimacy, it will more often cater to the preferences of powerful, well-organized interest groups than to those of the disorganized, fragmented general public. Thus, the supervisory powers of the supposed external constitutional arbiter are vastly diminished or transferred into the hands of a small fraction of those interested in quality legal services.

Fourth, although it can be argued that democratic elections infuse any given legal system with an element of diachronic competition, it has to be acknowledged that they still leave it devoid of any trace of synchronic competition. This is noteworthy insofar as it can be contended that diachronic competition is the less significant of the two – after all, a coercive monopoly whose managers are periodically replaced does not thereby cease to be a coercive monopoly, together with all of its undesirable characteristics.

Because the market data are in constant flux, especially with respect to consumer valuations, it is relatively unimportant to compare the performance of a number of service-providing agencies over time if at any given moment only one of them exists in operation. Can it be said, for instance, that if an administration X was voted out of office in favor of an administration Y and the latter managed to survive two terms, it indicates that the latter turned out to be unambiguously more successful in satisfying the wants of the voters than the former did? Insofar as the voters of yesterday need not be the same as the voters of today, the same being the case for the values endorsed and needs felt by those respective groups, we have to remain agnostic with regard to the answer to the earlier question. Strictly speaking, it cannot even be said that the latter administration turned out to be more adaptable to the changing social sentiments, because it might have just so happened that its terms in power overlapped with a period of unusual psychological stability among the public, triggered by factors completely independent of its choice of policies (such as, say, the emergence of a great entrepreneurial talent, capable of delivering cheap and high-quality goods to the masses, therefore greatly increasing their personal well-being).

The crucial point here is that, due to the absence of synchronic competition, at no point of time can it be said that a given democratically elected administration does its job better than its actual or potential competitors, because by definition there are none such, and thus the supposed external arbiter in the collective person of the voting public is at no point of time in a position to evaluate the performance of its representatives against a meaningful benchmark of efficiency (Mises 1962; Tullock 1965; Rothbard 2004, pp. 1070–4). In fact, to be more specific, the "voting public", treated as a monolithic social bloc, is, logically speaking, never in a position to engage in this kind of evaluation, because such an entity – due to its all-encompassing nature – necessarily locks itself in a world bereft of synchronic competition. It is only after it decomposes itself into individual customers capable of patronizing individual providers of legal services that this all-important element is brought into the picture, and with it the prudential yardstick of profit and loss.

Finally, there is the problem of delayed feedback (North 1993, p. 16; Sutter 2002) – under political democracy, the element of diachronic competition can be normally utilized only once every few years; to do it more often would, as both its proponents and critics agree, make the system too volatile to be practicable (Williamson 1976, p. 81). Market democracy (Mises 1978, p. 178), on the other hand, utilizes both diachronic and synchronic competition practically permanently, as a result of which some parts of the social system it creates are highly volatile, whereas some are consistently stable, neither being seen as its vice any more than volatility and stability can be seen as vices of individual characters. In other words, because entrepreneurs on the free market can survive only by adjusting their offers to the expectations and preferences of the consuming public, market democracy is bound to exhibit a tendency towards combining the fixity and flexibility of its various dimensions in the proportion consistent with the prevailing social time and risk preference (Kirzner 1973, 1997; Huerta de Soto 2010).

Thus, I have to conclude that the procedure of democratic elections fails to serve as an effective institutional guarantee of constitutional enforceability and fails to elevate the general public to the position of an efficient constitutional arbiter.

The second solution offered in this context by the supporters of legal monocentrism is to create an institutional structure based on the principle of checks and balances. As described by Barnett (1998, p. 253), "the essence of this strategy is to create an oligopoly or a 'shared' monopoly of power. This scheme preserves a monopoly of power but purports to divide this power among a number of groups". In other words, in connection with the issue of constitutional enforceability, the idea here is to make certain branches of a coercive legal monopoly the arbiters of the actions of its other branches.

The problem with this proposal is that, because any given monopoly of force aims at making its ability to deploy discretionary power maximally effective (even if, for the sake of argument, we were to assume that this power were to be used for what the representatives of the said monopoly regard as "the common good"), its separate branches have a natural incentive to cooperate with each other so as to form a close-knit cartel with uniform interests. As Barnett (1998, p. 254) puts it:

> Eventually, entrepreneurs of power – master politicians, judges, executives, or outsiders called "special interest groups" – figure out ways to teach those who share the monopoly that each has an interest in cooperating with the others in using force against those who are outside the monopoly. This process may take some time, but gradually what is originally conceived of as "checks and balances" eventually becomes a scheme more aptly described as "you don't step on my toes and I won't step on yours" or "you scratch my back, I'll scratch yours".

> Citing Buchanan (1968, p. 87), one might question this worry by saying that

> > it may prove almost impossible . . . to secure agreement among a large number of persons, and to enforce such agreements as are made. The

> reason for this lies in the "free rider" [problem]. . . . Even if an individual
> should enter into . . . [an] agreement, he will have a strong incentive to
> break his own contract, to chisel on the agreed terms.

However, the appeal to "chiseling" is inadmissible here. It could be made as an argument against the claim that free market cartels are sustainable arrangements, but it cannot be applied to a monopoly of force, because any attempt on the part of a segment of such a monopoly to become an independent provider of relevant services would be declared illegal by the institution in question. In other words, although it could be plausibly suggested that free riding has a beneficial effect on the consuming public insofar as it makes business cartels inherently unstable and operationally self-destructive (Armentano 1978; Pasour 1981),[12] the same phenomenon cannot be said to occur within bureaucratically rigidified structures of coercive monopolies.

Furthermore, even if we decide to analogize any given monopoly of force to a firm and its branch responsible for constitutional oversight to the said firm's supervisory department, we need to bear in mind that this analogy still leaves us with only one firm in the sector of lawmaking and law execution, and thus the efficiency with which the previously mentioned supervisory department performs its role still cannot be assessed against any intersubjective benchmark of entrepreneurial competence.

Finally, the inadequacy of the solution of checks and balances can be illustrated by appealing to the private language analogy mentioned earlier. This analogy suggested that one is capable of saying meaningfully that one follows a certain set of linguistic rules only if there is at least one external arbiter who can verify that person's claims. Now, let us assume that there exists a coercive monopoly that creates and enforces the binding linguistic rules within a given territory, organized according to the principle of check and balances – in other words, one of its branches creates the rules, whereas another verifies whether they are consistent with the body of the already existing ones. The crucial point here is that even if, on the most charitable interpretation, we were to accept that such an arrangement could be said to ensure that the language in question is used correctly from the point of view of the monopolistic institution under discussion, it cannot be cogently maintained that this assurance extends to any of this institution's "subjects". And this is a serious problem insofar as we agree that any given language is supposed to serve the purpose of effective communication among the whole population, not only among its rulers.

Likewise, the legal system is supposed to serve the purpose of peaceful conflict resolution among the whole society, not only among its lawmakers, law interpreters, and law enforcers. Hence, one might plausibly argue that whereas under a monopoly of force the relevant kind of freedom of association and choice of legal rules is granted only to its political and bureaucratic management, under a competitive, contractual, polycentric legal order the same freedom is extended to all members of society.

It might be suggested at this point that the earlier arguments simply reiterate standard points about the difficulty, if not impossibility, of limiting power in a centralized regime and that they do not raise any special Wittgensteinian problem about meaning. In order to illustrate this contention, the following example might be used: the commerce clause of the U.S. Constitution has been interpreted to give Congress very wide control over all economic activity. Efforts to limit the scope of the clause haven't been very successful. This doesn't show, though, the argument might go, that the question of whether the Supreme Court has correctly interpreted the commerce clause has no objectively correct answer. The clause's meaning can be debated in public language, and the fact that the power of the central government to act as it wishes cannot be blocked does not gainsay this. Hence, one might conclude, I have confused meaning and enforceability.

In response, I have to say that I find no disagreement with the content of the earlier example, but I do not agree that the critical conclusion derived from it applies to the arguments advanced in the present chapter. I never suggested that government-made law cannot be publicly debated or that it cannot thereby acquire intersubjective meaning. What I did argue is that under coercive legal monocentrism the meaning thus established is irrelevant from the point of view of law enforcement, because territorial monopolies of force set themselves up as exclusive lawgivers and law interpreters within the areas they control, and, as demonstrated in the preceding paragraphs, it is implausible to assume that the procedure of democratic elections can provide an effective external check on their actions. In other words, with regard to the actual operation of the legal system, as opposed to its public perception, the difficulty or impossibility of limiting power in a centralized regime does imply that its legal verdicts are objectively meaningless or effectively reduced to expressions of subjective whims of the regime's officials. To sum up, under coercive legal monocentrism, intersubjective legal meaning can still exist, but it cannot be translated into objective enforceability.

Thus, I have to conclude that both of the monocentric solutions analyzed earlier fail to resolve what was termed the "paradox of government". In distinct contrast, the voluntary, entrepreneurial alternative outlined in the introduction of this chapter offers hope to address it successfully. As Long (2007, 2008b), who describes the competitive order in question as "market anarchism", puts it:

> Market anarchists reject the concept of monopoly government, insisting that every legal institution must be subject to correction from without. It follows, of course, that any agency doing the correcting must also be subject to correction, and so on. This doesn't lead to an infinite regress, however, because while any legal institution is subject to correction from other legal institutions, those in turn are subject to correction from the first one; legal institutions check and balance each other.
>
> (Long 2008b, p. 137)

Thus,

> far from eschewing checks and balances, market anarchists take market competition, with its associated incentives, to instantiate a checks-and-balances system, and to do so far more reliably than could a governmental system.
>
> (Long 2008b, p. 141)

In other words, even though in the system under consideration there is no uniform, written constitution, there is a powerful mechanism of "constitutional" constraint, whereby the clients of any given arbitration agency can objectively evaluate to what extent it fulfills its contractual duty of resolving conflicts vis-à-vis its competitors in the same business. This kind of evaluation, it has to be noted, would appeal not to any rigid set of codified legal principles, but to a more amorphous criterion, composed of a number of elements: logical justifiability and commonsense character of the passed verdicts; their adequate grounding in the particular conditions of time and place of any given case; and, perhaps most importantly, their consistency with the customs, beliefs, conceptions of justice, and other aspects of the "soft" institutional framework of any given locality (or localities in cases of interlocal disputes). This I take to be the essence of what I described earlier as the soft variety of the critical rationalist approach to law interpretation and enforcement.[13]

Having defended contractual legal polycentrism as the only system capable of dealing adequately with the "paradox of government", let me now turn to considering some other, more disparate objections that can be raised against it.

4.4 Other objections to legal polycentrism

In this section I would like to address various other objections to legal polycentrism, including all those that do not fit into any larger category centered on a specific, overarching problem.

Let me start from a version of the "spillover effects" objection that I tackled in the previous chapter in the context of the claim that the non-excludable positive externalities of deterrence and incarceration of criminals might jeopardize the workability of the market for protection services. Here the argument is quite similar. According, for instance, to Landes and Posner (1979), "because the existence of definite and widely known rules of behavior provides a non-excludable benefit to all, private courts lack an incentive to establish the clear precedents that give rise to rules" (Hasnas 2008, p. 128). Because clear precedents

> would confer an external, an uncompensated benefit, not only on future parties, but also on competing judges, . . . judges might deliberately avoid explaining their results because the demand for their services would be reduced by rules that, by clarifying the meaning of the law, reduce the incidence of disputes.
>
> (Landes and Posner 1979, p. 238)

To answer this worry, it has to be noted that the precedents in question could be termed and considered "intellectual capital", akin to new technologies, inventions, specialist knowledge, entrepreneurial talents, and accumulated physical capital, all of which can likewise be said to confer uncompensated benefits on the public insofar as today's population enjoys a much larger supply of much cheaper and more advanced goods than its ancestors did. And yet, the realization that this will likely be one of the unintended effects of their efforts did not prevent those ancestors from specializing, innovating, accumulating capital, forecasting an uncertain future, and engaging in other kinds of wealth-generating activities, because doing so increased the productivity of their labor, thus raising their real wages and managerial rents, as well as allowed them to exploit ever new sources of entrepreneurial profit (Rothbard 2004, p. 1038). In view of this fact, it seems very implausible to assume that being aware of conferring uncompensated benefits on future generations could ever inhibit any given generation from trying to improve its well-being, materially or otherwise.

The same point applies to the judicial context mentioned earlier – although it is likely that in some unobservable, psychological sense the existence of clear precedents confers an external benefit on the public by making the law more unambiguous and transparent, it also, in a very observable, praxeological sense, increases judicial efficiency, because it allows the judges to base their decisions on a much larger body of accumulated legal knowledge, thus making them more productive in the business of solving conflicts. But being more productive, their services would, of course, attract higher, not lower, demand, thus contradicting the conclusion of Landes and Posner.

Another interesting objection to legal polycentrism comes from no less a supporter of decentralization, free competition, and unhampered entrepreneurship than F. A. Hayek, who explicitly endorsed legal monocentrism by suggesting that

> there is one convincing argument why you can't leave even the law to voluntary evolution: the great society depends on your being able to expect that any stranger you encounter in a given territory will obey the same system of rules of law. Otherwise you would be confined to people whom you know. And the conception of some of our modern anarchists that you can have one club which agrees on one law, another club [agrees on another law], would make it just impossible to deal with any stranger. So in a sense you have, at least for a given territory, a uniform law, and that can only exist if it's enforced by government.
>
> (Hayek 1978b)

This statement, however, seems to exhibit a rather simplistic or uncharitable understanding of the nature of polycentric, competitive legal order. To be more specific, it appears to assume that members of societies governed by different legal codes are necessarily strangers to each other, and thus no cooperative contact between them is possible. The main problem here lies with the fuzziness of the term "different". Admittedly, if the differences between any two legal codes are so vast as to make them incompatible on the most fundamental level, there might be very little scope for meaningful cooperation between any two individuals each of whom subscribes to a different code. However, the fact alone that there exists an enormous amount of mutually beneficial interaction between people on the international and supranational level indicates that the most successful and efficient legal codes overlap to a degree sufficient to allow "strangers" not only to "deal with each other", but to do so in a highly productive and reciprocally enriching manner.

Incidentally, and somewhat surprisingly, the recognition of this fact is a direct consequence of adopting Hayek's own theory of cultural evolution through group selection (Hayek 1988), according to which in the realm of human action there exists "some sort of crosscultural competition . . ., where certain sets of norms, beliefs, and rules could prove themselves to hold a comparative advantage over others such sets of norms, beliefs, and rules" (Zywicki 2000, p. 82). As soon as the existence of such competition is recognized,[14] it can be predicted that "societies that can create and maintain . . . 'group benefiting' rules will tend to prosper over those that do not" (p. 83). And because being able to interact with "strangers" in a mutually beneficial manner seems to be one of the most "group benefiting" rules that can be thought of, it does not appear plausible to suppose that a stable poly-centric legal order could consist overwhelmingly of the kind of legal codes and underlying cultural norms that would make fruitful intergroup contacts impos-sible or difficult.[15] Thus, it turns out that Hayek can successfully answer his own objection to legal polycentrism.

Finally, let us consider one relevant difficulty raised by Gordon Tullock (2005). By word of introduction, it should be noted that Tullock's criticism pertains not so much to legal polycentrism, but to the common law system. However, insofar as the common law system, in contrast to the civil law system, includes important elements of spontaneous ordering and competitive discovery of legal rules, and thus approximates polycentric legal order to a much greater extent than its legisla-tive counterpart does, most of the criticisms aimed at it that exhibit a preference for more centralized and non-competitive systems of law can be plausibly con-strued as aimed at legal polycentrism as well.

The essence of Tullock's argument is that the common law system is, admit-tedly, an example of a spontaneous order, but that it is a malign, not a beneficent, spontaneous order (Zywicki 2008, pp. 35–8) – an exercise not in entrepreneur-ial discovery, but in political rent seeking, whereby conflicted parties and their lawyers "essentially lobby government officials – judges and juries – much in the same way that special interest groups lobby the legislature" (Tullock 2005, p. 450). The civil law system, on the other hand, as Tullock sees it, reduces admin-istrative costs and the attendant social waste by centralizing the process of evi-dence gathering in the hands of the (presumably impartial) judge, as well as by channeling resources in the direction of truth finding rather than truth conceal-ment and diversion.

In response to this argument, I would argue that although the analogy between the common law adversarial system and the process of political lobbying and rent seeking has some logical appeal, it loses much of its strength in the case where judges and juries cannot be thought of as government agents, which is pre-cisely the case of genuine polycentric legal order. In other words, the operation of the adversary system can be construed as an exercise in rent seeking only if a coercive judicial monopoly is involved. Absent such a monopoly, a judge who is successfully "captured" by one of the competing litigants or who is completely unable to distinguish between useful evidence and diversionary "noise" is more than likely to have his reputation irreversibly tarnished, meaning that he will lose existing clients and have difficulty finding new ones, because his verdicts will from now on be considered unreliable. Hence, under the system in question there is no reason for a self-interested litigant to try to influence the judge's decision by way of obstructing the collection of evidence by the competing party or by collecting obfuscating pseudo-evidence, because pursuing such strategies would be self-defeating.

In addition, by hiring a lawyer who is very adept at collecting evidence, including evidence in favor of his client's position, one strengthens one's case only insofar as one makes the overall picture of the case clearer for all of the involved parties. In other words, if the collected evidence is to be of any use for a reliable judge, it has to be complete in the sense of fitting into the broader context of the investigated story (i.e., it cannot be selective in a biased and partial manner). To the extent that it seems deliberately fragmentary or visibly irrelevant, it is useless for a judge who cares about his reputation (and thus about his survival on the market for legal services). Hence, under the system of free judicial competition only evidence generated on the basis of visibly truth-seeking motives is useful in litigation, by the same token eliminating payoffs to rent seeking.

Finally, it seems by no means clear that even in the context of discussing monocentric legal monopolies a civil law–based system should be thought of as less susceptible to wasteful rent seeking than its common law–based counterpart. After all, there is no reason to suppose that legislators are any more resistant to lobbying than judges are. Furthermore, it appears plausible to assume that even the verdicts of judges successfully "captured" by lobbyists have to retain some meaningful connection to particular legal cases (and thus to the specific circumstances of particular legal disputes) in order to maintain some semblance of relevance, whereas legislative acts can be based entirely on the whims of politicians and the interests of their rent-seeking clients. This point is reinforced by the fact that judges are, by definition, specialists in the legal field, whereas the same need not be the case with respect to popularly elected politicians. In sum, there are plausible reasons to suppose that the ostensible rent-seeking tendencies of the common law system are only exaggerated under the civil law system, and it is somewhat surprising that these broadly public choice–style considerations are apparently lost on one of the founders of the public choice school (Tullock 1967). In any event, it looks as if, ironically enough, based on his own scholarly contributions Tullock could answer his doubts about spontaneous ordering and competitive discovery of legal rules just as well as Hayek could answer his on exactly the same grounds.

With this, let me conclude the present section and turn to the question of whether legal polycentrism may offer a unique solution to a type of chronic institutional failure known as "regime uncertainty", which cripples the legal framework necessary for the operation of effective entrepreneurship and whose occasional emergence may turn out to be an inherent feature of coercive legal monocentrism.

4.5 Legal entrepreneurship and regime uncertainty[16]

According to economic historian Robert Higgs, the main reason why the Great Depression lasted as long as it did was the prevalence of what he terms "regime uncertainty" (Higgs 1997), that is, the kind of uncertainty felt by businesspeople, investors, and entrepreneurs in the political and legal environment that threatens to tax and regulate their wealth-generating activities to the extent that it becomes unprofitable to engage in them in the first place. In other words, it is the uncertainty regarding not the behavior of consumers, but that of politicians and their bureaucrats.

However, insofar as the ability to forecast an uncertain future accurately can be seen as the main source of entrepreneurial profits[17] (Shackle 1958, 1968; Mises 1996; Salerno 2008a), it might be asked why the emergence of regime uncertainty should be considered a factor particularly destructive of entrepreneurship rather than as an obstacle that entrepreneurs should be uniquely suited to deal with.

It seems that the only satisfactory response to this question is the one capable of making a meaningful distinction between regime uncertainty and its "standard" counterpart.[18] It would be difficult to think of the former as simply a particularly intense and overwhelming degree of the latter, because that would suggest that the conditions of regime uncertainty simply make the standards of successful entrepreneurship more exacting, which is inconsistent with the fact that such conditions affect adversely the activities of all entrepreneurs, not just the supposedly insufficiently competent ones. Likewise, it would be hard to regard regime uncertainty as qualitatively different from its more familiar counterpart in the sense that it cannot be successfully borne by even the most acute entrepreneur, because then the emergence of the phenomenon in question would completely eradicate rather than just severely harm the activities of businesspeople.

Hence, the most promising answer in this context seems to be that regime uncertainty is not qualitatively different from "ordinary" market uncertainty, but it operates on a different level, the one normally removed from the ambit of entrepreneurial decision making. In order to illustrate this claim, let us refer to the hierarchy of levels of social analysis proposed by Williamson (1998, 2000). According to the said hierarchy, the first level is that of soft institutions – customs, traditions, norms, and religions – which emerge largely spontaneously and develop in an evolutionary manner, thus changing very slowly and leaving comparatively little scope for everyday uncertainty understood in the way discussed earlier. The second level is that of hard institutions, whose purpose is to specify "the formal rules of the game" (ibid., p. 597), that is, the ones referring to property rights, contract law, etc. The third level relates to the "play of the game", especially "aligning governance structures with transactions" (ibid.), that is, to the way in which entrepreneurs give their firms and projects an appropriate organizational structure. Finally, the fourth level deals with the strict essence of entrepreneurial activity – that is, with aligning the existing and future supply of consumer and producer goods of various orders, as well as the existing and future technological possibilities, with ever-changing consumer preferences.

Now, the crucial point to notice here is that entrepreneurship operates on levels three and four, which are composed almost exclusively of variables, but not on levels one and two, which are supposed to provide the underlying framework of constants. In other words, the content of particular contracts that any given entrepreneur concludes and the types of property that he purchases or sells during his daily activities can be – and usually are – in constant flux, but the nature of the underlying contract law and property rights have to be sufficiently fixed or at least predictable if there is to be any chance of conducting such activities profitably. Regime uncertainty prevents any such fixity or predictability from prevailing, and because it originates on level two of the aforementioned hierarchy, which typically lies outside of the usual scope of entrepreneurial decision making, there is relatively little that entrepreneurs can do qua entrepreneurs to overcome this predicament. It would seem that the only solution available to them under a system of coercive legal monocentrism is to infiltrate the realm of politics – either passively, by placing their informants in the appropriate legislative and judicial bureaus, or actively, by influencing the decisions made by such bureaus. This, however, can be seen as costly enough to be feasible only for the representatives of big business, in addition to being particularly likely to engender favoritism and other unhealthy phenomena characteristic of the overlap between business and politics, known under the umbrella term "political entrepreneurship" (Kolko 1963; DiLorenzo 1986, 1996; McCaffrey and Salerno 2011).

On the other hand, under a contractual, polycentric legal order, the notion of regime uncertainty, as defined on the basis of Williamson's hierarchy, does not even retain any logical meaning. This is because under such an order the establishment and maintenance of the requisite legal framework and the corresponding "rules of the game" are part of the job of market entrepreneurs, thus eliminating any qualitative difference between the uncertainty associated with the second level of the said hierarchy and that associated with its third and fourth levels. For the reasons mentioned in the earlier paragraphs of this chapter, it is exceedingly unlikely that the arrangements in question would allow for the appearance of arbitration and protection agencies that would actively try to hamper entrepreneurship by coercively meddling with those business projects that would involve no initiation of aggression against non-aggressors. In all probability, such institutions would quickly meet with widespread ostracism, retaliatory actions by non-aggressive protection agencies, and condemnatory verdicts by reputable arbitrators, which would swiftly drive them into bankruptcy.

Moreover, if at any given point the existing arbitration agencies would seem not so much prone to indicting victimless crimes, but to being whimsical and unpredictable to the point of their services becoming useless in settling any dispute among litigants in a mutually satisfactory manner, the element of synchronic competition built into the system under consideration would immediately trigger the market process aimed at weeding out the incompetent ("uncertain") arbitrators and replacing them with the more trustworthy and skillful ones.

Finally, if in this context one were to worry that polycentric law would have to be fragmented, chaotic, and internally conflicted due to a potentially large number of competing agencies being responsible for its oversight (thus necessarily creating rather than preventing the emergence of regime uncertainty), one needs to remember that it would be in the interests of all those agencies to make the general rules they would profess to uphold sufficiently uniform to reflect accurately the shared values and expectations of the society they would purport to serve (Boettke, Coyne and Leeson 2008). At the same time, however, one has to bear in mind that within this general framework of shared social values and expectations, they would have to adjust their verdicts to the specific circumstances of time and place of any given case, as well as to the fundamental principles of logic and commonsense prudence. Hence, polycentric law would, in all likelihood, constitute a combination of macro-scale fixity and micro-scale flexibility.

Thus, in addition to all of its advantages listed in the previous sections, legal entrepreneurship turns out to be the only realistic and decisive safeguard against the emergence of regime uncertainty.

4.6 Legal polycentrism and contractarianism[19]

The arguments presented in the previous sections of the present chapter allow for a critical analysis of a somewhat different and potentially more robust conception of public goods – the one advocated not by neoclassical economists, but by philosophical contractarians. According to the contractarian perspective, a public good can be thought of as not so much a good that meets the technical criteria of non-rivalness and non-excludability, but as one that is produced on a purely contractual basis, thus necessarily increasing the utility of all the involved parties. Thus, if it can be shown that a monopoly of force tasked with the provision of law and order can emerge on a purely contractual basis, it can be argued that it can produce the supposedly public good of law and order at least as effectively as any of its polycentric counterparts. A thorough investigation of this line of thinking should be of particular interest to the adherents of Austrian economics, because it suggests that it is possible to reconcile the monopolistic production of putative public goods with the strict requirements of methodological individualism and methodological subjectivism.

Nozick (1974, ch. 2) formulated one of the most popular and ingenious versions of this kind of argument. It is important to note, however, that his story is contractarian only in an indirect sense – he does not claim that the only contractually legitimate form of a monopoly of force (i.e., the minimal state) could arise through any sort of collective agreement, but that it could arise through an "invisible hand process" (i.e., through a series of decentralized, voluntary transactions whose outcomes do not violate anyone's individual rights). In other words, he provides a contractarian story of the "emergent" rather than the "teleological" variety (Schmidtz 1990). But the most controversial part of it consists in the way Nozick tries to justify banning all competing protection agencies by the dominant one as consistent with respecting individual rights. Nozick claims that until the dominant protection agency bans the activities of all of its actual and potential competitors, its clients will be exposed to "risky procedures" engaged in by the competitors in question (Nozick 1974, pp. 55–6). This, in turn, will presumably (though it is not stated directly) expose the clients of all protection agencies to the risk of living in the notorious Hobbesian jungle, thus violating their individual rights to life, liberty, and property. In sum, Nozick's justification of the minimal state is based on the claim that by banning the activities of competing protection agencies, the dominant protection agency-turned minimal state simultaneously insulates all of its inhabitants from "risky procedures" and compensates those among them who were clients of the alternative agencies in question.

Unsurprisingly, the notion of risk employed in the aforementioned train of thought turned out to be one of the most vigorously contested elements in the intellectual edifice of Nozick's minimal statism (Childs 1977; Rothbard 1977). It has been suggested that Nozick confuses quantifiable risk with unquantifiable uncertainty, thus rendering his notion of compensation logically meaningless and incompatible with the goal of individual rights preservation. It has been suggested that there are no reasonable grounds for believing that the activities of non-dominant protection agencies are inherently more risky than those of the dominant one, especially because the former are inherently leaner, more nimble, and more responsive to specific, local circumstances of time and place. And finally, it has been suggested that, far from shielding its inhabitants from the influence of risky activities, the dominant protection agency-turned minimal state is uniquely capable of subjecting them to the risk of gradually transforming itself into a maximal state and unleashing the horrors of totalitarian tyranny.[20]

I believe that the arguments presented in the previous sections of the present chapter provide further and even more serious doubts regarding the viability of Nozick's indirect contractarianism. First, they suggest that, regardless of what other kinds of uncertainties[21] it is able to eliminate, a monopoly of force tasked with the provision of law and order is uniquely capable of subjecting its "clients" to regime uncertainty, thus rendering inoperative the legal framework that was supposed to ensure the protection of their life, liberty, and property, especially in the context of specifically entrepreneurial activities. And second, they suggest that, even when it does not generate regime uncertainty, the monopoly of force under discussion still necessarily generates what has been called "the paradox of government", or what I called "the legal rule-following paradox", that is, the situation in which the meaning and thus also the efficiency of binding legal rules cannot be intersubjectively evaluated, again rendering them inoperative.

If these arguments are correct, then, in accordance with Nozick's own philosophical assumptions, the dominant protection agency-turned minimal state necessarily violates individual rights, and does so on many fronts, which controverts the notion that it might come into existence in an "emergently contractarian", invisible hand–driven manner. On the other hand, the correctness of these arguments would also imply that an entrepreneurial, polycentric legal order might arise in precisely such a manner, thus turning out to be far more compatible with Nozick's invisible-hand contractarianism than his preferred variety of the minimal state.

Let us now discuss another well-known contractarian proposal – that of Buchanan (1987). Buchanan argues that

> there are two levels of analysis in political economy – the pre-constitutional level of analysis and the post-constitutional level of analysis, [where] the pre-constitutional level . . . is focused on the choice over the rules of the game and the organizational arrangement that will enforce those rules, [while] the post-constitutional level . . . is focused on the choices made *within* a given set of rules.
>
> (Boettke 2014)

In other words, he argues that the purpose of arriving at a constitutional contract is to create a legal framework for orderly interpersonal interactions – his version of contractarianism is teleological rather than emergent insofar as what chiefly matters to him is not whether the contract in question is arrived at by an invisible-hand process, but whether it facilitates rule-based exchange relationships. And because Buchanan clearly adheres to the principles of methodological individualism and methodological subjectivism (Buchanan 1969), and thus to the principle that unanimity is a necessary condition of Pareto-superiority, his vision of an ideal constitutional contract is one that protects life, liberty, and property so that the members of society may enhance their well-being by entering into voluntary, mutually beneficial arrangements.[22]

However, Buchanan also claims that adhering to the strict rule of unanimity in the context of ratifying constitutional contracts is bound to generate prohibitive bargaining costs, and that is why reaching efficient outcomes on the pre-constitutional level may require a monopoly of force to impose the requisite framework of legal rules on any potential holdouts (Buchanan 1975). But because the existence of such a framework is a necessary prerequisite of engaging in mutually beneficial exchange relations on a regular basis, it can be assumed, the argument goes, that every member of society regards the establishment of such a framework as a positive development, and, were it not for the holdout problem, every member of society would freely consent to its creation. Thus, actual unanimity gives way to "conceptual unanimity". In other words, Buchanan's story assumes the form of a Hobbesian hypothetical contract, with the crucial caveat that the prerogatives of the sovereign are to be limited to protecting the life, liberty, and property of the members of society.

Unsurprisingly, this train of thought has been seen to involve a fatal departure from methodological subjectivism and praxeologically sound welfare economic and a rather conspicuous attempt at eating one's cake and having it too (Block and DiLorenzo 2000, 2001) – after all, a top-down imposition by a monopoly of force is the very opposite of a unanimous agreement, and any attempts to cloak it in the language of "hypothetical agreement" can be thought of as resorting to the kind of psychologizing that is completely at odds with the principles of methodological individualism.

However, even if we were to put this particular worry aside, it would still remain the case that, just as Nozick's minimal state, Buchanan's purely protective state based on a clearly specified constitutional contract would remain susceptible both to regime uncertainty and to the legal rule-following paradox. After all, as described in the previous sections of the present chapter, the monopolistic, coercive entity in question would be uniquely capable of refusing to abide by the constitutional rules (and backing its refusal with the threat of monopolized violence) (Higgs 1997) or reinterpreting them in a manner that would suit its exclusive interests to the detriment of society at large (Hasnas 1995). In other words, it seems reasonable to conclude that the alleged benefit of substituting conceptual unanimity for actual unanimity in the context of creating an effective, constitutionally constrained framework of legal and protective institutions does not exceed the associated costs.

This is not to say, however, that the benefits of contractually agreed constitutional limitations on the power of the institutions under consideration have to be abandoned. On the contrary, as I tried to show in the present chapter, within an entrepreneurial, polycentric legal order they could not only be maintained, but also reconciled with the principle of actual unanimity. Because, in order to generate value for their customers, competing private protection and arbitration agencies would have to present clearly specified sets of rules that they would be willing to uphold and enforce, and because, as free market institutions, they would have to be patronized on a purely voluntary basis, they would provide an example of what might be regarded as genuinely contractual governments. As Boudreaux and Holcombe put it:

> Competition among various contractual governments . . . provides a market mechanism that leads [them], as if by an invisible hand, toward the production of optimal rules. The contractual government is an institution that produces unanimous agreement in the real world that parallels the conceptual agreement postulated in the recent contractarian models.
>
> (Boudreaux and Holcombe 1989, p. 276)

In sum, insofar as we understand public goods as those that are produced on a purely contractual basis, it is plausible to argue that the free market (together with the institutional framework that sustains it) is the only real public good, because, as the sum total of voluntary interactions between people, it is the only good whose creation and perpetuation meet the criterion of strictly unanimous, and thus genuinely public, acceptance. And insofar as we understand the entrepreneurial, polycentric system of law and order as the best institutional framework for sustaining the free market, it is plausible to conclude that such a system is the paradigmatic example of a public good according to any form of contractarianism worthy of its name.

Now, having described the way in which entrepreneurial practice in the areas of competitive law and defense provision can provide the consuming public with the relevant goods in a manner whose efficiency is much superior to that offered by territorial monopolies of force, let me move to the considerations of the workability of the earlier proposals that start from a very different conception of why such monopolies exist than that advanced by the neoclassical club and common goods theorists and philosophical contractarians.

Notes

1 Territorial monopolies of force tend to be shielded from this accusation insofar as, though frequently called "evils", they are almost equally often regarded as "necessary" evils, that is, the only institutions capable of producing "public" goods efficiently, which is supposed to more than compensate for the dangers and detriments associated with their monopolistic character. As I already addressed this claim in Chapter 2, I shall not comment on it here any further.

2 And this is in fact what a substantial number of historical and contemporary empirical case studies illustrate (Benson 1988, 1990; Ellickson 1991; Friedman 1979; Anderson and Hill 2004; Leeson 2006, 2007a, 2007b, 2007c, 2008; Powell, Ford and Nowrasteh 2008; Adolphson and Ramseyer 2009).

3 In this context, the term "possession" must be used instead of the term "property", because property presupposes legitimacy, and the "outlaws" under consideration voluntarily reject the possibility of the existence of any procedure, be it purely logical, purely customary, or combining these two perspectives, aimed at establishing or proving the legitimacy of any property title. Just as a thief possesses but does not own the stolen goods, because he did not come into their possession by a legitimate procedure, the "outlaws" in question, who reject the legal system altogether, complete with the category of ownership, admittedly do not thereby become thieves by default, but render themselves legally and socially defenseless against any thief or fraudulent self-proclaimed owner who would make an effort to appropriate their possessions.

4 Although it is still better than the scenario in which a given population is simply stuck with a monopoly of force, without being able to enjoy at least a brief interval of legal contractuality and polycentricity between the said monopoly's dissolution and later re-establishment.

5 It might be worth adding in closing that even if the circularity argument were correct, the argument that the advantages of market competition make a polycentric legal order preferable to a monocentric one has not been refuted. The circularity argument would show only that a state is necessary to establish a legal system. It would not show that, once a legal system exists, the monocentric order should be retained.

6 This section incorporates material from Wisniewski (2013c).

7 Some of the points elaborated in this section are in certain respects parallel to those made by Leeson (2011) and Leeson and Coyne (2012), although these authors focus primarily on analyzing the relative efficiency of various sources of social rules, whereas I concentrate on advancing the claim that there is a more fundamental, logical contradiction embedded in the notion that a monocentric legal system can avoid falling prey to the paradox of government.

8 In keeping with our methodology of investigating the institutional robustness of various systems of political economy, we may even suppose that the judicial monopoly of force under consideration is composed exclusively of perfectly well-intentioned and absolutely incorruptible individuals.

9 Another economically relevant illustration of the original Wittgensteinian rule-following paradox is, of course, the theorem of the impossibility of economic calculation under socialism (Mises 1996, ch. 26), which says that in the absence of the intersubjective benchmark of efficiency afforded by the market price structure, which results from the fact that all the factors of production are in the hands of a monopoly of force, no logically meaningful distinction can be made between the said monopoly allocating resources rationally (i.e., efficiently from the point of view of consumer sovereignty) and it only claiming to do so. In this context, "private" prices (i.e., prices set by a single

coercive agency) are as praxeologically meaningless as "private" linguistic rules (i.e., linguistic rules set by the only user of a supposed language). Consequently, the rational allocation of resources under socialism turns out to be as logically impossible as the rational use of a private language. Kripke (1982, p. 89) also draws attention to this point.

10 One might suggest that I cannot use Hasnas's point to support my claim that a polycentric system is needed for objective legal rules, because Hasnas isn't saying that under such a system we would have the rule of law, but that no such thing as the objective rule of law exists (even though a polycentric system is still desirable, because it allows for serving the interests of others besides the group which dominates a centralized system). I do not find such an interpretation of Hasnas's claims problematic. What matters from my point of view is that I can use his contentions to illustrate the essence of what I termed the legal rule-following paradox. Beyond that, I do not need to agree with his views regarding the nature and possibility of the rule of law. Thus, I believe that the potential criticism mentioned earlier is misplaced.

11 See Vanberg (2011) on the importance of constitutional enforcement.

12 Cowen and Sutter (1999) raise the point that there might be a tension between saying that, on the one hand, cartels are unstable because they face a collective action problem, and yet, on the other hand, that collective action problems can be solved to privately produce public goods. We believe that Caplan and Stringham (2003) successfully answer their worry by pointing out the fact that, in the context under discussion, Cowen and Sutter seem to mistake (self-enforcing) coordination game scenarios with (non–self-enforcing) prisoner's dilemma scenarios.

13 Although it has to be noted that even strict adherence to this particular approach leaves space for elements of constructive rationalism insofar as arbitrators have to construct logical justifications for their verdicts, that is, engage in acts of intellectual creation. It appears to me that in this sense every kind of entrepreneurial activity combines "critical" elements, associated with discovering the specific needs and desires of one's prospective customers, and "constructive" elements, associated with designing one's products and services, their advertising techniques, effective methods of staff management, etc. The crucial point here, however, is that the latter category is subordinate to the former, and that is why I regard entrepreneurship (including legal entrepreneurship) as falling squarely into the area of critical rationalism (as opposed to, e.g., politics and all sorts of self-directed intellectual activities).

14 For the literature on biological group selection among humans, which can be thought of as a plausible model for the phenomenon of cultural group selection, see, e.g., Sober and Wilson (1988) and Ridley (1996).

15 In this connection, see the following quotation from none other than Hayek himself: "instinctual aggressiveness towards outsiders must be curbed if identical abstract rules are to apply to the relations of all men, and thus to reach across boundaries – even the boundaries of states" (Hayek 1988, p. 13).

16 This section incorporates material from Wisniewski (2012a).

17 The reason why successful entrepreneurship is such a comparatively rare phenomenon is that it involves dealing not just with risk (i.e., measurable and statistically predictable "uncertainty", which one can insure against), but also with "real uncertainty", characteristic of those areas of knowledge in which there are no constants and no experimentally separable variables, the prime example of which is the area of human action. For more on the distinction between risk and uncertainty, as well as the corresponding kinds of probability, see Mises (1996, pp. 105–18); Knight (1985); and Hoppe (2007).

18 For an extended analysis of the relationship between regime uncertainty and "regular" market uncertainty, see Bylund and McCaffrey (2012).

19 This section incorporates material from Wisniewski (2017).

20 As a particularly telling illustration of this point, it is worthwhile to imagine how self-described individualist anarchists would react to hearing that they will be compensated

for being deprived of the services of competing protection agencies by being offered the services of a monopolistic, coercive state and how convinced they would be that none of their individual rights have been violated in the process (Rothbard 1977, p. 51).

21 From now on, I shall call "uncertainty" what Nozick calls "risk", because I agree that he confuses these two concepts, whereas only the former is applicable to theorizing about the realm of human action (Knight 1985; Hoppe 2007).

22 It is also the case that Buchanan considered himself a "philosophical anarchist" and supported secession as a means of curtailing governmental predation and inefficiency (Buchanan and Faith 1987). The endorsement of legal polycentrism can be regarded as taking the next step and bringing the secession-based argument in question to its ultimate logical conclusion. What prevented Buchanan from taking this step is likely to have been his support for the neoclassical public goods framework, which has been criticized in the preceding chapters.

Bibliography

Adolphson, M. and Ramseyer, J. M. (2009), 'The Competitive Enforcement of Property Rights in Medieval Japan: The Role of Temples and Monasteries', *Journal of Economic Behavior and Organization*, 71, 660–8.

Anderson, T. L. and Hill, P. J. (2004), *The Not So Wild, Wild West: Property Rights on the Frontier* (Stanford: Stanford University Press).

Armentano, D. T. (1978), 'A Critique of Neoclassical and Austrian Monopoly Theory', in L. M. Spadaro (ed.), *New Directions in Austrian Economics* (Kansas City: Sheed Andrews and McMeel), 94–110.

Barnett, R. (1998), *The Structure of Liberty* (New York: Oxford University Press).

Benson, B. L. (1988), 'Legal Evolution in Primitive Societies', *Journal of Institutional and Theoretical Economics*, 144, 772–88.

Benson, B. L. (1990), *The Enterprise of Law: Justice without the State* (San Francisco, CA: Pacific Research Institute for Public Policy).

Block, W. (1977), 'Austrian Monopoly Theory: A Critique', *Journal of Libertarian Studies*, 1 (4), 271–9.

Block, W. and DiLorenzo, T. (2000), 'Is Voluntary Government Possible? A Critique of Constitutional Economics', *Journal of Institutional and Theoretical Economics*, 156 (4), 567–82.

Block, W. and DiLorenzo, T. (2001), 'Constitutional Economics and *The Calculus of Consent*', *Journal of Libertarian Studies*, 15 (3), 37–56.

Block, W. (2008), 'Market Monopoly Is Apodictically Impossible', *Corporate Ownership & Control*, 5 (3), 385–9.

Boetie, E. de la (1997) [1576], *The Politics of Obedience: The Discourse of Voluntary Servitude* (Montrèal/New York/London: Black Rose Books).

Boettke, P. J., Coyne, C. J. and Leeson, P. T. (2008), 'Institutional Stickiness and the New Development Economics', *The American Journal of Economics and Sociology*, 67 (2), 331–58.

Boettke, P. J. (2014), 'Entrepreneurship, and the Entrepreneurial Market Process: Israel M. Kirzner and the Two Levels of Analysis in Spontaneous Order Studies', *Review of Austrian Economics*, 27 (3), 233–47.

Boudreaux, D. J. and Holcombe, R. G. (1989), 'Government by Contract', *Public Finance Quarterly*, 17 (3), 264–80.

Brennan, G. and Buchanan, J. M. (2000) [1980], *The Power to Tax: Analytical Foundations of a Fiscal Constitution* (Indianapolis: Liberty Press).

Buchanan, J. M. (1968), *The Demand and Supply of Public Goods* (Chicago: Rand McNally).

Buchanan, J. M. (1969), *Cost and Choice* (Chicago: Markham Publishing Company).

Buchanan, J. M. (1975), *The Limits of Liberty: Between Anarchy and Leviathan* (Chicago: University of Chicago Press).

Buchanan, J. M. (1987), 'The Constitution of Economic Policy', *American Economic Review*, 77 (3), 243–50.

Buchanan, J. M. and Faith, R. L. (1987), 'Secession and the Limits of Taxation: Toward a Theory of Internal Exit', *American Economic Review*, 77 (5), 1023–31.

Bylund, P. L. and McCaffrey, M. (2017), 'A Theory of Entrepreneurship and Institutional Uncertainty', *Journal of Business Venturing*, 32 (5), 461–75.

Caplan, B. (2000), 'Rational Irrationality: A Framework for the Neoclassical-Behavioral Debate', *Eastern Economic Journal*, 26, 191–211.

Caplan, B. and Stringham, E. P. (2003), 'Networks, Law, and the Paradox of Cooperation', *Review of Austrian Economics*, 16 (4), 309–26.

Caplan, B. (2007), *The Myth of the Rational Voter: Why Democracies Choose Bad Policies* (Princeton, NJ: Princeton University Press).

Childs, R. A., Jr. (1977), 'The Invisible Hand Strikes Back', *Journal of Libertarian Studies*, 1 (1), 23–33.

Cowen, T. and Sutter, D. (1999), 'The Costs of Cooperation', *Review of Austrian Economics*, 12, 161–73.

DiLorenzo, T. (1986), 'Competition and Political Entrepreneurship: Austrian Insights into Public Choice Theory', *Review of Austrian Economics*, 2 (1), 59–71.

DiLorenzo, T. (1996), 'The Myth of Natural Monopoly', *Review of Austrian Economics*, 9 (2), 43–58.

Downs, A. (1957), *An Economic Theory of Democracy* (New York: Harper).

Ellickson, R. C. (1991), *Order without Law: How Neighbors Settle Disputes* (Cambridge, MA: Harvard University Press).

Fielding, K. T. (1978), 'The Role of Personal Justice in Anarcho-Capitalism', *Journal of Libertarian Studies*, 2 (3), 239–41.

Friedman, D. (1979), 'Private Creation and Enforcement of Law: A Historical Case', *Journal of Legal Studies*, 8, 399–415.

Gumplowicz, L. (1899), *The Outlines of Sociology* (Philadelphia: American Academy of Political and Social Science).

Hasnas, J. (1995), 'The Myth of the Rule of Law', *Wisconsin Law Review*, 199, 199–233.

Hasnas, J. (2008), 'The Obviousness of Anarchy', in R. T. Long and T. R. Machan (eds.), *Anarchism/Minarchism: Is a Government Part of a Free Country?* (Burlington, VT: Ashgate), 111–32.

Hayek, F. A. (1944), *The Road to Serfdom* (Chicago: University of Chicago Press).

Hayek, F. A. (1960), *The Constitution of Liberty* (Chicago: University of Chicago Press).

Hayek, F. A. (1967), 'Kinds of Rationalism', in *Studies in Philosophy, Politics and Economics* (Chicago: University of Chicago Press).

Hayek, F. A. (1978b), *Tom Hazlett Interviews Friedrich A. Hayek, November 12, 1978, UCLA Oral History Program and the Pacific Academy of Advanced Studies*, retrieved December 12, 2010, from www.hayek.ufm.edu.

Hayek, F. A. (1979), *Law, Legislation and Liberty, Vol. 3: The Political Order of a Free People* (Chicago: University of Chicago Press).

Hayek, F. A. (1988), 'The Fatal Conceit: The Errors of Socialism', in W. W. Bartley III (ed.), *The Collected Works of F. A. Hayek* (Chicago: University of Chicago Press).

Heertje, A. and Middendorp, J. (2006), *Schumpeter on the Economics of Innovation and the Development of Capitalism* (Edward Elgar Publishing).

Higgs, R. (1987), *Crisis and Leviathan: Critical Episodes in the Growth of American Government* (New York: Oxford University Press).

Higgs, R. (1997), 'Regime Uncertainty', *Independent Review*, 1 (4), 561–90.

Holcombe, R. G. (2011), 'Consent or Coercion? A Critical Analysis of the Constitutional Contract', in A. Marciano and R. G. Holcombe (eds.), *Constitutional Mythologies: New Perspectives on Controlling the State* (New York: Springer).

Hoppe, H.-H. (1989b), *A Theory of Socialism and Capitalism* (Boston: Kluwer Academic Publishers).

Hoppe, H.-H. (2007), 'The Limits of Numerical Probability: Frank H. Knight and Ludwig von Mises and the Frequency Interpretation', *Quarterly Journal of Austrian Economics*, 10 (1), 3–21.

Huerta de Soto, J. (2010), *Socialism, Economic Calculation and Entrepreneurship* (Edward Elgar Publishing).

Hume, D. (1740), *A Treatise of Human Nature* (London: John Noon).

Hume, D. (1971) [1742], 'On the First Principles of Government', in *Essays: Moral, Political and Literary* (Oxford: Oxford University Press).

Jouvenel, B. de (1949), *On Power* (New York: Viking Press).

Kirzner, I. M. (1973), *Competition and Entrepreneurship* (Chicago: University of Chicago Press).

Kirzner, I. M. (1997), 'Entrepreneurial Discovery and the Competitive Market Process: An Austrian Approach', *Journal of Economic Literature*, 35, 60–85.

Knight, F. H. (1985) [1921], *Risk, Uncertainty and Profit* (Chicago: University of Chicago Press).

Kolko, G. (1963), *The Triumph of Conservatism: A Reinterpretation of American History, 1900–1916* (New York: Free Press).

Kripke, S. (1982), *Wittgenstein on Rules and Private Language* (Oxford: Blackwell Publishing).

Landes, W. M. and Posner, R. A. (1979), 'Adjudication as a Private Good', *Journal of Legal Studies*, 8 (2), 235–84.

Leeson, P. T. (2006), 'Cooperation and Conflict: Evidence on Self-Enforcing Arrangements and Heterogeneous Groups', *American Journal of Economics and Sociology*, 65, 891–907.

Leeson, P. T. (2007a), 'An-Arrgh-Chy: The Law and Economics of Pirate Organization', *Journal of Political Economy*, 115, 1049–94.

Leeson, P. T. (2007b), 'Better Off Stateless: Somalia before and after Government Collapse', *Journal of Comparative Economics*, 35, 689–710.

Leeson, P. T. (2007c), 'Trading with Bandits', *Journal of Law and Economics*, 50, 303–21.

Leeson, P. T. (2008), 'The Laws of Lawlessness', *Journal of Legal Studies*, 38, 471–503.

Leeson, P. T. (2011), 'Government, Clubs, and Constitutions', *Journal of Economic Behavior & Organization*, 80 (2), 301–8.

Leeson, P. T. and Coyne, C. J. (2012), 'Wisdom, Alterability, and Social Rules', *Managerial and Decision Economics*, 33 (5–6), 441–51.

Leoni, B. (1972), *Freedom and the Law* (Los Angeles: Nash Publishing).

Locke, J. (1967) [1689], *Two Treatises of Government*, P. Laslett (ed.) (2nd ed., Cambridge: Cambridge University Press).

Long, R. T. (2007), 'Anarchy Defended: Reply to Schneider', *Journal of Libertarian Studies*, 21 (1), 111–21.

Long, R. T. (2008a), 'Corporations versus the Market: Or, Whip Conflation Now', *Cato Unbound*, retrieved from https://www.cato-unbound.org/2008/11/10/roderick-t-long/corporations-versus-market-or-whip-conflation-now.

Long, R. T. (2008b), 'Market Anarchism as Constitutionalism', in R. T. Long and T. R. Machan (eds.), *Anarchism/Minarchism: Is a Government Part of a Free Country?* (Burlington, VT: Ashgate), 133–51.

Matsusaka, J. (1995), 'The Economic Approach to Democracy', in M. Tommasi and K. Ierulli (eds.), *The New Economics of Human Behavior* (Cambridge: Cambridge University Press).

McCaffrey, M. and Salerno, J. T. (2011), 'A Theory of Political Entrepreneurship', *Modern Economy*, 2 (4), 552–60.

Miller, E. F. (1976), 'Hayek's Critique of Reason', *The Modern Age*, 20 (4), 383–94.

Mises, L. von (1962), *Bureaucracy* (New Haven: Yale University Press).

Mises, L. von (1978), *On the Manipulation of Money and Credit* (Dobbs Ferry, NY: Free Market Books).

Mises, L. von (1996) [1949], *Human Action* (4th ed. revised, San Francisco: Fox and Wilkes).

Nielsen, K. S. (2008), *The Evolution of the Private Language Argument* (Aldershot: Ashgate).

Nock, A. J. (1935), *Our Enemy, the State* (New York: William Morrow & Company).

North, D. (1993), 'Institutions and Credible Commitment', *Journal of Institutional and Theoretical Economics*, 149 (1), 11–23.

Nozick, R. (1974), *Anarchy, State, and Utopia* (Basic Books: New York).

Olson, M. (1971) [1965], *The Logic of Collective Action: Public Goods and the Theory of Groups* (Cambridge, MA: Harvard University Press).

Oppenheimer, F. (1922) [1914], *The State* (New York: B.W. Huebsch).

Osterfeld, D. (1989), 'Anarchism and the Public Goods Issue: Law, Courts, and the Police', *Journal of Libertarian Studies*, 9, 47–68.

Ostrom, E. (1990), *Governing the Commons: The Evolution of Institutions for Collective Action* (Cambridge: Cambridge University Press).

Pasour, E. C., Jr. (1981), 'The Free Rider as a Basis for Government Intervention', *Journal of Libertarian Studies*, 5 (4), 453–64.

Powell, B., Ford, R. and Nowrasteh, A. (2008), 'Somalia after State Collapse: Chaos or Improvement', *Journal of Economic Behavior and Organization*, 67, 657–70.

Ridley, M. (1996), *The Origins of Virtue: Human Instincts and the Evolution of Cooperation* (New York: Viking Press).

Rothbard, M. (1977), 'Robert Nozick and the Immaculate Conception of the State', *Journal of Libertarian Studies*, 1 (1), 44–57.

Rothbard, M. (2004), *Man, Economy, and State: A Treatise on Economic Principles with Power and Market* (Scholar's ed., Auburn, AL: Ludwig von Mises Institute).

Salerno, J. T. (2008a), 'The Entrepreneur: Real and Imagined', *Quarterly Journal of Austrian Economics*, 11 (3), 188–207.

Schmidtz, D. (1990), 'Justifying the State', *Ethics*, 101 (1), 89–102.

Schumpeter, J. (1975) [1942], *Capitalism, Socialism and Democracy* (New York: Harper).

Shackle, G. L. S. (1958), *Time in Economics* (Amsterdam: North Holland Publishing Company).

Shackle, G. L. S. (1968), *Expectations, Investment, and Income* (2nd ed., Oxford: Oxford University Press).

Sober, E. and Wilson, D. S. (1988), *Unto Others: The Evolution and Psychology of Unselfish Behavior* (Cambridge, MA: Harvard University Press).

Stringham, E. P. (1999), 'Market Chosen Law', *Journal of Libertarian Studies*, 14 (1), 53–77.

Stringham, E. P. and Zywicki, T. (2011), 'Hayekian Anarchism', *Journal of Economic Behavior & Organization*, 78 (3), 290–301.

Sutter, D. (2002), 'The Democratic Efficiency Debate and Definitions of Political Equilibrium', *The Review of Austrian Economics*, 15 (2–3), 199–209.

Thierer, A. D. (1994), 'Unnatural Monopoly: Critical Moments in the Development of the Bell System Monopoly', *The Cato Journal*, 14 (2), 267–85.

Tilly, C. (1985), 'War Making and State Making as Organized Crime', in P. Evans, D. Rueschemeyer and T. Skocpol (eds.), *Bringing the State Back* (Cambridge: Cambridge University Press).

Tullock, G. (1965), *The Politics of Bureaucracy* (Washington, DC: Public Affairs Press).

Tullock, G. (1967), 'The Welfare Costs of Tariffs, Monopolies, and Theft', *Western Economic Journal*, 5, 224–32.

Tullock, G. (2005), 'The Case against the Common Law', in C. K. Rowley (ed.), *The Selected Works of Gordon Tullock*, Vol. 9 (Indianapolis: Liberty Fund), 399–455.

Vanberg, G. (2011), 'Substance vs. Procedure: Constitutional Enforcement and Constitutional Choice', *Journal of Economic Behavior & Organization*, 80 (2), 309–18.

Weingast, B. (1995), 'The Economic Role of Political Institutions: Market-Preserving Federalism and Economic Development', *Journal of Law, Economics, and Organization*, 11 (1), 1–31.

Williamson, O. E. (1976), 'Franchise Bidding for Natural Monopolies: In General and with Respect to CATV', *Bell Journal of Economics*, 7, 73–104.

Williamson, O. E. (1998), 'Transaction Cost Economics: How It Works: Where It Is Headed', *De Economist*, 146 (1), 23–58.

Williamson, O. E. (2000), 'The New Institutional Economics: Taking Stock, Looking Ahead', *Journal of Economic Literature*, 38 (3), 595–613.

Wisniewski, J. B. (2012a), 'On Regime Uncertainty and Legal Entrepreneurship', *Independent Review*, 17 (2), 253–6.

Wisniewski, J. B. (2013c), 'Legal Monocentrism and the Paradox of Government', *Quarterly Journal of Austrian Economics*, 16 (4), 459–78.

Wisniewski, J. B. (2017), 'Legal Polycentrism and Contractarianism', *Ekonomia: Wroclaw Economic Review*, 23 (2), 75–82.

Wittgenstein, L. (1953), *Philosophical Investigations* (London: Blackwell Publishing).

Zywicki, T. J. (2000), 'Was Hayek Right about Group Selection after All?', *Review of Austrian Economics*, 13, 81–95.

Zywicki, T. J. (2008), 'Spontaneous Order and the Common Law: Gordon Tullock's Critique', *Public Choice*, 135, 35–53.

5 Ideas, institutions, and preferences

5.1 Predation, not protection: the inevitabilist challenge

Political theorists as different as Hobbes (1991), Rawls (1971), and Buchanan (1975) argue that the emergence of territorial monopolies of force should be thought of in terms of contractual bargaining, whereby individuals renounce their natural right to self-governance in exchange for protection of life and property ensured by the said monopolies. Translated into the language of neoclassical economics, the contractarian story describes the process whereby a certain amount of private goods is sacrificed in order to establish the institutional framework necessary to provide the supposedly public goods of law, domestic order, and national defense.

In the previous three chapters I endeavored to show that the category of public goods is, from the economic point of view, artificial and arbitrary, and thus the goods that allegedly belong to it can be effectively produced in the absence of institutional coercion. However, a non-contractarian might claim that my whole preceding analysis is irrelevant, because it stems from the false assumption that territorial monopolies of force (i.e., governments) are created in order to supply public goods, whereas, in fact, "they are created and imposed on people by force, most often for the purpose of transferring resources from the control of those outside government to the control of those within it" (Holcombe 2004, p. 326).

In other words, a case for the inevitability of government can be made on the basis of recognizing the predatory nature of power-hungry human beings. The course of events leading to its unstoppable and ubiquitous emergence may be thought of as a perverse equivalent of the Smithian invisible-hand procedure – just as a competitive natural selection process removes inefficient entrepreneurs from the market and allows the efficient ones to survive and prosper, the same process operating in the state of nature is supposed to allow one "protection agency" (the one most skillful not so much at defense, but at deploying aggressive force for predatory purposes) to subjugate all others and thus effectively destroy the very prerequisites of a competitive market environment in the provision of law and defense (Cowen 1992), which, in turn, paves the way for any further coercive intervention in the economy that such an organization might wish to employ.

Holcombe bolsters his argument with what might be thought of as inductive evidence, according to which the history of mankind seems to show consistently that consensual and voluntary legal and protective agreements do not survive and therefore that a framework of coexisting, maximally limited territorial monopolies of force is the best practically available choice. In a similar vein, Cowen and Sutter (2005) argue that "we must take seriously the fact that governments exist all around the world, for better or worse. . . . History shows that 'cooperating to coerce' is relatively easy to establish, regardless of the exact path to that final state of affairs" (p. 113). This might be taken to be an example of a worst-case interpretation of the relevant historical records, in this case, a reading of historical data that supports the conclusion that legal voluntarism and polycentrism is not a robust system. Implicit in such an interpretation is the assumption that predatory actions are (or are generally considered to be by the would-be wielders of coercive monopolies) more profitable for those who commit them, even in the long run, than integrating oneself with the system of peaceful cooperation under division of labor and unhampered entrepreneurial activities (North 1993; Olson 2000).

Why should the peaceful, productive part of any given society be bound to fail in its efforts to repel the predators? Two main reasons are usually adduced in this context. The first of them is the dark underside of the phenomenon of specialization and division of labor, known under the name of the "iron law of oligarchy":

> Oligarchic rule is rendered practically inevitable by the law of comparative advantage. The tendency toward division of labor and specialization based on the unequal endowment of skills pervades all areas of human endeavor. Just as a small segment of the population is adept at playing professional football or dispensing financial advice, so a tiny fraction of the population tends to excel at wielding coercive power.
>
> (Salerno 2008b, p. 449)

This, one might plausibly claim, is an insufficient explanation, because the aforementioned principle also implies that individuals who excel at offering protection services should exist and there are no grounds for assuming that the gains from looting must always, or even in general, exceed those from providing one's clients with an efficient and reliable service.

This is where the second of the aforesaid reasons comes into the picture. One of the greatest social advantages of the free market order is that, being a composition of innumerably many, individual, dovetailing conscious plans and designs, it allows for coordinating the demonstrated preferences of individuals with diverse value scales and preference rankings. Thus, it achieves the aim of coordination and efficient allocation of resources without subjecting its constituent members to any overarching, vertically organized structure created to pursue a single goal. However, one might argue that precisely because the free market order does not normally exhibit any substantial degree of "thick" ideological unity,[1] its structural features do not make it particularly easy for its participants to overcome the macro-scale collective action problem (Olson 1971; Ostrom 1990) and deal effectively with harmful free riders bent on parasitically exploiting the work of productive individuals and their voluntary associations.

The task of the parasitically inclined free riders, on the other hand, is relatively facile in comparison, because their potential payoffs from successfully establishing a territorial monopoly of force are highly concentrated, their interest in creating such an entity is highly uniform, and monitoring potential free riders within their group is comparatively manageable due to its limited size. In sum, the collective action problem of defense against organized predation coupled with the iron law of oligarchy is alleged to ensure the inevitability of the existence of exploitative governments.

5.2 Answering the challenge: the importance of preferences[2]

The fundamental weakness of the earlier reasoning, as plausible as it otherwise sounds, is that it is based entirely on the analysis of incentives while treating the underlying preferences as fixed. Preferences, however, are crucial in the context of solving the collective action problem (Hummel 2001; Stringham and Hummel 2010), and there is plenty of evidence of substantial preference change throughout history (North 1981, 1990), sometimes within surprisingly short time frames.

After all, it appears fair to assume that in a world in which incentives were the sole non-material influence on the shape of societies, due to the combination of the collective action problem and the iron law of oligarchy, "nearly all humankind would still be slaves groaning under the Pharaohs of Egypt" (Hummel 2001, p. 531).[3] It would not do to reply to this observation by suggesting that over time predators learn that decreasing the size, scope, and intensity of their predation enhances the productive incentives of their victims and thus leads to the creation of more wealth to loot, because then the logical endpoint of such a learning process would be the realization that peaceful cooperation under the division of labor is infinitely more wealth generating than predation is. This, in turn, would lead to the disintegration of territorial monopolies of force and their transformation into private protection agencies operating in a voluntary society. And if one were to suggest that this is in fact the direction history is moving, then one could ask why it seems to be taking so many destructive detours, with periods of relative freedom interspersed with periods of intolerably overwhelming predation. Finally, it might be asked how the predators could conceivably learn about the incentive-enhancing effects of reducing their predation unless their victims were capable of upsetting the initial predatory equilibrium and making it somewhat less so, thus demonstrating to their oppressors the superior productivity of the free exchange system.

The answer to these puzzles and the lynchpin of the earlier observations is that preferences matter just as much as incentives do. Notice that arguments such as that of Holcombe (2004), which suggest that limited government is the best one can realistically hope for when it comes to law and defense provision, make implicit and perhaps unwitting assumptions about preferences. For instance, Holcombe's endorsement of limited government as the least bad solution to the problem of effective protection and law enforcement implies, obviously enough, the viability of limited government. But the viability of limited government implies, in turn, that the "battle of ideas" in the realm of social values can be tipped in favor of the notion that less rather than more predation is better for prosperity (including the prosperity of the predators). And although ideas both influence and are influenced by incentives, it would be rather implausible to argue that they are reducible to them, and the only other viable candidate for their creation are preferences.

In response, Holcombe might suggest that his argument does not deny the importance of preferences, but does not presuppose any major shifts in preferences or any radical ideological commitments either. What it does instead is to uncontroversially assume as constant the preference of most for more over less prosperity plus the preference of some for predation over production and then propose that the institutional framework that generates an incentive structure capable of optimally accommodating these conflicting preferences within a relatively stable legal order is that of limited government. Furthermore, he might add that the reason why the majority of the world's governments are hardly limited stems not so much from the prevalence of preference for heavy predation or from the domination of statist ideologies, but from widespread economic ignorance, which results in the emergence of inefficient incentive structures. Hence, those who would like to bring into existence a stable and reliable though maximally unobtrusive legal order should not try to achieve the psychologically unlikely goal of establishing a voluntary system of competitive legal polycentrism by means of radically changing the preferences of the public, but rather the much more psychologically likely goal of establishing a limited government by means of influencing the incentives of the public through economic education.

Would such a reformulation of the inevitability argument allow it to retain its strength? I do not think that it would. It seems far from obvious that given sufficient knowledge about all the indirect, unintended, and hidden effects of governmental intrusions into the free workings of the extended order of society (Hayek 1988), the members of any such order would continuously strive to keep territorial monopolies of force constrained to the minimal size they are supposedly bound to reach as natural monopolies of violence. In other words, even under the conditions of hypothetical enlightened contractarianism, whose preemptive adoption Holcombe advocates as an alternative to being subjugated by external predatory invaders, it is unclear whether the following description would hold true: "In any social contract, individuals obviously would not choose to form an all-powerful leviathan government that could exploit them. Instead, they would want to form a government limited to enforcing their agreement not to steal from each other" (Powell and Coyne 2003, p. 24).

If, as Holcombe and other "inevitabilists"[4] argue, governments are created for the purpose of transferring resources from the control of producers to the control of predators, then, assuming constancy of the few general, uncontroversial preferences mentioned earlier, it can be expected that at best only those governments will remain limited that are based on a clear distinction between the ruling predators and the ruled producers. However, because, by definition, it is in the interest of those who have a comparative advantage in violence (North 1981, p. 21) to increase their predation towards the subjugated population as its wealth grows, it is reasonable to assume that over time the predators will evolve forms of government where the distinction between the rulers and the ruled is highly blurred.

Some argue that, in its various aspects, democracy is precisely an example of such a form of government (de Jouvenel 1949; Hoppe 2001; Rothbard 2004), a system in which and through which, to borrow a phrase from Frédéric Bastiat (1998, p. 77), "everyone tries to liv+e at the expense of everyone else", i.e., participate in the predatory process and share in its proceeds. Thus, it is far from obvious that "if government is inevitable, and if some governments are better than others, then citizens have an incentive to create and maintain preemptively a government that minimizes predation and is organized to preserve, as much as possible, its citizens' liberty" (Holcombe 2004, p. 335). Again, this observation indicates that whether attempts at limiting government, let alone successful ones, will be undertaken depends primarily not on incentives, but on preferences, with detailed knowledge about the results of acting on them being of secondary importance.[5]

As long as people at large prefer more government to less because its comparatively large size coupled with its democratic form increases their chances of becoming more prosperous in the short term quickly and effortlessly by voting themselves the property of others or forming a powerful lobby group (i.e., unionized workers calling for minimum wage laws; big corporations calling for subsidies, protective tariffs, and monopoly privileges, etc.), no amount of economic knowledge will be able to direct their incentives towards establishing a Holcombian limited government or a Buchananite purely "protective" (Buchanan 1975, pp. 68–70) as opposed to "redistributive" (Buchanan, Tollison and Tullock 1980) state. And regardless of whether one is willing to admit it or not, a preference for redistributive democracy equals a preference for less liberty, less free enterprise, fewer voluntary interactions, less thrift, less providence, less capital accumulation, less smooth functioning of the price system, and more possibilities of snatching resources from the forcibly created "common pool", even if that increases the risk of becoming one of those whose resources will be routinely snatched by others.

In fact, a number of well-described phenomena exist that illustrate how adopting the set of preferences mentioned earlier generates corresponding rational (that is, logically justifiable and appropriately informed) sets of incentives, even if their rationality might seem misdirected and counterproductive to those whose own preferences are very different. Take the phenomenon of rational ignorance (Downs 1957; Matsusaka 1995), which consists of it being economically rational for voters to vote at random given the time commitment of obtaining all the relevant information about the candidates and the unlikelihood that a single vote can make any difference on the outcome of any given election. There does not seem to be anything logically or even psychologically contradictory about a rationally ignorant voter with a preference for redistributive democracy conceived as a form of lottery or political game of chance. How would Holcombe convince such a person to modify her preferences and embrace purely protective, minimal government by appealing to her incentives alone?

Or take the phenomenon of rational irrationality (Caplan 2000, 2007), which consists of it being economically rational for voters to indulge in making irrational choices (i.e., choices based on implausible or incoherent beliefs) due to their cheapness, which results from the democratic possibility of dispersing the costs of their unsavory effects among the whole electorate. Again, how would an inevitabilist proponent of minimal government convince a rationally irrational voter to abandon her preference for acting on implausible beliefs in favor of a preference for peaceful prosperity that comes with economic rationality? Or how would he go about educating someone who votes primarily for expressive purposes, that is, in order to signal her emotional support for certain ideas and policies, regardless of their truth and efficiency (Brennan and Lomasky 1993)? Needless to say, the same difficulty applies with particular force to any attempts to educate a rent seeker for whom significant profits achieved through political machinations are preferable to even more significant profits achievable through honest economic activity (Tullock 1967).

In sum, although I am far from denying the didactic importance of appealing to the effectiveness (or lack thereof) of one's incentives, I am skeptical of the persuasiveness of this approach unless it is firmly grounded in the underlying structure of preferences of the person to be convinced, or unless it attempts to influence this structure first. In other words, I believe that Holcombe would be able to succeed in persuading the proponents of redistributive democracy to abandon it in favor of purely protective limited government only if he were to start from reorienting their preferences toward long-term thinking, far-sightedness, prospective planning, developing the ethos of an industrious entrepreneur rather than that of a cunning rent seeker, etc.

Let us recall at this point that the purpose of the preceding four chapters of the present work was to demonstrate that there is nothing logically and economically incoherent in the notion of a purely voluntary polycentric system of law and order. This implies that the difference between such a system and that of Holcombian limited government, Buchananite protective state, and Nozickian night-watchman state is one of degree, not of kind. Such a conclusion, coupled with the commonsense observations that preferences are at least as important as incentives and that preferences, including those of large groups of people, can undergo changes, sometimes radical, suggests that if there is nothing inevitable about the ascent of predatory redistribution, there is nothing inevitable about the survival of predatory "protection" either. In other words, if the earlier content suggests that maximal government is not inevitable, then neither is its minimal counterpart.

In fact, if the proponents of the thesis of governmental inevitability accept the earlier two commonsense observations, then their position becomes doubly shaky, because, as demonstrated in the preceding paragraphs, it can not only be pushed toward non-governmental legal polycentrism in an optimistic scenario, but, more importantly, it does not offer any reasonable hope for the survival of minimal government in a pessimistic scenario, especially given their doubts about the prospects of successfully opposing large-scale, organized predation on a voluntary, decentralized basis (Leeson and Stringham 2005).

In essence, the proponents of the earlier thesis are bound to hold the view that limited governments can be designed and restricted in their scope only by groups of individuals who exhibit a marked preference for personal liberty over that for predatory redistribution. However, any process of governmental design must, by definition,

> involve political agents, but once we admit political agents, these agents' self-interest enters the picture. In light of this ruler self-interest, coupled with [their] superior strength . . ., does any hope remain for limits on government? Rather than creating the minimal state . . ., these political actors will deliver much more than anyone bargained for. If we agree . . . that government is created by force, why then would we assume that its creators will produce the minimal state?
>
> (Leeson and Stringham 2005, p. 547)

This observation creates a dilemma for the inevitabilist supporters of minimal government. If they concede that ideological unity can allow any given society to overcome the collective action problem and successfully constrain the power hunger of political actors, then they cannot consistently argue that the same unity cannot allow the society in question to get rid of political actors (i.e., "stationary bandits" [Olson 2000]) altogether. If, on the other hand, they want to argue that the collective action problem makes it exceedingly unlikely that the will of a liberty-minded society can outweigh the will of its ruling class, then for the same reason they should regard it as exceedingly unlikely that any given minimal state is not bound to morph over time into a maximal state. As Leeson and Stringham put it:

> If the public agrees on the principles of liberty and can act in concert to maintain the minimal state, the public can act in concert also to maintain libertarian anarchy. Just as the public can constrain the minimal state from becoming more coercive, the public can constrain private protection agencies from becoming more coercive.
>
> (2005, p. 547)

The inevitabilists might attempt to escape this dilemma by suggesting that phenomena such as rational ignorance, rational irrationality, and the logic of special interest groups make the establishment of libertarian anarchy far more difficult than the establishment of a minimal state (Holcombe 2005, p. 552). However, although in all likelihood true, this assertion fails to prove that there is a qualitative rather than just quantitative difference in the difficulty of establishing these respective social orders. The phenomena mentioned earlier are just the other side of the familiar collective action problem, and although there is no question that the collective action problem makes the establishment of either of these social orders very difficult, there is no logical or even psychological reason to suppose that it makes the failure to create one of them inevitable.

Another objection that the inevitabilists might decide to fall back on consists of questioning the relevance of the historical evidence adduced by the proponents of libertarian anarchy:

> The historical presence of long-standing, primitive, anarchic societies spans the globe. Consider, for example, societies such as the Eskimo tribes of the North American Arctic, Pygmies in Zaire, the Yurok of North America, the Ifugao of the Philippines, the Land Dyaks of Sarawak, the Kuikuru of South America, the Kabyle Berbers of Algeria, the Massims of East Paupo-Melanesia, and the Santals of India – none of which had governments. Many stateless societies also populated precolonial Africa; a few encompassed significant numbers of people. Consider, for example, the Tiv, which included more than one million individuals; the Nuer, whose population has been estimated at four hundred thousand; or the Lugbara, with more than three hundred thousand members. In Africa, the Barabaig, Dinka, Jie, Karamojong, Turkana, Tiv, Lugbara, Konkomba, Plateau Tonga, and others long existed as stateless or near-anarchic orders as well. Today Somalia is essentially stateless and has remained effectively so since its government dissolved in 1991 despite predictions that a new government would emerge immediately.
>
> (Leeson and Stringham 2005, p. 544)

Upon being presented with this list of well-functioning non-governmental societies, an inevitabilist might reply that they avoided being subjugated by territorial monopolies of force precisely because they were primitive and poor, thus giving predatory organizations little incentive to exploit them on a regular basis (Holcombe 2005, p. 553). In other words, he could suggest that a significant positive correlation exists between the poverty and primitiveness of a given region and its likelihood of remaining in the state of peaceful, functional anarchy. The problem with this suggestion, however, is that it is factually incorrect. After all, some of the most oppressive governments currently in existence rule over some of the most "primitive" (i.e., economically underdeveloped and materially destitute) regions of the world. And contrariwise, the majority of the most materially prosperous and economically advanced countries of the world are ruled by relatively non-predatory governments (Gwartney, Lawson and Hall 2012; The Heritage Foundation 2013).

This observation also contradicts what Cowen (2007) referred to as the "Paradox of Libertarianism", that is, the putative phenomenon of increasing social demand for coercive governmental redistribution prompted by growing social wealth, which, in turn, is initially caused by growing economic liberty and government retrenchment. Cowen's argument, just like that of Holcombe's, is reasonable and describes a tendency that no doubt exists in many cases. However, the premises on which it is based are too contingent and particular to support the degree of necessity and universality of the conclusion he derives from it. Whether those societies in which economic freedom causes some of its members to become fantastically wealthy will turn in the direction of redistributive predation depends crucially on the ethical and cultural values predominant in them. If these suggest, for instance, that successful individuals should be emulated rather than expropriated, and that economic liberty is a necessary prerequisite of their successful emulation, then their growing presence in any given society will most likely lead to even more, not less, liberty.

In fact, the only value that would have to be widely respected in any given society to prevent its descent into redistributive predation, and that might be better characterized as prudential rather than moral, is patience. Neither a patient predator nor any of his patient clients would opt for expropriating their victims to the point of increasing their present income at the expense of destroying the capital value of their victims' assets or of breaking their entrepreneurial spirit. Their mode of action would be predicated on the notion that limited predation, as opposed to unbridled predation, does not prevent a steady growth of the pool of resources that they may subsequently prey upon. In sum, Cowen's contention that the more eggs a golden hen will lay, the more intensely she will be preyed upon has some initial plausibility, but both logical analysis and historical evidence suggest that it is by no means universally applicable.

A variation on Cowen's "Paradox of Libertarianism" is the claim that government is inevitable simply because organized coercion generates large positive payoffs that are not subject to any external constraints (Cowen and Sutter 2005), which is amply evidenced by how wealthy government officials all around the world are. However, it is crucial to note in this context that "the payoffs themselves are at least partly a function of institutions and hardly constant for all time. Altering the institutions can alter the level and even the ranking of the payoffs" (Stringham and Hummel 2010, p. 38). To take a concrete example, in today's world, which is almost unanimously opposed to slavery, slave owners and traders are unlikely to acquire significant wealth and political power, because their activities are confined to the black market. If they were to leave these relatively narrow confines, they would be immediately ostracized and criminalized. It is essential to note here, however, that their relatively restricted and thus rather weak position does not stem from their inferior organization or their limited ability to wield coercive power. Insofar as these aspects play a significant role, they are derivative of how little ideological support slave owners and traders can muster in today's cultural and moral environment.

My claim here is quite strong: I take it that firm ideological unity among the majority always trumps superior organization of coercive means among the minority (Hume 1971; Higgs 1987; Mises 1996, pp. 188–91; Boetie 1997). Could the governments of the world reinstate slavery? Yes, they could. They possess sufficient coercive power at their disposal. But would they dare to do it? No, they would not. The prevalent social attitude toward slavery makes such an action uneconomic from the point of view of the calculus of power. Similarly, could warlords and mafias destroy a stateless order and replace it with a statist one? Yes, they could. They might possess sufficient coercive power at their disposal. But they would dare to do it only if the prevalent social attitude toward statism made such an action profitable from the point of view of the calculus of power. And there is nothing inevitable as to what this attitude will be.

In any event, there is no reason to suppose that, given a sufficiently strong commitment to a particular set of preferences, maintaining a social order based on those preferences is bound to be more challenging than establishing it in the first place. If the members of a given society were to establish a stateless order not through violent overthrow of their erstwhile rulers, but through their commitment to voluntary methods of, say, peaceful non-compliance and grey market entrepreneurship, the resulting situation would be unlikely to generate a conflict over a power vacuum, because "the same social consensus, the same institutions, and the same ideological imperatives that had gained them liberation from their own state would be automatically in place to defend against any other states that tried to fill the vacuum" (Hummel 2001, p. 533).

Furthermore, because preferences crucially influence the shape of the institutional framework within which they find expression, a peacefully established polycentric, stateless legal order would by definition contain no state structures that would-be Olsonian stationary bandits might want to take over in their quest to create a territorial monopoly of force. This, in turn, would make their predatory efforts much more costly from the organizational point of view (Rothbard 1973a).

More specific difficulties associated with establishing a stable coercive apparatus in a politically virgin land include the costs of holding out against the possible retaliatory actions of a decentralized local opposition (e.g., guerilla troops) (Stromberg 2003). Such an opposition, usually being amorphous, horizontally organized, and much more knowledgeable about the contested territory (in the Hayekian sense of being familiar with the specific circumstances of time and place), is very likely to be much more effective in undermining the power of the usurper than the usurper is likely to be in undermining the power of it. A related point is that if the subjugated population resorts to using the services of clandestine, private protection agencies operating on the black market, the would-be monopolistic predator would have to expend additional costs on infiltrating and dismantling such organizations, which might be extremely expensive and onerous (Childs 1977). Again, it is essential to notice here that all of the difficulties accruing to the actions of predators stem not from the superior coercive power of their would-be victims, but from the organizational-institutional structure adopted by the latter, which, in turn, derives from their preferences and ideological convictions.

Let us now turn back to the historical evidence of well-functioning non-governmental societies mentioned earlier and consider yet another inevitabilist suggestion as to why it is ultimately irrelevant. An inevitabilist might try to modify his initial reply and suggest that all of the stateless societies from the aforementioned list turned out to be comparatively stable and long-lasting not so much because they were poor and primitive (and thus offered little concentrated wealth to loot by potential predators), but because they were all relatively small (and thus offered little total wealth to loot), the largest including just around 1 million individuals.

There are two problems with this reply, one theoretical and one empirical. Starting with the latter, there is, as in the context of the original inevitabilist interpretation of the data in question, no significant positive correlation between the size of a given region and its likelihood of being taken over by a particularly predatory monopoly of force. Admittedly, a number of exceptionally wealthy small countries seem to owe their prosperity partly to the fact that their governments are relatively non-predatory (e.g., Hong Kong, Liechtenstein, Luxembourg), but there are also many large countries whose residents enjoy much greater freedom from institutional predation than the residents of their much smaller counterparts (e.g., Canada compared to Cuba or Australia compared to Burundi).

Now let us move to the theoretical problem, which is, in an important sense, more fundamental than its empirical companion. Even if we were to assume for the sake of argument that there does indeed exist a significant positive correlation between the size of a given region and its likelihood of being taken over by a particularly predatory monopoly of force, it would by no means establish the conclusion that monopolies of force are inevitable. After all, because governments come in all kinds of sizes, and because, presumably, all inevitabilists would agree that secession is not only possible, but sometimes even plausible, they should also agree that there is nothing fundamentally implausible about the occurrence of a thoroughgoing secessionist process whose culmination would be strict alignment of "political" borders with those of private property. As Carl Watner put it:

> If the inhabitants of the world may secede from the universe, why not the inhabitants of North America from the world? And if North Americans may secede, why not inhabitants of the United States, New York, or Manhattan? Each neighborhood? Each block? Each house? Each person? The right of secession for groups of people logically ends by recognizing the right of secession for the individual and his property. If each person may secede then we have arrived at individualist-anarchism based upon self-ownership and homesteading rights.
>
> (Watner 1982, p. 312)

In other words, even if big states are to be thought of as necessarily highly predatory, there is nothing inevitable about big states staying big, and a sufficiently small state is no longer a state, but rather a plot of private property governed by its owner or owners in a completely unanimous, voluntary manner. A global polycentric, competitive, entrepreneurial system of law and order would be precisely a world composed of tens or even hundreds of millions of such independent plots of land, presumably often integrated into homeowner and neighborhood associations.

One final issue that should be mentioned in this section is the non-existence of world government. Let us recall that according to the inevitabilists, a competitive natural selection process operating in the state of nature is supposed to lead to one "protection agency" (the one that enjoys the greatest comparative advantage in deploying aggressive force for predatory purposes) to subjugate all others and thus effectively destroy the very prerequisites of a competitive market environment in the provision of law and defense. Logically speaking, the ultimate culmination of such a process should be the establishment of a world government. And yet no such institution exists, and there are hardly any indications that it is likely to emerge in the near future. The dominant form assumed by territorial monopolies of force in today's world is that of so-called "nation-states", whose borders are coterminous with the borders of territories inhabited by different ethnic, cultural, and linguistic groups. This observation appears to be yet another corroboration of the main claim advanced in this chapter – namely, that it is the influence of preferences and ideologies (in this case, the ideology of nationalism or patriotism) rather than the possession of a comparative advantage in violence that ultimately determines the extent to which any given territorial monopoly of force will be able to expand and subdue those unwilling to accept its control. In sum, because world government is clearly not inevitable, and because preferences and ideological convictions, including those that currently support the existence of nation-states, can undergo changes,[6] sometimes radical, it seems that national governments are not inevitable either (Block 2005).

To counter this conclusion, an inevitabilist would have to argue that there is a relevant difference between national and world government that makes the former, but not the latter, inescapable. This is precisely what Holcombe (2007) tries to accomplish by accusing Block (2005) of committing the fallacy of composition. In order for this accusation to be correct, the inevitabilist needs to point out what makes the sum (the world) non-governable by a single coercive entity, while making its constituent parts (individual countries) governable in such a manner, let alone inescapably so. Perhaps the relevant difference consists in national governments being, for the most part, nationally homogeneous, whereas a world government would have to be highly multinational. Perhaps the inevitabilist can eat his cake and have it too by suggesting that ideologies indeed matter, so much so that no political ideology is likely to transcend national differences and serve as the foundation of a world state, while still claiming that within any given national group occupying a given piece of land a territorial monopoly of force is unavoidably going to emerge.

This reply does not seem convincing insofar as many presently existing governments rule over multinational, multiethnic, and multilingual regions, successfully subsuming diverse social groups under the common denominator of "national identity". And if national governments are clearly capable of forging such identities, why shouldn't it be possible for a world government to create a global nation and a corresponding global national identity? Asking such a question appears particularly legitimate in view of the existing historical evidence for the theory that national identities are deliberately invented rather than spontaneously evolved phenomena (Anderson 1983; Melman 1991).

Another reply that the inevitabilist might give in this context is that world government, unlike national governments, does not face any external political competition, and that political diseconomies of scale make it unlikely that any territorial monopoly of force could expand so much as to eliminate all of its competitors in the entire world. The problem with this suggestion is that no such diseconomies seem to exist, or if they do, they are outweighed by political economies of scale. After all, the more territorially extensive a given monopoly of force is, the bigger its tax base is, the higher are the taxes that it can impose on the inhabitants of the area that it controls (because it faces fewer governmental competitors capable of enticing people to relocate to areas whose inhabitants are subject to less political predation), the longer it can engage in the process of inflationary redistribution of the purchasing power of politically controlled fiat money before bringing about an economically ruinous crack-up boom (Mises 1996, p. 427), the more difficult it makes overcoming the collective action problem among those of its victims willing to mount an opposition to it, etc. As Hülsmann (1997) puts it, explaining the political benefits of advancing the process whose culmination would be the establishment of a world government:

> The driving force [behind political unification] is the necessity and the will of governments to extend their power, and to survive in times of crisis. This force leads to political unification, because bankrupt *and* not-yet-bankrupt governments have a common interest in bargaining financial assistance against political influence.
>
> (p. 92)

In addition, as noted by Cuzán (1979), political competition occurs not only between territorial monopolies of force, but also within the ruling class of each of them. In other words, governments, especially democratic ones, only shift the problem of eliminating an anarchic order onto a higher level, because anarchy (i.e., absence of any overarching coercive authority) always persists between the members of a newly emerged ruling order. As Cuzán describes it:

> In their relations among each other, [the rulers] remain largely "lawless." Nobody *external to the group* writes and enforces rules governing the relations among them. At most, the rulers are bound by flexible constraints imposed by a "constitution" which they, in any case, interpret and enforce among and upon themselves.
>
> (1979, p. 153)

This suggests that the inevitabilists overexpose the problem of the possible imposition of a coercive order on a given society by the outsiders at the expense of underexposing the remaining problem of predatory competition between the political forces within any given coercive monopoly. In any event, these reflections show that it is by no means the case that the phenomenon of political competition disappears with the establishment of a world government. If, contrary to the claim considered earlier, some political ideologies might transcend national differences and serve as the foundation of a hypothetical world state, the institution in question, and in particular its ruling class, would in all likelihood still consist of many conflicting groups, each catering to its own interests, including those of national or ethnic character. To sum up, the existence or lack thereof of political competition cannot be treated as a difference between national and world government that makes the former, but not the latter, inevitable, because, as I tried to demonstrate earlier, political competition exists both between and within governments, including the ones so big that they encompass the entire world.

In conclusion, it appears that the anti-inevitabilist argument from the nonexistence of world government cannot be undermined by accusing its proponents of committing the fallacy of composition. This, in turn, further strengthens the chief contention of this chapter – namely, that the influence of preferences and ideologies ultimately trumps the influence of organized violence and coercion, thus implying that the emergence of territorial monopolies of force is not inevitable.

5.3 Collective action, cooperation, and collusion[7]

Let us now consider one of the more theoretically sophisticated varieties of the inevitabilist challenge, which relies on a supposed symmetry between Pareto-superior and Pareto-inferior solutions to the collective action problem.[8] The challenge in question says the following: assuming that voluntary cooperation can successfully solve the collective action problem, it has to be capable of solving it regardless of the moral qualities of the motives that drive the solution. Thus, if it is possible to successfully produce public goods on a voluntary, decentralized basis, it must also be possible on the same basis to create stable cartels capable of reaping monopoly gains and frustrating consumer sovereignty. Conversely, if harmful cartels are to be thought of as inherently unstable and thus short-lived, it must also be concluded that the temptation of underselling one's competitor will thwart any attempts to successfully produce public goods on a voluntary, decentralized basis (Cowen and Sutter 1999). In sum, either governments are inevitable or private production of public goods is impossible.

I believe that the solution to this challenge lies in recognizing that there is, in fact, a fundamental asymmetry between the viability of beneficial and malevolent cooperation. In short, the former is normally profitable both in the short and the long run, whereas the latter is profitable only in the short run. And conversely, opposing the latter is normally profitable both in the short and the long run, whereas opposing the former is profitable only in the short run. To illustrate: if X bundles the production of private goods with the production of public goods, his offer is more attractive than the offer of those who focus exclusively on the production of private goods, thus generating short-term profits for him (Long 1994). But apart from tangible profits, such a business approach also generates favorable reputation, which gives X an additional competitive edge and makes his business even more profitable in the long run (Klein 1997).

Conversely, cooperating with a cartel generates short-term profits for its members, but it by the same token makes their activities very disreputable, which further aggravates the inherent instability of their association, makes them subject to social ostracism, undermines their trustworthiness and thus reduces the number of their potential business allies, gives outside competition extra incentive to put the cartel out of business, etc. Breaking the cartel agreement, however, allows the breaker not only to gain short-term profits by underselling his erstwhile partners, but also to gain a favorable reputation, the reputation of an honest businessman who opposes collusion, which is likely to generate additional long-term profits for him.

In sum, overcoming the collective action problem to benefit oneself by harming others pays in the short run but backfires in the long run, whereas overcoming it to benefit oneself by benefiting others pays in the short run and in the long run. Thus, there is a good reason to believe that, on the whole, voluntary cooperation can not only successfully solve the collective action problem, but also make the effects of the majority of voluntarily undertaken collective actions unambiguously beneficial.

Of course, as is consistent with the main theme of the present chapter, whether such an outcome will actually obtain this depends crucially on whether the majority of a given society exhibit a relatively low time preference, a penchant for long-term thinking, and at least an elementary predilection for peace over conflict. However, given how transparent and easily understandable are the benefits of adopting such a preference structure, and how equally transparent and easily understandable are the costs of adopting the opposite one, it seems by no means inevitable that at least minimally reasonable individuals will always opt for the latter. In sum, contra the challenge considered in this section, if governments are not inevitable, effective private production of public goods is still possible.

5.4 The circularity problem[9]

The last issue that I would like to touch upon in this chapter is the so-called "circularity problem" (Morris 1998; Lee 2008; Buchanan 2011), which can be summarized as follows:

> To show that competition between protection agencies would have beneficial consequences, [legal] polycentrists often cite results from price theory about market competition. But there is a circularity problem here: markets presuppose a legal framework; hence before polycentrists can employ price theoretic arguments about market competition, they must first show that the legal requirements of markets are satisfied, that is, that property rights and contracts are enforced. If these requirements are not satisfied, it is illegitimately circular to draw on market competition as an argument for legal polycentrism.
>
> (Wiebe 2012, p. 1)

The implicit worry here is that price theoretic arguments about market competition and other efficiency-enhancing features of free-enterprise–based institutional arrangements depend on, but do not prove, the existence of the requisite legal framework in a stateless environment.

In response, it has to be noted that the difficulties ostensibly raised by the circularity argument are by no means unique to legal polycentrism. An argument of a very similar structure can be deployed against, for instance, the supposed contractarian justification for governmental legal monocentrism: it might be claimed that if the social contract can be made in the state of nature, then the state (understood as a contract enforcer) is redundant, but if the social contract cannot be made in the state of nature, then the state is impossible. In sum, either the contractarian position is viciously circular or the social contract, needing no meta-state to enforce it, effectively becomes a self-enforcing anomaly.

The reason why I mention this parallel is because I believe that it illustrates the fact that the circularity alluded to in the context of both of the previously mentioned legal systems does not point to any fundamental unworkability of either of them. Where a proponent of legal polycentrism claims that "a functioning market and a functioning legal order arise together" (Long 2008, p. 141), a proponent of coercive legal monocentrism can equally justifiably claim that a functioning state and a functioning legal order arise together. The parallel under discussion seems to me to point to the fact that incipient legal orders, regardless of their more specific characteristics, such as monocentricity or polycentricity, are necessarily grounded in the underlying soft legal institutions (customs, traditions, general social norms, etc.).[10] In other words, if by "state of nature" one means a state of affairs in which there are no hard legal institutions, then legal systems do, in fact, emerge directly out of the state of nature.

This is illustrated, for instance, by the fact that "roving bandits" (Olson 2000) can rely on the soft, informal institutions of trust and ostracism to solve their own prisoner's dilemma, successfully police or eliminate free riders, etc., and eventually become stationary bandits. The same applies to "anarchic" communities that manage to survive for at least some time without being subjugated by roving-bandits-turned-stationary-bandits but also generate wealth sufficient to become attractive prey for them.

In sum, what ultimately accounts for the stability and workability of any given set of hard legal institutions (be it monocentric or polycentric, coercive or voluntary, monopolistic or competitive, etc.) is the underlying set of corresponding soft legal institutions, that is, the ones rooted in custom, tradition, religion, etc., or, more broadly speaking, the ones ultimately dependent on preferences rather than incentives. They are, in an important sense, and for all practical purposes, an ultimate given, because they originate over very long periods in an endogenous, evolutionary manner. The familiar message of de la Boetie, Hume, Mises, and their modern successors is that any territorial monopoly of force that fails to tap into these institutions, or at least make peace with them, is ultimately bound to collapse (Hume 1971; Higgs 1987; Mises 1996, pp. 188–91; Boetie 1997). According to the theory of legal polycentrism, the same goes for any rogue protection or arbitration agency, that is, an agency whose mode of operation fails to reflect accurately the shared values and expectations of the society it purports to provide with protective or legal services.

One of the unique features of a competitive, contractual, polycentric legal order is that the role it assigns to hard legal institutions is merely to make the enforcement of rules based on the underlying soft legal institutions more effective. In other words, in such an order hard legal institutions do not establish the rules of social cooperation, but rather allow the process of their enforcement to benefit from specialization, division of labor, economic calculation, capital accumulation, greater incentive compatibility, and other efficiency- and welfare-enhancing features of free-enterprise-based arrangements. As I see it, the chief, non-circular claim of the legal polycentrist is that market competition in the area of law and defense provision generates precisely these beneficial features, whereas state monopoly in this area necessarily prevents their emergence. This is so especially insofar as the idea behind coercive legal monocentrism is essentially to override the aforesaid soft legal institutions rather than consult them, which results in what I called earlier the legal rule-following paradox, that is, the impossibility of making a logically meaningful distinction between the coercive monopolist enforcing the law and merely claiming to enforce it, which, in turn, makes the whole concept of law empty or arbitrary.[11]

There exist numerous historical examples of the previously mentioned process of the development of hard legal institutions on the foundation of their soft counterparts, some of which point to monocentric and some to polycentric results. The list of examples belonging to the former category is admittedly much longer, but this should not be surprising, because it is a well-known and well-understood fact that overcoming the collective action problem is much easier for roving bandits than for aspiring market entrepreneurs.

As I have emphasized repeatedly throughout this chapter, institutional efficiency is a function of the underlying incentive structure, which, in turn, is largely a function of the underlying ideological conditions. As it happens, the praxeological features of collective action imply that minorities can undertake it with much greater facility than majorities, because within small groups benefits are more highly concentrated, interests are more uniform, and effective monitoring of free riders is more feasible. This, coupled with the iron law of oligarchy (Mosca 1939; Michels 1959), implies that it is much easier for bands of roving bandits to generate incentive structures favorable to undertaking successful collective actions than it is for peaceful members of extended societies to accomplish the same task. In other words, it is much easier to establish a territorial monopoly of force than to create a network of private, competing protection and arbitration agencies that could safeguard a given society from the depredations of such a would-be monopoly.

However, as the present chapter tries to demonstrate, the difficulty of the latter task by no means implies its impossibility – instead, it points to the crucial link between incentives and preferences and to the crucial fact that successfully modifying the latter can substantially alleviate the collective action problem. Thus we get what might be called the regression theorem of institutional development, whereby the development of higher-level (hard) institutions is conditioned by the development of lower-level (soft) institutions.[12] No alleged circularity seems to make this process inoperative.

In response, the defender of the circularity objection might suggest that the earlier solution is of limited value, because "informal institutions are limited in their ability to scale up", that is, in their ability "to function effectively as population size increases. For example, reputational mechanisms might break down in large anonymous groups, since communicating information about cheaters becomes prohibitively costly" (Wiebe 2012, p. 8). I believe that this suggestion rests on a misunderstanding of the role of informal institutions in the process of establishing a robust system of polycentric governance. The scalability objection would work if the role of informal institutions was to replace their formal counterparts rather than to provide the necessary foundation for their emergence. This, however, is not the case – as soon as formal institutions emerge against the background of their informal counterparts, the scalability of the latter (or lack thereof) becomes irrelevant.

This is best illustrated by Menger's (1976) famous description of the bottom-up evolutionary process whereby the most marketable commodity assumes the role of a universal means of exchange upon outcompeting all of its less marketable rivals, thus transforming a barter economy into a monetary economy. Now, although the initial existence of barter arrangements is necessary for the initiation of the aforementioned process that culminates in the emergence of money, together with the complex, formalized institutional framework that allows for its effective operation, the scalability of the former setting is in no way identical or even proportional to that of the latter. A barter economy is clearly limited in its ability to scale up, but a monetary economy is not. Likewise, "soft" reputational mechanisms might be limited in their ability to create a sufficiently scalable set of legal and protective institutions, but the same need not apply to "hard" frameworks that develop on their foundation. A different conclusion may be reached only if one mistakenly thinks of soft and hard institutions as substitutes rather than complements.

In sum, there does not seem to be any insurmountable problem of circularity confronting the position of legal polycentrism. Falling back on the hierarchy of levels of social analysis described in the new institutionalist literature (Williamson 1998, 2000) allows us to generate a regression theorem of institutional development which disposes of any troublesome circularity in this context. Scalability also does not seem to be an overwhelming problem here. The reason why voluntary, competitive institutions in the area of law and defense have a harder time scaling up than coercive, centralized ones follows from the praxeological features of collective action, but this is a well-known observation, long appreciated by the theorists of legal polycentrism, who clearly recognize the indispensable role of ideology and preference change in rectifying this asymmetry.

With this, let us conclude our examination of the inevitabilist challenge and the ways in which it can be addressed and proceed to the penultimate chapter of the present book.

Notes

1 As opposed to "thin" ideological unity, which manifests itself in general respect for private property rights and the principle of free exchange of goods and services.

2 This section incorporates material from Wisniewski (2014a).

3 On the same issue, see also the following remarks of Block (2002): "if [the] public-choice-based theory were a correct explanation of increasing government encroachment, there would be no possibility of the existence of the economies of Hong Kong or Singapore, which are not earmarked by excessive government, at least relative to most other countries in the world. . . . Nor would this [theory] apply to the U.S. in its early days, where rarely was there to be found a government program that would be considered excessive, at least by today's standards. . . . If public choice considerations were definitive, these nations, areas and epochs of relative economic freedom could not have occurred, for we would have had to, in effect, bribe bureaucrats with the proceeds of excessive governmental 'rent seeking' to induce them to produce needed statist programs" (pp. 65–6).

4 This is the name I shall henceforth apply to the proponents of the thesis that the existence of territorial monopolies of force, although not necessary for the production of public goods, is nonetheless inevitable.

5 At the same time, it has to be remembered, especially in this context, that incentives and preferences are usually highly interdependent, with changes in incentives contributing to changes in preferences and vice versa. To take an illustrative example: if, due to the existence of social networking websites, the members of a given society realize that overcoming the collective action problem is easier than it used to be, they might start to view political ways of creating supposedly public goods as increasingly less attractive, more cumbersome, etc. Similarly, if they have a strong preference for liberty, it is likely to give them extra encouragement to try to devise effective ways of overcoming the collective action problem.

6 It has to be borne in mind in this context that the nation-state, as well as the state as such, are relatively recent historical developments (Pierson 1996; Van Creveld 1999).

7 This section incorporates material from Wisniewski (2015).

8 The former meaning "beneficial to all of the affected agents" and the latter meaning "beneficial to those agents who participate in collective action, but harmful to at least some of the affected non-participants".

9 This section incorporates material from Wisniewski (2014b).

10 Unless a legal system is imposed on the inhabitants of a given territory by conquest, but even then its long-term survival depends on the ability of conquerors to integrate it with the local soft institutions to a sufficient degree.

11 It has to be stressed that this observation does not contradict my earlier claim that any territorial monopoly of force that fails to tap into the soft institutions existing in a given society, or at least make peace with them, is ultimately bound to collapse. This is because, first, overriding such institutions is not tantamount to ignoring them altogether, and second, as territorial monopolies of force consolidate their power over time, their dependence on such institutions may loosen.

12 A somewhat similar solution is suggested by Friedman (1996), who claims that the formal arrangements of a polycentric legal and protective order can piggyback on the pre-existing equilibrium generated on the basis of a past sequence of mutual threat games. I believe that the narrative described here complements and improves upon Friedman's proposal insofar as it explicitly grounds it in the distinction and mutual relationship between incentives and preferences, as well as between qualitatively different kinds of institutions.

Bibliography

Anderson, B. (1983), *Imagined Communities: Reflections on the Origin and Spread of Nationalism* (London: Verso).

Bastiat, F. (1998) [1850], *The Law* (Irvington-on-Hudson, NY: Foundation for Economic Education).

Block, W. (2002), 'All Government Is Excessive: A Rejoinder to "in Defense of Excessive Government" by Dwight Lee', *Journal of Libertarian Studies*, 16 (3), 35–82.

Block, W. (2005), 'Governmental Inevitability: Reply to Holcombe', *Journal of Libertarian Studies*, 19 (3), 71–93.

Boetie, E. de la (1997) [1576], *The Politics of Obedience: The Discourse of Voluntary Servitude* (Montrèal/New York/London: Black Rose Books).

Brennan, G. and Lomasky, L. (1993), *Democracy and Decision: The Pure Theory of Electoral Preference* (Cambridge: Cambridge University Press).

Buchanan, J. M. (1975), *The Limits of Liberty: Between Anarchy and Leviathan* (Chicago: University of Chicago Press).

Buchanan, J. M., Tollison, R. P. and Tullock, G. (eds.) (1980), *Towards a Theory of the Rent-Seeking Society* (College Station: Texas A&M University Press).

Buchanan, J. M. (2011), 'The Limits of Market Efficiency', *Rationality, Markets, and Morals*, 2, 1–7.

Caplan, B. (2000), 'Rational Irrationality: A Framework for the Neoclassical-Behavioral Debate', *Eastern Economic Journal*, 26, 191–211.

Caplan, B. (2007), *The Myth of the Rational Voter: Why Democracies Choose Bad Policies* (Princeton, NJ: Princeton University Press).

Childs, R. A., Jr. (1977), 'The Invisible Hand Strikes Back', *Journal of Libertarian Studies*, 1 (1), 23–33.

Cowen, T. (1992), 'Law as a Public Good: The Economics of Anarchy', *Economics and Philosophy*, 8, 249–67.

Cowen, T. and Sutter, D. (1999), 'The Costs of Cooperation', *Review of Austrian Economics*, 12 (2), 161–73.

Cowen, T. and Sutter, D. (2005), 'Conflict, Cooperation and Competition in Anarchy', *Review of Austrian Economics*, 18 (1), 109–15.

Cowen, T. (2007), 'The Paradox of Libertarianism', *Cato Unbound* (March 11).

Cuzán, A. (1979), 'Do We Ever Really Get Out of Anarchy?', *Journal of Libertarian Studies*, 3 (2), 151–8.

Downs, A. (1957), *An Economic Theory of Democracy* (New York: Harper).

Friedman, D. (1996), 'Anarchy and Efficient Law', in J. Sanders and J. Narveson (eds.), *For and against the State* (Rowman and Littlefield).

Gwartney, J., Lawson, R. and Hall, J. (2012), *Economic Freedom of the World: 2012 Annual Report* (Fraser Institute), retrieved September 20, 2012, from www.freetheworld.com.

Hayek, F. A. (1988), 'The Fatal Conceit: The Errors of Socialism', in W. W. Bartley III (ed.), *The CollectedWorks of F. A. Hayek* (Chicago: University of Chicago Press).

The Heritage Foundation (2013), *Index of Economic Freedom*, retrieved August 20, 2013, from www.heritage.org/index/.

Higgs, R. (1987), *Crisis and Leviathan: Critical Episodes in the Growth of American Government* (New York: Oxford University Press).

Hobbes, T. (1991) [1651], *Leviathan: Cambridge Texts in the History of Political Thought* (Cambridge: Cambridge University Press).

Holcombe, R. G. (2004), 'Government: Unnecessary but Inevitable', *Independent Review*, 8 (3), 325–42.

Holcombe, R. G. (2005), 'Is Government Inevitable? Reply to Leeson and Stringham', *Independent Review*, 9 (4), 551–7.

Holcombe, R. G. (2007), 'Is Government Really Inevitable?', *Journal of Libertarian Studies*, 21 (1), 41–8.

Hoppe, H.-H. (2001), *Democracy: The God That Failed: The Economics and Politics of Monarchy, Democracy, and Natural Order* (New Brunswick, NJ: Transaction Publishers).

Hülsmann, J. G. (1997), 'Political Unification: A Generalized Progression Theorem', *Journal of Libertarian Studies*, 13 (1), 81–96.

Hume, D. (1971) [1742], 'On the First Principles of Government', in *Essays: Moral, Political and Literary* (Oxford: Oxford University Press).

Hummel, J. R. (2001), 'The Will to Be Free: The Role of Ideology in National Defense', *Independent Review*, 5 (4), 523–37.

Jouvenel, B. de (1949), *On Power* (New York: Viking Press).

Klein, D. B. (ed.) (1997), *Reputation: Studies in the Voluntary Elicitation of Good Conduct* (Ann Arbor: University of Michigan Press).

Lee, J. R. (2008), 'Libertarianism, Limited Government, and Anarchy', in R. T. Long and T. R. Machan (eds.), *Anarchism/Minarchism: Is a Government Part of a Free Country?* (Burlington, VT: Ashgate), 15–20.

Leeson, P. T. and Stringham, E. P. (2005), 'Is Government Inevitable? Comment on Holcombe's Analysis', *Independent Review*, 9 (4), 543–9.

Long, R. T. (1994), 'Funding Public Goods: Six Solutions', *Formulations*, 2 (1).

Long, R. T. (2008), 'Market Anarchism as Constitutionalism', in R. T. Long and T. R. Machan (eds.), *Anarchism/Minarchism: Is a Government Part of a Free Country?* (Burlington, VT: Ashgate), 133–51.

Matsusaka, J. (1995), 'The Economic Approach to Democracy', in M. Tommasi and K. Ierulli (eds.), *The New Economics of Human Behavior* (Cambridge: Cambridge University Press).

Melman, B. (1991), 'Claiming the Nation's Past: The Invention of an Anglo-Saxon Tradition', *Journal of Contemporary History*, 26 (3–4), 575–95.

Menger, C. (1976) [1871], *Principles of Economics* (New York: New York University Press).

Michels, R. (1959) [1915], *Political Parties* (New York: Dover).

Mises, L. (1996) [1949], *Human Action* (4th ed. revised, San Francisco: Fox and Wilkes).

Morris, C. (1998), *An Essay on the Modern State* (Cambridge: Cambridge University Press).

Mosca, G. (1939), *The Ruling Class* (New York: McGraw-Hill).

North, D. (1981), *Structure and Change in Economic History* (New York: W.W. Norton).

North, D. (1990), *Institutions, Institutional Change and Economic Performance* (Cambridge, MA: Cambridge University Press).

North, D. (1993), 'Institutions and Credible Commitment', *Journal of Institutionaland Theoretical Economics*, 149 (1), 11–23.

Olson, M. (1971) [1965], *The Logic of Collective Action: Public Goods and the Theory of Groups* (Cambridge, MA: Harvard University Press).

Olson, M. (2000), *Power and Prosperity* (New York, NY: Basic Books).

Ostrom, E. (1990), *Governing the Commons: The Evolution of Institutions for Collective Action* (Cambridge: Cambridge University Press).

Pierson, C. (1996), *The Modern State* (London and New York: Routledge).

Powell, B. and Coyne, C. (2003), 'Do Pessimistic Assumptions about Human Behavior Justify Government?', *Journal of Libertarian Studies*, 17 (4), 17–37.

Rawls, J. (1971), *A Theory of Justice* (Cambridge, MA: Belknap).

Rothbard, M. (1973a), 'Police, Law and the Courts', in E. P. Stringham (ed., 2007), *Anarchy and the Law: The Political Economy of Choice* (New Brunswick/London: Transaction Publishers).

Rothbard, M. (2004) [1962], *Man, Economy, and State: A Treatise on Economic Principles with Power and Market* (Scholar's ed., Auburn, AL: Ludwig von Mises Institute).

Salerno, J. T. (2008b), 'Imperialism and the Logic of War Making', *Independent Review*, 12 (3), 447–57.

Stringham, E. P. and Hummel, J. R. (2010), 'If a Pure Market Economy Is So Good, Why Doesn't It Exist? The Importance of Changing Preferences vs. Incentives in Social Change', *Quarterly Journal of Austrian Economics*, 13 (2), 31–52.

Stromberg, J. R. (2003), 'Mercenaries, Guerrillas, Militias, and the Defense of Minimal States and Free Societies', in H.-H. Hoppe (ed.), *The Myth of National Defense: Essays on the Theory and History of Security Production* (Auburn, AL: Ludwig von Mises Institute).

Tullock, G. (1967), 'The Welfare Costs of Tariffs, Monopolies, and Theft', *Western Economic Journal*, 5, 224–32.

Van Creveld, M. (1999), *The Rise and Decline of the State* (Cambridge: Cambridge University Press).

Watner, C. (1982), 'The Proprietary Theory of Justice in the Libertarian Tradition', *Journal of Libertarian Studies*, 6 (3–4), 289–316.

Wiebe, M. (2012), 'Legal Polycentrism and the Circularity Problem', unpublished manuscript, last modified September 30, 2012. PDF file.

Williamson, O. E. (1998), 'Transaction Cost Economics: How It Works: Where It Is Headed', *De Economist*, 146 (1), 23–58.

Williamson, O. E. (2000), 'The New Institutional Economics: Taking Stock, Looking Ahead', *Journal of Economic Literature*, 38 (3), 595–613.

Wisniewski, J. B. (2014a), 'Defense as a Private Good in a Competitive Order', *Review of Social and Economic Issues*, 1 (1), 3–35.

Wisniewski, J. B. (2014b), 'Legal Polycentrism, the Circularity Problem, and the Regression Theorem of Institutional Development', *Quarterly Journal of Austrian Economics*, 17 (4), 510–8.

Wisniewski, J. B. (2015), 'A Note on Collective Action, Cooperation, Collusion, and Voluntary Production of Public Goods', *Ekonomia: Wroclaw Economic Review*, 21 (2), 55–8.

6   The ethics of legal and protective polycentrism

6.1 Introduction

In the preceding chapters I endeavored to show that 1) the category of public goods is, from the economic point of view, artificial and arbitrary, and thus the goods that allegedly belong to it can be effectively produced in the absence of institutional coercion and that 2) monopolized, institutional coercion is not necessary to produce the alleged public goods, but neither is its existence necessitated by the collective action problem coupled with the iron law of oligarchy.

However, even at this point one might argue that there are some substantial benefits to be derived from having territorial monopolies of force around, because their coercive power, even if generally economically inefficient, can be useful in compelling certain desirable outcomes in cases of emergency. One might suggest that this, due to the existence of a tradeoff between efficiency and equity, is likely to secure important ethical gains that could not be otherwise achieved, chief among them being the provision of certain vital goods to the least well-off. After all, could it not be argued that one of the most important public goods, construed not in economic, but in ethical terms, is the availability of an emergency subsistence fund that someone who fell on hard times through no fault of his own could draw on until he gets back on his feet? And could it not be plausibly suggested that monopolized, institutional coercion is uniquely suited to guarantee the existence of such a fund, even if only at the cost of some degree of economic efficiency?

As I indicated in the project overview in Chapter 1, at this point one might wonder whether it is not a mistake to postpone the discussion of such crucial considerations until the last chapter. My view is that, on the contrary, it is impossible to discuss these issues in a serious manner without first circumscribing the relevant normative analysis with a thorough investigation of pertinent economic questions, which I hope to have conducted over the preceding five chapters. It seems to me that one of the most important roles of economics is to explain the difference between the possible and the desirable, and in this sense to serve as the perimeter of rational ethics. Thus, I regard the content of the previous chapters as indirectly but significantly contributing to the ethical analysis of legal and protective polycentrism along the lines suggested by Rothbard:

> Praxeology – economics – provides no ultimate ethical judgments: it simply furnishes the indispensable data necessary to make such judgments. . . . And

yet praxeology may be extended beyond its current sphere, to criticize ethical goals. This does not mean that we abandon the value neutrality of praxeological science. It means merely that even ethical goals must be framed meaningfully and, therefore, that praxeology can criticize (1) existential errors made in the formulation of ethical propositions and (2) the possible existential meaninglessness and inner inconsistency of the goals themselves. If an ethical goal can be shown to be self-contradictory and *conceptually impossible* of fulfillment, then [it] should be abandoned by all.

(Rothbard 2004, p. 1297)

In sum, there is an indirect but crucial link between positive economic theorizing and normative considerations, which, as I see it, makes the content of the preceding chapters highly relevant to the issues of a more directly normative character that are to be explored in what follows. In other words, the task of the present chapter is no longer to explore the perimeter of the relevant ethical area, but to focus on the area itself – rather than circumscribing the relevance of certain ethical concepts, it will investigate directly their potential for justifying the existence of territorial monopolies of force insofar as their relevance can be accepted as a given.

6.2 Moral philosophy, Austrian economics, and rationality[1]

One of the central concepts employed in the subsequent sections of this chapter is that of (normatively understood) rationality, both in its prudential and moral variety. I believe that the philosophical foundations of Austrian economics offer some unique insights into its nature, including an illumination of the ways in which modern moral philosophy and its views on rationality have been (in many respects unfortunately) influenced by the methodological assumptions of neoclassical economics. Thus, I also believe that substantive moral considerations involving the notion of rationality should be preceded by a methodological introduction containing a relatively brief but comprehensive exposition of the intellectual gains from trade between the fields of Austrian economics and moral philosophy. It is my hope that an introductory set of reflections of this kind will provide the reader with yet another potent illustration of the contention that positive economic theorizing – though itself value free – can indirectly shed light on normative issues.

With these few words of preliminary explanation, let me proceed to investigating the ways in which praxeological analysis can elucidate such central concepts in moral philosophy as rationality and well-being, whose clear understanding will prove essential in the context of substantive ethical considerations in the subsequent sections.

According to one of the central figures of the Austrian tradition, Ludwig von Mises, "For acting man there exists primarily nothing but various degrees of relevance and urgency with regard to his own well-being" (Mises 1996, p. 119). To paraphrase, every human action is aimed at the attainment of some end, and human well-being consists of the satisfaction of chosen ends. Thus, I take it that the majority of Austrians would not object to endorsing the unrestricted desire-satisfaction account of prudential well-being.[2] There is, however, a strong tendency in modern moral philosophy to impose restrictions on the range of desires that are to count as genuinely contributive to the desirer's welfare. Perhaps the most frequent among such proposals is that only appropriately "informed" or "rational" desires are to count.

The terms mentioned earlier bring in a flurry of issues and interpretations, oftentimes very different from those constitutive of Austrian praxeology: some understand entertaining irrational desires in terms of not being sufficiently informed with regard to broadly empirical matters; some in terms of thinking in a logically defective manner or relying on a muddled conceptual apparatus; some others do not bring in the issue of rationality at all, but simply contend that one's desires are not informed (and hence not conducive to one's well-being) if they are not in an appropriate sense related to one's life.

All these proposals require disentangling and will be analyzed in turn. I shall argue that the philosophical assumptions that underlie them suffer from the influence of equilibrium methodology and thus fall prey to the same shortcomings as it does. I shall also point out that what could have been long learned from the Austrian methodology is only now slowly creeping into moral philosophy in the form of the concept of "satisficing" (under a particular interpretation).

Let us then start our analysis from examining the suggestion that one's desires are rational only if they are related to one's life in an appropriate manner. First, let us consider how some modern moral philosophers characterize the issue in question. Derek Parfit, for instance, draws the distinction between what he calls the Unrestricted Desire-Fulfillment Theory and the Success Theory. According to the former, one's well-being is best increased by the satisfaction of all of one's desires, regardless of the way in which they are connected to one's life. Parfit dismisses this theory rather quickly and without much substantiation:

> Suppose that I meet a stranger who has what is believed to be a fatal disease. My sympathy is aroused, and I strongly want this stranger to be cured. We never meet again. Later, unknown to me, this stranger is cured. On the Unrestricted Desire-Fulfilment Theory, this event is good for me, and makes my life go better. This is not plausible. We should reject this theory.
>
> (Parfit 1984, p. 494)

The Success Theory, on the other hand, is supposed to include as conducive to one's well-being only those desires that are in the relevant sense related to one's life. What sense is that? I take it to be the sense in which one's desires are made crucially self-regarding. This seems to follow from Parfit's remarks that the life of an exile, who wants his children's lives to go well, but whose lives (unbeknownst to him) actually go very wrong, is not to that extent worse. However, as soon as the exile's other-regarding desire "I want my children's lives to go well" is replaced with the self-regarding desire "I want to be a successful parent", Parfit agrees that the exile's offspring's' misfortunes decrease his own level of well-being. One can plausibly infer that he takes the changes produced in the exile's existence by the events that do not impinge on his self-regarding desires to be mere Cambridge-changes, changes in the true statements that can be made about him, which have nothing to do with his welfare.

James Griffin, on the other hand, voices doubts about the possibility of severing the link between utility and experience:

> Indeed, without the Experience Requirement, why would utility not include the desires of the dead? And would that not mean the account had gone badly awry?
>
> (Griffin 1986, p. 17)

Admittedly, Griffin concedes later on that there is a good case for honoring wishes expressed in wills, but only to the extent that their realization benefits the living or does justice to the dead in the moral sense (which need not have any prudentially positive effects). So the concession in question aims at preserving the experiential link that Griffin is so concerned about.

I disagree with both of these suggestions – I do not think that in order to contribute to one's well-being, one's desires need either to be related experientially to one's life or contain a substantial element of self-regardingness. Both of these claims seem to me to fall prey to what Mises identified as "materialism"[3] (understood as opposed to "formalism") – namely, the approach whereby subjective human aims are judged against some pre-conceived, objectified benchmark of value.

With regard to the former, let me say the following: some desired states of affairs might remain forever beyond the reach of our experience, and yet, it does not imply that they thereby do not add to our welfare. It is useful to think about such states of affairs in counterfactual terms – if a given person could rise from the dead and learn that her will was ignored, she would conclude that her life didn't go well after all. If, on the other hand, she were to find out that her will was honored, she would have to conclude that her life did go well, and it seems intuitively plausible that she might remark: "And it would go well, regardless of whether I knew". Thinking otherwise appears to make well-being overly mind-dependent. For instance, would it be plausible to suggest that, in some science fiction world of eugenic dystopia, a person bred specifically for the purpose of developing strong and healthy organs for certain pre-arranged recipients, who lived a convincing semblance of a normal and happy life until she was suddenly and painlessly killed (i.e., had no experience of dying and of the attendant fear and pain) in one's prime, did enjoy a good life after all? Most importantly, would it be plausible to claim that no loss of well-being follows from the fact that the person in question can no longer realize the desires associated with her future plans, because now they count among the desires of the dead? My view is that both of these questions should be answered negatively.

Now let me turn to the suggestion that one's well-being cannot be augmented by the satisfaction of those of one's desires that are not in any sense self-regarding.

Let us imagine a man who regularly and profusely gives to charity, but, as a method of avoiding the danger of falling into self-pride, complacency, and vanity, he explicitly refuses to receive any information regarding the lives of those whom he helped. And let us suppose that the size of his charitable contributions sufficed for putting a lot of people out of misery. So even though the man under consideration might well derive some psychological benefits from the very activity of giving to charity (i.e., from the satisfaction of his self-regarding desire of the form "I want to give to charity"), he does not derive any psychological benefits from the fact that others are helped by him (i.e., from the satisfaction of his other-regarding desire of the form "I want people in the third world countries to be relieved from poverty"), because he does not know (and does not want to know) to what degree this is in fact the case. And yet, can it be said that to the extent that his other-regarding desire is actually satisfied his life does not go better? This seems to me very implausible. On the contrary, his attitude appears to me to represent the paradigm of disinterestedness and selflessness, which are typically deemed not only as moral virtues, but also as prudential advantages[4] (unlike some other putative virtues, e.g., self-sacrifice and martyrdom).

Furthermore, even though the philanthropic desire in question contains no element of self-regardingness, it seems very counterintuitive to think of the changes brought about by its satisfaction vis-à-vis the philanthropist as mere Cambridge-changes – after all, it is not the case that satisfying his other-regarding desire makes him live simply in the world in which more Third World people are being helped, but in the world in which precisely his charitable intentions and their diligent implementation are largely responsible for this help. These are by no means merely changes in the true statements that can be made about the philanthropist – these are changes that bear as clear an axiological relation to his person as there can be.

On the basis of these considerations, I have to conclude that neither the desires that are detached from the possibility of experiential verification of their satisfaction nor the desires that are not in any sense self-regarding vis-à-vis the desirer can be called irrational or uninformed and thus not conducive to the desirer's well-being.

Before moving to the analysis of the relationship between irrationality and acting on information insufficient to produce a workable means–ends structure, let us first focus on the interesting cases where regret (or perhaps guilt, reluctance, or disgust) is simultaneous with the action or even with the intention to act. These I take to be the cases of what is called *akrasia*, weakness of will, where the person is unwilling to do X (perhaps even strongly opposed to doing X), and yet does X, apparently voluntarily. Would that constitute an example of irrationality, understood as actualizing the wrong kind of desires, desires uncontributive to one's well-being?

I think not. What seems uncontroversially accepted about the phenomenon of *akrasia* is that it involves a conflict of desires. It is clearly not an irresolvable conflict, because the akratic agent is not suspended in the state of permanent hesitation, but makes a definite decision. Now the question is: If one desire wins out in a competition with another desire, why should acting on the dominant desire be called irrational? Harry Frankfurt (1971) suggests that the aforementioned accompanying feelings of regret and reluctance are the voice of one's second-order desires (desires to have [or not to have] certain first-order desires), which are supposedly constitutive of one's real, albeit suppressed, personality. But I find the talk of second-order desires somewhat puzzling and perhaps incompatible with the principle of not multiplying entities beyond necessity.

First, as soon as we postulate the existence of higher-order volitions, what can stop one from suggesting that just as Z's actions are opposed to Z's second-order desires, Z's words are opposed to Z's third-order desires, which constitute his real, albeit totally suppressed, personality? Could such a suggestion be considered guiltier of speculative psychologizing than Frankfurt's original claim?[5]

And second, in what sense is the suppressed personality supposed to be our *real* personality? Can words really speak louder than actions? Consider an analogy: someone who is a bouncer at a night club could insist that what he really desires is to become a computer scientist. But then, why did he not undertake any actions towards becoming a computer scientist? Perhaps due to the lack of necessary skills or financial resources, but in that case his decision to become a bouncer was not irrational – it was attuned to the possibilities at hand. Likewise, the fact that a drug addict who insists that he would prefer to quit continues to take drugs does not make his actions irrational. What distinguishes a willing addict (who either has no second-order desires, or whose second-order desires coincide with his first-order desires) from an "unwilling" addict is that the latter is aware of the opportunity costs of taking drugs, whereas the former sees none (or is not concerned about them). What is irrational in the psychological makeup of the latter is at most his tendency to assert that he genuinely prefers something that he acts against – there seems to be a kind of self-deception involved, and self-deception is irrational insofar as it indicates the incapability of grasping the logical concept of evidence (a belief is irrational if it is not proportioned to the available evidence, and in this case the evidence of willed and executed action is overwhelming). However, this particular ratiocinative flaw does not interfere with the possibility of acting on what I take to be one's genuine, dominant desires, thus it does not make them in any sense ill informed and unworthy of pursuing.

Let us now turn to the question that I gestured towards earlier: the question of the relationship between irrationality and acting on information insufficient to produce a workable means–ends structure. Here, it seems to me, we need to distinguish between two substantially different ways of being informed: being informed about the methods of cogent reasoning, necessary to give any means–ends structure the proper logical and conceptual shape, and being informed in the sense of possessing the empirical data required for translating the said structure into a set of practically implementable solutions. Both of these kinds of information appear to me to be gained a posteriori – the latter uncontroversially so, but even the former, insofar as it operates with communally established and utilized concepts, starts by picking up such concepts and their meanings in an experiential way (i.e., through social interaction). Now the question is: Does acting while being deficient with regard to either or both of the earlier mentioned kinds of information make one's actions irrational? If not, then we should conclude that rationality and ill-informedness are fundamentally different concepts, with no necessary connections between them. This is indeed what I wish to argue.

We live in a world of far-reaching uncertainty, both synchronic and diachronic, both with respect to ourselves and with respect to others, and there should be nothing surprising or implausible in the conclusion that, at any given moment, we cannot possibly know all the factors relevant to making even relatively simple decisions. Each decision we make is, to some degree, a leap in the dark. Thus, it appears that those philosophers who would wish to equate rationality with well-informedness, understood as having complete knowledge with regard to any given choice (and the desire motivating it), fall prey to the same mistake as the economists who take general equilibrium models (where information is perfect) to be an accurate representation of real-world economies. As was notably remarked by Hayek:

> In ordinary language we describe by the word "planning" the complex of interrelated decisions about the allocation of our available resources. All economic activity is in this sense planning; and in any society in which many people collaborate, this planning, whoever does it, will in some measure have to be based on knowledge which, in the first instance, is not given to the planner but to somebody else, which somehow will have to be conveyed to the planner.
>
> (Hayek 1945, p. 520)

This remark can be generalized from economics and knowledge relevant to business plans into the all-encompassing epistemological problem of uncertainty, which, in our context, might be phrased thus: one will never have full information with regard to his desires, because one will never have full information with regard to the surrounding world. Every choice confronts one with the task of determining tradeoffs between spending time on gathering information and acting on this (however limited) information. The ineradicable scarcity of time implies that one cannot postpone making a decision indefinitely and at some point one has to act given the data one possesses, however incomplete or dubious these might be.

Unfortunately, this predicament cannot be alleviated by listening to nuggets of wisdom such as "plan first, act later" or "in every plan, the first priority is always gathering the relevant knowledge", because, given the ubiquity of uncertainty, no plan can be executed without trial and error: admittedly, we might be eager to learn in advance how to execute plan P1, but in order to do so, we also have to learn how to learn how to execute plan P1 (which would be plan P2, whose successful implementation would in turn require formulating plan P3), and so on ad infinitum. So action aimed at information gathering will start, out of necessity, as soon as we formulate any specific goals or desires. It is mistaken to think that we can conduct any sort of extensive, sterile inquiry into various possible means of accomplishing our ends and gather all the relevant information without making any less than fully informed choices that will influence the likelihood of attaining those ends (Kirzner 1984).

These remarks seem to find corroboration in the introduction of the concept of "satisficing" into the rational choice literature (Simon 1955). Satisficing is supposed to be a more reality-oriented (rather than model-oriented) counterpart of maximizing. Whereas maximizing appears to require that perfect information and infinite time belong to the background of any rational decision-making process, satisficing is more suited to acting in a world of ubiquitous scarcity:

> Satisficing is rational as a time- and other resource-saving strategy: Given our limited resources, we sometimes settle for what's good enough in order to devote resources elsewhere. We could hold out for the best price when buying or selling a car, but that could consume a lot of time and energy that we would prefer to spend elsewhere.
>
> (Byron 2004, p. 5)

In other words, satisficing emerges as maximizing those factors in the inescapable constraints of essential resources. This is the so-called "instrumental conception of satisficing" (Slote 2004, p. 14), which I think of as the only compatible view with my contention that irrationality should be decoupled from uninformedness. An alternative view, which conceives of satisficing as intrinsically valuable, suggests that it consists of exercising the virtue of moderation (p. 16). Let me say very briefly why I find this view implausible. Slote characterizes moderation as the virtue of being satisfied with what one already has, even though having more would not be a bad thing. I, on the other hand, think of moderation as the virtue of not exceeding the limit beyond which good becomes bad – for instance, not eating the fourth piece of cake if my organism can safely digest only three. But if my organism can safely digest ten pieces of cake, then there is nothing immoderate about eating ten pieces of cake and nothing moderate about eating, say, only four. Relatedly, but somewhat differently, if I can (and I want to) win the swimming championship without exerting my organism to the point of permanent health damage, then putting into it only as much effort as is sufficient to get the second place is not moderation, but laziness. Thus, contra Slote, I do not see any intelligible role to play for satisficing understood as intrinsically rational – as I argued in the preceding paragraphs, satisficing always aims at maximizing, but takes account of the pertinent constraints.

I do not think, however, that the two need always converge (into "maxificing"), which is the view held, for example, by Jan Narveson (2004). His motivation for holding it is, I presume, his vision of life as a constant exercise in bounded rationality and the appraisal of budgetary limitations. I am very sympathetic to such a vision, yet I believe that there are cases in which a stroke of good luck removes the said limitations and thus allows one to maximize *simpliciter*. Imagine that I visit a foreign province and I want to stay in the best hotel available. I do not know which is best, but I do know that the natives do not like choosy visitors and that they will become very hostile towards me if I make a reconnaissance into three consecutive hotels and stay in none of them. So if in three attempts I will not find the best hotel, I will settle for the best of what I have found – that is, I will satisfice. But it might also fortunately happen that the first hotel I will stumble upon will turn out to be the best hotel in the province, which will give me a chance to maximize. The former procedure need not necessarily overlap with the latter, and there is clearly no difference in rationality between the two.

Thus, so far I have attempted to establish that neither being less than fully informed, nor being acted upon by an akratic agent, nor being detached from experiential verification, nor being insulated from any element of self-regardingness should be taken as indicative of any given desire's irrationality. Does that mean that I take rationality to be a defining feature of human action? Do I claim that, by definition, there can be no irrational desires? This is certainly the line endorsed by most Austrians, most notably by Mises:

> Human action is necessarily always rational. The term "rational action" is therefore pleonastic and must be rejected as such. . . . The opposite of [rational] action is not *irrational behavior*, but a reactive response to stimuli on the part of the bodily organs and instincts which cannot be controlled by the volition of the person concerned.
>
> (Mises 1996, pp. 19–20)

I myself, however, cannot fully agree with this view. In my preceding discussion of *akrasia* and intertemporal volatility of preferences, some clear candidates for ratiocinative flaws and deficiencies did crop up – first, self-deception, and second, inconsistency, that is, lack of maintenance of a transitive order of rank on one's preference scale. I do believe, nonetheless, that when it comes to the formation and subsequent actualization of one's desires, the most serious potential deficiency of rationality is the inability to grasp the logical relationship between the concepts that comprise the content of those desires. Indeed, without such basic logical and conceptual skills it is probably impossible to construct any effective means–ends structure. Note, however, that this is different from not understanding the relevant concepts and their logical interrelations in the first place – as discussed earlier, such an initial lack of understanding is an indication not of irrationality, but of being badly instructed (or uninstructed).

In this connection, it should perhaps be added that every end, apart from any of one's ultimate ends, can be considered a means as well. And although instruction and persuasion might be effective in changing one's lower-level ends (treated as a means to the attainment of one's higher-level ends), I do not think that they can change one's ultimate ends. I believe that one's ultimate ends might be challenged on moral grounds, but (again, this is the standard Austrian line) not on prudential grounds – it seems that with regard to the latter, the most one can achieve is to help another person spell her final goals out more clearly or point to the fact that they are not really her *final* goals.

Let us consider the following example for the purpose of illustration: X says that his ultimate goal is to beat all of his neighbors on the head and his means to that end is buying a sufficiently big bludgeon. Presumably, an appropriate thing to ask him would be: but why do you want to beat them? Perhaps he would reply: because I want to earn their respect. At that point it would be worthwhile to explain to X that bullying people cannot earn one respect and that primitive violence rarely engenders fearful admiration, but almost always breeds hatred and resentment. That crucial bit of information might well discourage him from going on a violent rampage – his rejection of a badly chosen means would indicate that it is possible to reason with him after all. Worse still, X could not be branded irrational if he clearly identified bullying people as his ultimate end and chose means appropriate for attaining it.[6] But if, despite being taught the requisite logical and conceptual skills over and over again, he were to continue bullying people and expressing surprised disappointment at learning that pursuing this strategy consistently fails to make him more respectable, I believe it would be plausible to conclude that his rational faculties are in some sense dysfunctional.

It might be objected at this point that presumably Mises does not wish to claim that all actions are rationally related to the actor's previous actions or to what he might reasonably have been expected to learn. This sounds plausible, but if the actor is visibly immune both to deductive argument and to highly reliable inductive evidence (as he is in my example), I think it likely that he might be unable to comprehend, even implicitly, the crucial concepts involved in the very process of acting, such as means, end, choice, causality, data, etc., and thus be effectively incapable of acting in the strict Misesian sense. This incapability, however, does not seem to deprive him of the status of a purposive, reflective, desire-entertaining, and decision-making being, which would indicate that possessing such characteristics might not be sufficient for being a rational agent.

To sum up, let us return to the basic question: Can there be irrational desires? My answer is "no" with regard to their content, but "yes" with regard to their relation to the means presumed capable of those desires' satisfaction. Further, the potentially irrational character of the said relation can consist not in the desirer's empirical ignorance, but in his (persistent) inability to comprehend the conceptual interrelations between various parts of the means–ends structure that he (unsuccessfully) employs for the accomplishment of his goals.

In conclusion, it is pointless to criticize the content of specific desires as (prudentially) irrational, but it is quite appropriate to point out that unless one is able to construct a logically cogent means–ends structure (regardless of the amount of instruction one received), one will not be able to satisfy any of one's desires – and that, if anything, deserves the name of irrationality. Thus, if I am right, this is perhaps a significant point that is missing from most descriptions of Austrian praxeology and its characterization of human action and that should be included in their future elaborations.

This, however, is a task for another occasion. For the time being, having investigated the ways in which praxeological analysis can illuminate our understanding of moral philosophy in general and the nature of rationality in particular, let us proceed to the section dealing with the closely related concept of moral objectivity and its relationship with the issue of public goods.

6.3 Well-being and objectivity[7]

Let us suppose that, having thoroughly familiarized himself with the content of the previous chapters, our critic were to agree that the purely economic, neoclassical definition of public goods is untenable and that the criteria it consists of lack sufficient logical coherence. This, however, he might argue, is irrelevant from the normative point of view, because, in addition to the economic one, there is the ethical definition of public goods, which does not conceive of them in subjective, but rather in objective terms, that is, terms independent of anyone's individual desires, interests, and preferences. And although weighing the respective values associated with subjective and objective goods and aggregating them into a result characterized by any degree of quantitative precision is an extremely tricky issue, it might be enough for our critic to plausibly suggest that objective goods do in fact exist, and because their objectivity implies that it is desirable for everyone to enjoy them, he might argue that territorial monopolies of force may be uniquely suited to provide them in a sufficient amount so that "no one is left behind".

However, in order for this line of argumentation to proceed in a potentially promising direction, what constitutes an objective good has to be defined with the requisite degree of conceptual precision. Let us look at some possible avenues for reaching such a definition.

In embarking on this task, some authors start by claiming that the belief that there is an objective element of well-being figures prominently in our moral practices. This suggests that its existence is implied by our deep-seated moral intuitions. Scanlon (1975), for instance, argues that "it seems clear that the criteria of well-being that we actually employ in naming moral judgments are objective" (p. 658). Further, he suggests that in the case of duties of mutual aid the strength of a stranger's claim on us depends not on the strength of his desires and preferences, but on the urgency of his needs. In such scenarios, preference is taken to represent the subjective aspect of one's interests, whereas urgency is supposed to stand for its objective aspect.

If urgency is to take precedence over desire, then it clearly is a powerful notion that needs to be cashed out in detail. Thus, we need to establish the reasons to see any given interest as urgent – in other words, we need to know the possible sources of urgency. Two approaches to this issue suggest themselves: naturalistic and conventional.

One promising version of the former approach postulates that urgency consists of the duty to preserve the life and life functions of purposive agents. Because a sufficiently healthy life is a prerequisite of forming and acting on any desires whatsoever, life and health preservation seems to be a good candidate for an objective requirement of well-being, provided that we can define health in terms independent of anyone's subjective understanding of it. This suggestion also fits well with the notion that law and order is an objective public good, because a society cannot function unless its members are healthy, and none of its members can preserve their health if they are unable to rely on the requisite protective and legal services.

On the other hand, the latter approach, which grounds urgency in society-wide agreements, dispenses with objectivity and contents itself with intersubjectivity. The price to pay here is mind independence, but the gain is protection from moral error; because intersubjective evaluative facts are to be thought of as social or institutional facts, there is no problem with conceiving of them as cognitively accessible and ontologically intelligible. I leave it up to the reader to decide whether this is a worthwhile tradeoff.

Having defined both approaches, let us now analyze them in more detail, starting with the former. Perhaps the most significant attempt to define health naturalistically is Christopher Boorse's Biostatistical Theory, hereafter BST (Boorse 1977, 1997). According to a paraphrase of BST, provided by Elselijn Kingma (2007): "health is normal species functioning, which is the *statistically typical* contribution of all the organism's parts and processes to the organism's overall goals of survival and reproduction" (p. 128). A group of organisms with respect to which the contribution in question is statistically typical is dubbed the *reference class*. BST then specifies the relevant reference classes in terms of the following characteristics: age, sex, and race (Boorse 1977, p. 555). This is the crucial point of Boorse's account, because introducing "wrong" reference classes (e.g., those comprising heavy drinkers and diabetics) or dispensing with them altogether (i.e., assuming that healthy functions are statistically typical species-wide *simpliciter*) would produce very counterintuitive results not at all consonant with the present-day conception of medicine. To give just one example, it would allow for thinking of the liver functions of a heavy drinker as healthy, because they are statistically typical within the reference class of heavy drinkers.

Obviously enough, BST has not gone unchallenged. A recent interesting critique by Kingma (2007) concerns the perceived inadequacy of the way in which Boorse defines appropriate reference classes: that is, as natural classes of organisms of uniform functional design (Boorse 1977, p. 562). Kingma discusses all three pivotal elements of this definition (natural, uniform, and design) before concluding that none of them succeeds in demarcating healthy from diseased features. For instance, if "natural" is to be understood as "occurring in nature", then, clearly, we would have to count as healthy many naturally occurring characteristics that medicine classifies as diseased (diabetes, Down's syndrome, etc.). Likewise, uniformity is just as prevalent among Boorse's preferred reference classes as it is among those that he would like to exclude (consulting an atlas of pathology proves the point in question). Finally, an appeal to design, understood as nature's intent, does not fare any better, because natural selection can maintain both healthy and diseased traits (e.g., sickle-cell anemia). Hence, the argument goes, contrary to the claims of Boorse, BST cannot be a naturalistic, value-free account of health, because counting only his preferred reference classes as appropriate is a value-laden choice, determined by social judgments rather than by empirical facts alone.

Even though it is by no means obvious that these worries conclusively invalidate BST, they nonetheless indicate that considerable prima facie problems exist with formulating a satisfactory naturalistic conception of urgency. In view of this, let us now investigate whether the second of the approaches mentioned at the outset of this section – the conventional approach – fares better in the matter at hand.

The kind of convention that seems particularly relevant in the present context is that established by means of social consensus. To the extent that any given society arrives at an unanimous consensus, the criterion of urgency practically coincides with the criterion of subjective desire satisfaction – what is most urgent is what I (as well as others) desire most strongly. Thus, in such situations there is no danger of making tradeoffs detrimental to moral minorities. Unfortunately, the variation of individual preferences is so great, and the transaction costs of aggregating them are so insurmountable, that there are no truly unanimous social agreements. The question, then, is: What, if not unanimity, can ground the validity of any intersubjective, conventional understanding of urgency? Perhaps the will of reasonable and knowledgeable members of society can do the task. Such a proposal, however, seems to break with the conventional character of our approach – reason and knowledge are not group-relative or society-relative features, and by following this train of thought one could equally well suggest that the standards of urgency should be set by the totality of reasonable and knowledgeable people, regardless of whether they belong to any given society.

Another proposal would be to claim that the requisite normative authority could stem from some sort of majoritarian bargaining process. Would a dissident have an objective, or at least intersubjective, reason to follow this kind of authority? I find it difficult to see one. Admittedly, it might be prudent of him to respect the will of the majority out of fear of being punished for disobedience, but this is a paradigmatic agent-relative, not intersubjective, let alone objective, reason. In order to become binding in the sense sought in this section, the reason under consideration would have to appeal to the content of the values agreed upon, not to the mere fact that their acceptance stems from a majoritarian consensus.

In addition, what I take to be a major problem with the conventional approach is that, qua communal beings, we are normally expected to follow a variety of different and oftentimes mutually incompatible conventions, and our membership in any given society does not tell us which of these conventions should trump others and in what circumstances. To phrase it differently, we normally belong to a number of different "societies", both micro and macro, and it is ultimately up to us to decide how to rank the importance of our membership in each in relation to the rest. For example, given any pair of people who are both deeply religious and deeply patriotic, it appears that it is the task of their subjective mind-sets to weigh the importance of their allegiance to the divine against the importance of their allegiance to the nation, and, obviously enough, the results of such weighing can be very different in their respective cases.

In sum, even though, again, these worries need not be thought of as conclusively fatal to any attempt to formulate a satisfactory conventional conception of urgency, they nonetheless suggest that it might be more worthwhile to seek a potential source of the objectivity of well-being elsewhere.

Perhaps, then, an appropriate strategy in this context is not to try to establish that there is some privileged group of desires counting as "urgent", but to examine more meticulously the very prerequisites of being able to formulate and act on any desires. As I argued in the previous section, the conceptual ability to construct a logically cogent means–ends structure appears to be one such prerequisite. But there also seem to be others that suggest themselves quite naturally. A question that might bring us closer to identifying at least one of them is the following: What is it that really matters in well-being? Is it desire satisfaction per se, regardless of what particular desires we happen to entertain, or is it the satisfaction of precisely those particular desires? In order words, if we could immediately and effortlessly change our present desires (e.g., by swallowing a psychology-altering pill) and replace them with desires that are easier to satisfy, then should we do this? Could we do this?

Issues of personal identity aside (let us suppose for the sake of simplicity that the alteration of one's psychology would not alter one's identity), it appears that the answer to these questions depends crucially on what one really wants, on what kind of general regulative meta-desires one subscribes to – if one has nothing against being classified as a Rawlsian "bare person" (Rawls 1971, p. 152), who is not committed to the accomplishment of any specific ends, then one should swallow the pill and thereby make one's desires cheaper and easier to satisfy; if, on the other hand, one feels that pursuing certain concrete aims is constitutive of his personality and world outlook, one should not try to cheapen his desires for the sake of making them more readily realizable. In sum, what appears to be of crucial significance here is not the shape of one's specific goals, but the fact of them being chosen *autonomously*. Thus, autonomy, that is, living one's life by one's own lights, emerges as a sine qua non for desire satisfaction, and hence as an objective element of well-being.

To drive this point home, consider our natural intuition that nobody is entitled to shove a psychology-altering pill down somebody else's throat in order to change his desires and make them less expensive (think, for example, of a mother doing that to her extremely fastidious child). I take it that the reason for having such an intuition is that the action in question would imply that one's psychological makeup is altered by an involuntary external influence, comparable, for instance, to forcible drugging or lobotomy. It clearly differs from the forms of influence that respect autonomy (e.g., non-coercive teaching or persuasion), because the psychological changes induced by these can be voluntarily accepted or rejected, as well as interpreted in a free manner.

Having then established that the satisfaction of any given desire can contribute to one's well-being only if it stems from a preceding autonomous intention and action, we should ask whether by implication we can find some other objectively valuable characteristics in the structure of such action.

It seems to me that we can – if it is plausible to claim that one of them is autonomy, then, by extension, exclusive ownership rights in one's body and one's mind appear to emerge as objective values as well, because every purposeful and voluntary action is coupled with an implicit recognition of the universal validity of such rights. This point is captured by the so-called Principle of Generic Consistency (hereafter PGC), which might be likened to a kind of latter-day Categorical Imperative, and which says the following: "Act in accord with the generic rights of your recipients as well as of yourself"[8] (Gewirth 1978, p. 135). According to Roger Pilon's elaboration of PGC, because voluntariness and purposiveness are generic features of all action, no intentional agent can maintain normative consistency without valuing these features and making a rights-claim to them (Pilon 1979). This, in turn, implies that he has to disvalue and make a rights-claim against aggression, coercion, and violence. Finally, because all human beings are equal qua intentional and purposive agents, these rights-claims have to be treated as universalizable. In other words, every agent is required to presuppose and respect them, regardless of his subjective interests, preferences, or whims.

In other words, if we are to understand persons as "purposeful rational agents, in possession of means of action that embody their active powers and faculties" and a person's rights as "his means of action and the actions in which he employs them" (van Dun 2003, p. 5), then initiating physically aggressive behavior or verbal threats of such behavior emerges as a clear candidate for an instance of an objectively unacceptable rights violation. Whenever one argues in favor of a doctrine that condones initiation of aggression and whenever one acts aggressively, one implicitly recognizes that the aforementioned fundamental rights hold with respect to oneself, but at the same time denies that they hold with regard to others. In view of the requirement of universalizability, the result is a performative contradiction, evidenced by a lack of fit between the content and the performance of a given speech act or physical act. Thus, all such behavior can be called *morally* irrational, and all desires whose realization prevents other people from realizing their own desires (provided that the latter are not similarly obstructive) can be called objectively bad.

To sum up, in this section I have analyzed a number of different accounts of moral objectivity. Out of these, the one that I find most intellectually robust is the account whose cornerstone is rationality (understood specifically as the ability to construct effective means–ends structures),[9] as well as respect for autonomy and voluntariness, represented by exclusive ownership rights in one's body and one's mind, rights held by all purposive agents.

What this implies in the context of employing a satisfactory definition of objective goods to justify the existence of territorial monopolies of force as entities uniquely suited to provide such goods to everyone is somewhat ambiguous. On the one hand, one might accept that law and order are valid examples of such goods if one is convinced by the traditional Lockean, Hobbesian, or neoclassical story, according to which it is precisely territorial monopolies of force that are responsible for creating protective frameworks within which individuals can enjoy their autonomy and enter all kinds of voluntary transactions. On the other hand, if one is persuaded by the conclusions of the preceding chapters (especially Chapter 5) and comes to believe that, far from being uniquely effective in protecting individual rights from aggression, territorial monopolies of force are uniquely effective in violating these rights, and are indeed necessarily founded upon their violations, then one is bound to regard the notion that such entities can produce objective public goods as highly implausible.

Because the purpose of the preceding chapters was to investigate whether the Lockean, Hobbesian, and in particular neoclassical story hold up to critical scrutiny and the conclusion of this investigation was predominantly negative, I am strongly inclined to side with the latter interpretation of the implications of this section. In other words, even assuming that there exist objective public goods in the ethical sense of the term, the existence of territorial monopolies of force should not be thought of as conducive to their provision.

6.4 Robust political economy and the question of motivations[10]

As I mentioned in Chapter 1, one of the main elements of the methodology employed throughout the present work is the investigation of the so-called institutional robustness of various systems of political economy. To reiterate briefly, the concept in question stands for the ability of a given system of social organization to pass the test of "hard cases", that is, hypothetical scenarios under which the ideal assumptions concerning, for example, information and motivation possessed by the members of a given society are relaxed (Boettke and Leeson 2004; Leeson and Subrick 2006). Drawing on this notion and the attendant framework of testing various forms of political economy against scenarios involving less-than-optimal conditions, it might be argued that, for instance, contractual legal polycentrism[11] is always more robust than coercive social democracy (or vice versa), even if an institutional setup based on the former (or latter) is introduced into a community populated by individuals who are generally selfish and ignorant, whereas that based on the latter (or former) is introduced into a community controlled by selfless and wise statesmen.

This brief reminder of the methodological approach utilized in the current work is important in this context, because if it turns out that even under optimal conditions social democratic politicians cannot improve upon the results generated by the spontaneous order of polycentric, entrepreneurial production and exchange, then there is no plausible reason to believe in the desirability of territorial monopolies of force as institutions uniquely capable of balancing efficiency and equity.

I believe that the most important point to be raised in this connection is that some doubts may be entertained as to whether selfishness should be rated as suboptimal and selflessness as optimal on the motivational spectrum, and thus as to whether selfless social democrats should be thought of as motivationally and morally superior to "selfish", profit-driven entrepreneurs. It is worthwhile to remember that the pursuit of profit is, after all, essentially nothing else than the willingness to substitute a more satisfactory state of affairs for a less satisfactory one, which can be taken as the defining feature of acting man (Mises 1996, pp. 13, 19). If this view is correct, why should the essence of rational agency be regarded as in some sense morally defective? Because it concerns itself with the relationship between means and ends, not with the normative evaluation of any specific means or end, it seems morally neutral at worst.[12] Moreover, only if the desire one aims to satisfy is, strictly speaking, self-centered (i.e., aimed at achieving something exclusively for the desirer, not for others) can a meaningful subjective value be attached to it. This is because only intrapersonal appraisals of utility can be made in the context of direct exchange, and only through the mutual interplay of such appraisals, made by individual consumers, producers, and entrepreneurs, does a tool that allows for making cardinal, interpersonal appraisals of utility – namely, the price system – have a chance to emerge (Herbener 1996; Reynolds 1998). Thus, only selfish adherence to the profit-and-loss system enables one to allocate resources rationally, so that one's customers can receive what they want and reciprocate by giving their supplier what he wants.

A totally selfless individual, on the other hand, willing to give away all the fruits of his labor, is unlikely to generate the wherewithal necessary to produce a steady stream of valuables ready for welfarist distribution. To put it very simply, one cannot give away what one did not produce first, and there seems to be no other compass for sustainable production than the market procedure of profit and loss.

To sum up the preceding paragraphs, it appears impossible to disentangle and analyze separately the motivational and the informational (or calculational) aspects of any given system of political economy. Another conclusion that follows from my remarks is that in the context of investigating the institutional robustness of contractual legal polycentrism versus that of coercive social democracy, any scenario of pure selfishness is actually better than any scenario of pure selflessness, even though the best-case scenario would probably involve some balanced combination of the entrepreneurial penchant for (monetary) profit seeking and Samaritan benevolence. Insofar as institutional robustness is, broadly speaking, a utilitarian criterion, that is, a criterion concerned with the resilience and prosperity of any given system of political economy, it needs to be pointed out that, far from being a drag on the economic development of any given society, the culture of charity contributes to it by creating an atmosphere of mutual trust, respect for entrepreneurship, and opportunity for the impoverished to better their situation (Porter and Kramer 2006). This observation alone suggests that the alleged tradeoff between efficiency and equity is illusory,[13] although it also emphasizes the point that the two reinforce each other only when combined in appropriate proportions.

As was noted earlier, the development and execution of charitable initiatives is, in an important sense, removed from the ambit of rational economic calculation, because it is also removed from the ambit of monetary appraisal by the totality of market participants. This, however, is not an insurmountable problem for private firms and other market entities as long as they treat their charitable projects as purchases of psychic satisfaction or investments the returns on which are so intangible and so dispersed that it is impossible to quantify them in any financially meaningful manner. Because such entities operate within the nexus of economic calculation and the profit-and-loss system, they know what proportion of their funds they can allocate to such projects without impairing their financial stability, and by doing so they in no way distort or diminish the ability of their business allies and competitors to do likewise. Thus, they will never be able to determine the ideal proportions for combining selfish profit seeking and philanthropic generosity, but the discovery procedure of entrepreneurial competition (Hayek 2002) will continuously inform them as to which of these combinations are financially sustainable and conducive to the emergence of an atmosphere of mutual trust and a healthy work ethic.

On the other hand, a monopoly of force with welfarist ambitions, being an organization that coercively externalizes the costs of its operation onto private firms and other market entities (thus effectively insulating itself from the nexus of economic calculation and the profit-and-loss system), cannot realize its ambitions without distorting the aforementioned discovery procedure (and possibly also the competitive incentive structure that drives it). Hence, it can neither objectively evaluate its actions from the point of view of economic efficiency, nor, a fortiori, can it point out the instances where such efficiency goes hand in hand with moral improvement. This, it is important to add, is the case even if those in charge of any given monopoly of force and its welfare policy are full of the best and most public-spirited intentions and motivations.

What about a system that is not only controlled by selfless and wise statesmen, but also populated by entrepreneurs whose motivation is not diminished by the absence of monetary incentives? In other words, what about a system in which entrepreneurs are free to collect their managerial wages and reinvest a substantial portion of their profits so that their business ventures may grow and prosper, but the rest of their profits (those that they would otherwise spend on additional consumption) is taxed away for welfarist purposes without causing any disincentivizing effects? Some argue that this would be precisely the kind of system that would most fully embody the spirit of social democracy or market socialism and represent their most institutionally robust form (Cohen 2009).

I believe that the crucial problem with this proposal is that it fails to grasp the precise nature of entrepreneurship. Entrepreneurship is the exercise of business judgment under the conditions of uncertainty (Salerno 2008a; Klein 2008b), and as such it cannot operate successfully on the basis of any formulaic rules. Thus, an outside observer cannot credibly separate an entrepreneur's productive and non-productive activities – given sufficient creativity on his part, what an entrepreneur initially buys as a tool of amusement (i.e., a consumption good) may be used later on as a factor of production – his apparently leisurely travels to exotic places can inspire him to undertake innovative ventures (especially in the places he visits), etc. In other words, it is logically impossible to construct a system in which the personal consumption of entrepreneurs is politically capped but their incentive structures are not distorted, regardless of how ascetic and workaholic we can imagine them to be – every coercive interference with an entrepreneur's spending patterns exerts a disruptive influence on the profit-and-loss system of economic calculation, appraisement, and discovery, thus sacrificing efficiency without increasing equity.

A variation on this proposal has been suggested by Carens (1981). Analyzing it is particularly worthwhile insofar as it visibly exhibits the internal contradictions inherent in all similar schemes. Under Carens' system, everyone's income available for personal consumption is coercively equalized, but individual incomes available for other purposes – that is, saving, investment, or hoarding – can remain unequal, even greatly so, in order to preserve the process of business competition, capital accumulation, entrepreneurial speculation, and other market-based sources of economic growth and development. Such a solution, in Carens' opinion, allows for promoting the spirit of economic equality without damaging the spirit of economic efficiency and innovation.

It appears clear that the key difficulty in implementing the system in question would be to induce people to become as motivated by "social duty satisfactions" as they are currently motivated by "income-consumption satisfactions" – in other words, to induce them to become as motivated by contributing to the growth of the equally divided wealth pie as they are currently motivated by contributing to the growth of the unequally divided wealth pie insofar as their share of it is proportional to their contribution. One might, unsurprisingly and justifiably, doubt whether such a motivational shift is even remotely psychologically feasible; as noted by Steele (1992, pp. 216–36), because Carens stipulates that the members of his ideal society still clearly care about income-consumption satisfaction (after all, they all want the wealth pie to grow), because it seems inevitable that some of them will differ in their relative evaluations of income-consumption satisfaction and social duty satisfaction, and because under Carens' system more of the former can be achieved without more of the latter, the system in question is, ceteris paribus, bound to be less efficient than one in which individual incomes available for personal consumption are not coercively equalized.

But there is actually an even more fundamental conceptual difficulty with the viability of the arrangement under discussion. As I noted in relation to Cohen's suggestion, in the context of entrepreneurial creativity and alertness to profit opportunities, it is economically meaningless to draw a strict separation between consumption and production, or value destruction and value creation. Applying this observation to Carens' egalitarian simulated market, we may likewise conclude that, when discussing the activities of market entrepreneurs, it is economically meaningless to draw a strict separation between income-consumption satisfaction and social duty satisfaction, because the former is inextricably connected with the latter when it comes to contemplating entrepreneurial ventures. In other words, again, it turns out that trying to curb the market entrepreneurs' capacity to consume value while maintaining their capacity to produce it is a logically incoherent endeavor.

To sum up the present section, what all of these considerations suggest is, first, that the profit-oriented, contractual activities undertaken within the spontaneous order of polycentric, entrepreneurial production and exchange contribute both to efficiency and equity, and, second, that even the most well-intentioned administrators of any given monopoly of force governing even the most well-motivated population would not be able to replicate the beneficial results of such activities.

In other words, the considerations under discussion provide a potent illustration of the fact that a spontaneous social order cannot generate useful goods and services if they are to be coercively diverted to purposes other than those originally intended by its members (Buchanan 1982).

6.5 Legal polycentrism, the veil of ignorance, and brute luck

Let us begin the present section by deciding, for the sake of argument, to discount the discussion of objectivity from Section 6.3, as well as the discussion on motivations from Section 6.4, and simply assume – as we did at the outset of the present chapter – that a coercive mechanism capable of redistributing basic goods and services in the direction of the least well-off is a viable prima facie candidate for an ethically understood, objective public good. If, having put aside the philosophical difficulties with arriving at a conception of objectivity that would mandate such an assumption, as well as the considerations of institutional robustness from the previous section, we find that there are still further problems with the assumption in question, we might conclude with an even higher degree of conviction that the alleged tradeoff between efficiency and equity does not exist, thus invalidating the ostensible ethical justification for the desirability of territorial monopolies of force.

Perhaps the most famous recent attempt at providing such a justification on exactly this basis is that of John Rawls (1971), which is built around the device of the so-called "original position" (pp. 15–19). The original position is supposed to be "a fair and impartial point of view" where "we are to imagine ourselves [as] free and equal persons who jointly agree upon and commit themselves to principles of social and political justice" (Freeman 2012). The parties that are supposed to reach the agreement in question are placed behind "the veil of ignorance", that is, an analytical device that deprives them "of all knowledge of their personal characteristics and social and historical circumstances" (ibid.). Rawls contends that under such fair conditions the most rational choice that the negotiating parties can make is to establish a political system that "secures for all a guaranteed minimum of the all-purpose means (including income and wealth) that individuals need to pursue their interests and to maintain their self-respect as free and equal persons" (ibid.).

More specifically, Rawls claims that in such a system "economic inequalities, for example inequalities of wealth . . ., are just only if they result in compensating benefits for everyone, and in particular for the least advantaged members of society" (Rawls 1971, p. 13). Further, he argues that such an arrangement "rule[s] out justifying institutions on the grounds that the hardships of some are offset by a greater good in the aggregate" and that it follows the notion that "it may be expedient but it is not just that some should have less in order that others may prosper" (p. 13). In other words, he clearly endorses the claim that there exists a tradeoff between efficiency and equity and that a just social system needs to keep balancing these two conflicting values via redistributive means.

Numerous objections can be raised against the Rawlsian proposal. First of all, it presumes, without argument, that social institutions – and, in particular, legal institutions – have to come into existence according to the conception of what I referred to in Chapter 4 as "constructive rationalism" – that is, according to over-arching, top-down plans whose scope encompasses the whole of a given society. As I argued in Chapter 4, I find it highly unlikely that such plans could be agreed on as a result of reaching a genuine social consensus, because members of any given society are typically very diverse with respect to their unwritten legal and moral customs, their beliefs concerning justice and fairness, etc., and thus highly unlikely to decide voluntarily to patronize a single provider of legal services. It appears much more likely, and this is in fact what the relevant historical evidence indicates (Gumplowicz 1899; Oppenheimer 1922; Nock 1935; Jouvenel 1949; Tilly 1985), that such overarching plans have to be coercively imposed by the self-proclaimed ruling class on the rest of a given society, thus making it very difficult to honestly call the resulting system "a cooperative venture for mutual advantage" (Rawls 1971, p. 4). If such a system were to genuinely reflect the dif-fering social and, in particular, legal needs of a given group of individuals, I find it much more plausible that it would have to assume the form of a contractual, polycentric order "brought about by the mutual adjustment of many individual economies in a market" (Hayek 1978a, pp. 108–9).

If true, this conclusion by itself does not prove that there is no tradeoff between efficiency and equity, but it at least drives home the point that the existence of such a tradeoff cannot be presumed by default, thus implying that the desirability of establishing a monopoly of force supposedly capable of addressing it cannot be presumed by default either.

This observation leads us to the second problem with Rawls's proposal: even assuming that creating an institutional framework based on his preferred prin-ciples of justice is a rational thing to do, it does not follow that those who refuse to participate in its creation and subsequent operation can be coerced to do so. As Huemer (2012) puts it:

> There is a wide gap between what hypothetical agreement might plausibly be taken to establish, such as the fairness or reasonableness of some arrange-ment, and what the defender of political authority needs to establish: the right to impose an arrangement by force, including the right to intentionally and coercively harm those who fail to cooperate and the obligation of individuals to accede to that arrangement.
>
> (p. 52)

In other words, even assuming that there is a tradeoff between efficiency and equity and that it is rational to address it in a systemic manner, it does not follow that the conception of rationality that advocates any such solution can coercively trump all available alternatives. After all, because, as was indicated earlier, mem-bers of any given society typically differ with respect to their preferences con-cerning legal services, they also differ with respect to their conceptions of legal rationality, and although the coexistence of such differing conceptions can be accommodated within a bottom-up, contractual framework of legal polycentrism, it cannot be accommodated within Rawls's top-down, coercive system of political redistribution.

Furthermore, even assuming that the ends aimed at by the social system based on Rawls's preferred principles of justice are not just rational, but more rational than any other social ends that can be pursued in this context, it still does not follow that they can be pursued by means of institutionalized coercion. This is due not only to deontological reasons (e.g., those suggesting that initiatory coercion is wrong because it is a violation of human nature, whose defining characteristic is the ability to act freely, an ability that cannot be exercised when hampered by physical force), but, perhaps less controversially, also to consequentialist reasons (i.e., those suggesting that the selected means are unsuitable in attaining the chosen goals).

The desirability of the use of coercive redistribution in the context at hand is predicated on the premise that a territorial monopoly of force is an entity uniquely capable of guaranteeing the provision of basic subsistence goods to the least well-off. This premise, however, is in turn based on an unwarranted causal assumption that the threat of institutional coercion is a tool that can automatically command obedience without heavily distorting the incentive structures of those expected to obey, as well as of those expected to benefit from their obedience. Contrary to this assumption, it seems reasonable to suppose that, in the strict sense of the term, a territorial monopoly of force cannot really guarantee anything, or at least cannot do so any more than voluntary social institutions can. In fact, it is plausible to conclude that it is in a much worse position to guarantee anything than a charitable institution or a business enterprise is. This is because the latter two kinds of institutions have a reliable source of income, whereby "reliable" I mean a source based on consensual support and unambiguous enthusiasm for the services they offer. In other words, as long as they continue to provide their patrons with goods and services of sufficient quality, they can expect their income to remain steady or even grow, which allows them to give as good a guarantee as possible that they will keep delivering on their entrepreneurial and charitable promises.

A monopoly of force, on the other hand, does not have any such reliable source of income. Its situation is ever precarious in this respect – it is ever threatened by the possibility of its involuntary donors "voting with their feet", moving into the grey market, or ceasing entrepreneurial activity altogether. At the same time, its declaration of guaranteeing the provision of basic subsistence goods to the least well-off is likely to skew the relevant incentive structures in the direction of ever more individuals joining the group of the least well-off (Murray 1994; Niskanen 1996; Bradley and Rector 2010), both voluntarily (due to considering the utility of being able to live at the expense of others as greater than the utility of enjoying an independent life at a higher material level) and involuntarily (due to the previously mentioned flight to safety of the involuntary donors of the monopoly of force and the resulting diminution of opportunities for gainful employment). In sum, this leads to ever fewer resources being at its disposal and ever more entitlement claims being made on them, which is the paradigmatic situation of operational unsustainability. Hence, regardless of how rational we take Rawls's preferred principles of justice to be, it is difficult to take institutional coercion as a rational means to their implementation.

On a charitable interpretation, it might be suggested that the proposal to employ coercive redistribution in the context at hand is motivated by the assumption that society produces its goods and services collectively, and thus has the right to distribute them on the basis of collective decision making, where individual objections can be overruled by the representatives of the will of the majority. This assumption, however, seems inferior to the one suggesting that, rather than having any sort of collective identity, society is simply a collection of voluntary, mutually beneficial transactions and institutions that allow for and facilitate their conclusion. The following passage describes the notion in question in a clear fashion:

> The characterization of a society as a cooperative venture for mutual advantage seems to imply that the society has some sort of collective identity. Instead, a society may be seen as the sum total of a vast number of cooperative interactions, including a variety of interlinked ventures. We can speak of a general pattern in accordance with which social cooperation leads to mutual advantage; but that's quite different from a social contract in which people agree to engage in a shared enterprise and determine how best to divide the proceeds of the enterprise.
>
> (Chartier 2014, pp. 144–5)

If we adopt this particular understanding of what society consists of, then it appears plausible to conclude that the social system that would best satisfy Rawls's preferred principles of justice would not be coercive social democracy, but voluntarist legal polycentrism. Such a system, in which there is no territorial monopoly of force and thus no possibility to undertake legally sanctioned initiatory coercion against others, can offer no guarantee that basic subsistence goods will be provided to the least well-off. However, contrary to what it may seem to imply on the surface, this very fact, coupled with all the efficiency-enhancing features of a competitive, entrepreneurial order, offers the best possible approximation of such a guarantee, that is, the availability of as great a number as possible of basic subsistence goods, and, better still, of opportunities to leave the ranks of the least well-off.

Furthermore, given that, for the sake of argument, our guiding assumption is that individuals deliberating behind the veil of ignorance genuinely wish to create a society based on Rawls's preferred principles of justice, and supposing that they share our doubts about institutional coercion being a feasible, let alone effective, means of implementing them, it seems clear that, next to entrepreneurship, the means they will choose for that purpose will be various forms of charity. Such a combination makes the competitive, entrepreneurial order of legal polycentrism uniquely capable of bettering the situation of the least well-off for a number of reasons.

First, due to its efficiency-enhancing features described over the course of the preceding chapters (the competitive incentive structure, heightened capital accumulation and technological innovation, the possibility of using the unhampered price system to calculate the profits and losses of one's actions, etc.), under such a system the productive rich are richer, so they have more resources to contribute to charity. Second, these same features of the system in question make the productive poor richer as well, which, in turn, makes them less reliant on charity and thus able to leave more charitable resources for the involuntarily nonproductive poor (i.e., those genuinely unable to engage in any productive activities through no fault of their own). Third, under legal polycentrism all productive individuals, being able to keep all the fruits of their labor and thus feeling that their liberty and dignity is genuinely respected, have not only the means, but, more importantly, also a genuine incentive to contribute to charity, rather than fleeing with their resources into the grey market or looking for loopholes through which to squeeze them into financial safety. Finally, in the system under consideration the voluntarily non-productive poor (i.e., those able but unwilling to engage in productive activities), knowing that they have no "guaranteed" right to live at the expense of others, have a strong incentive to become productive, thus, again, leaving more charitable resources for the involuntarily non-productive poor.

In sum, if the deliberators behind the veil of ignorance were to choose not only the most rational ends available (again, for the sake of argument let us suppose that they are the ones that follow from Rawls's principles of justice), but also the most rational means for their implementation (which, as I argued, would be the establishment of voluntarist legal polycentrism), they would find out that they created an institutional structure that simultaneously promotes efficiency and equity. In other words, if we assume that a social mechanism capable of providing the least well-off with basic goods and services is a viable candidate for an ethically understood, objective public good, we have to conclude that no monopoly of force is needed to bring this good into existence, whereas a contractual, entrepreneurial order of legal polycentrism is more than likely to do so.

Let us conclude the present chapter by moving to the analysis of one final candidate for an ethically understood, objective public good – that is, a social mechanism that ensures that "people enter the market on equal terms", where what is meant by "equal terms" is not that they should enter the market with equal resources, but that they should be compensated to the extent that their relative inability to accumulate resources stems from instances of bad "brute luck" (Dworkin 2000, p. 70), that is, handicaps and misfortunes that, for various reasons, cannot be insured against. Because everyone is a potential victim of bad brute luck, it might be argued that the existence of such a social mechanism would be to everyone's advantage, thus indicating that it would indeed be an objective public good. Furthermore, it might be argued that, in order to make the compensatory scheme aimed at countering the effects of bad brute luck sufficiently comprehensive, a monopoly of force should be tasked with its administration.

What appears to be the most significant problem with this proposal is that the notion of measuring objectively how lucky or unlucky (in the "brute" sense) one is seems extremely controversial. If the underlying assumption is that bad brute luck translates into reduced ability to accumulate resources, and reduced ability to accumulate resources translates into losses of utility, then implementing the scheme in question commits us to making interpersonal comparisons of utility, which, as I noted several times over the preceding chapters, is a very dubious endeavor, because utility is a subjective, agent-relative, psychological, and intensive (Robbins 1935, pp. 138–40; Rothbard 1956; Herbener 1997), rather than an objective, agent-independent, physical, and extensive magnitude. Furthermore, even if utility were uncontroversially measurable, it would be by no means clear how to translate gains and losses of utility into instances of good and bad brute lack. Even if in this context one were to help oneself to the notion of opportunity costs expressed in terms of objective (monetary) exchange values, it would remain unclear what specific goods of certain total exchange value a given victim of a given instance of bad brute luck had to pass up precisely and exclusively due to her uninsurable handicaps. After all, "in every market action luck is interwoven inextricably and is impossible to isolate" (Rothbard 2004, p. 1333).

In addition, there seems to be no necessary logical connection between compensating others for the effects of bad brute luck and allowing them to enter the market on equal terms (understood in terms of resource distribution). In fact, under some circumstances handing out such compensation may make these terms more unequal. As Rothbard puts it:

> [T]here is no justification for saying that the rich are luckier than the poor. It might very well be that many or most of the rich have been *unlucky* and are getting less than their true DMVP [discounted marginal value product], while most of the poor have been *lucky* and are getting more.
>
> (ibid.)

In other words, it appears that the "aim to neutralize interpersonal bad luck begs the question of justification and just helps itself to the goal of equality" (Hurley 2003, p. 157).

I tried to argue that the earlier difficulties with the compensatory scheme under consideration follow from the very idea of attempting to reduce the inequality of resource distribution by means of countering the results of bad brute luck, but a still further difficulty presents itself once we assume that such a scheme is to be organized on the basis of monopolized, institutional coercion. If a monopoly of force tasked with its administration is to be thought of as powerful enough to coerce every inhabitant of a given territory to participate in it, then being subject to its confiscatory actions can be considered by unwilling participants as another instance of uninsurable bad luck – that is, of bad brute luck. Thus, the scheme in question turns out to simultaneously neutralize and intensify its influence. One might argue that this is justifiable insofar as the amount of bad brute luck generated through such confiscatory actions is smaller than the amount of bad brute lack neutralized by them, but making such a claim brings us back to the notion of measuring luck, comparing it interpersonally, and translating it into interpersonally comparable utility, all of which appear to be insurmountable or perhaps even conceptually incoherent tasks.

Finally, if one attempts to circumvent all of these problems by treating the condition resulting from bad brute luck as a vague shorthand for the condition of being the underdog, or a member of the worst-off social group, then the compensatory scheme under consideration becomes practically indistinguishable from the Rawlsian approach discussed earlier and equally susceptible to the conclusion that the optimal conditions for implementing it are the ones existing under voluntarist legal polycentrism. In sum, here, too, the supposed objective public good capable of being provided only by a territorial monopoly of force turns out to be either illusory or, provided a slight reconsideration of its nature, more likely to be provided in such a monopoly's absence.

At this point, one might argue that I am repeatedly circumventing the main concern that motivates redistributivists such as Rawls and Dworkin, which has to do with justifying property titles in the first place, and only later envisioning a socioeconomic system that would assign property titles in accordance with the appropriate justification. Thus, the critic might say, in order to make my argument complete, I would have to put forward an alternative justification for property titles that would provide a foundation for the polycentric, contractual system that I am describing.

This, I believe, would be an incorrect assessment of my position. What I regard as one of the main advantages of the arguments expounded in this section is that their validity does not depend on the acceptance of any particular theory and justification of property rights. This, in turn, implies that they remain valid even if, for the sake of argument, one is willing to assume that their only correct justification is one of the Rawlsian or the Dworkinian variety, that is, one that morally accepts a given distribution of property titles only insofar as it is conducive to the increased well-being of the worst-off or capable of mitigating the effects of bad brute luck. As I argued in the preceding paragraphs, the latter is either conceptually unachievable[14] or reducible to the former, whereas the former is best served under voluntarist legal polycentrism. Thus, rather than arguing for the notion that the ethical justifiability of the spontaneous distribution of property titles under voluntarist legal polycentrism depends on the validity of a specific deontological (Rothbard 1998), consequentialist (Friedman 1989), eudaemonist (Long 2000), or intuitionist (Huemer 2012) theory of property rights, I can assume the validity of the theory of property rights embraced by representative egalitarian redistributivists and still reach the conclusion defended throughout the previous sections of the present chapter and the previous chapters of the present book. I take this to be yet another indication of the institutional robustness of the contractual, entrepreneurial, polycentric framework under consideration.

With this, let me now move to the concluding chapter, where I investigate and summarize what I take to be the main intradisciplinary developments and interdisciplinary ramifications associated with the key findings of the present work.

Notes

1 This section incorporates material from Wisniewski (2009).
2 There is, however, no necessity for the Austrians to be committed to such an account. This commitment follows only insofar as one accepts that what is rational is prudentially

desirable, which I do not think of as an unlikely position for an Austrian to endorse. Praxeology in itself is value free and implies no commitment to any particular moral or prudential stance.

3 A prime example of which is hedonism, where pain and pleasure are given an exclusively "material and carnal meaning" (Mises 1996, p. 15).

4 After all, selflessness is likely to command respect, and even though the charitable man does not know whom exactly he helps, those helped by him might know the identity of their benefactor and be ready to aid him whenever a contingency arises. Moreover, the family and friends of the person in question might revere and support him precisely because they know him to be a paragon of disinterestedness, which would not be the case if his philanthropic desire were not fully other-regarding.

5 Frankfurt could perhaps respond that the person's words are evidence for the existence of second-order desires. Third-order desires, likewise, would have to have some evidential basis, and because they seem to have none, their existence cannot be postulated as easily as that of second-order desires. I believe, however, that such putative evidence could be found in, for example, conflicts of statements made by the person in the state of *akrasia* and in the state of hypnosis. One could then argue that the person's real desires are neither the ones acted upon nor the ones expressed verbally in her normal state of consciousness, but the ones voiced under hypnosis. Subsequently, one might perhaps attempt to induce deeper and deeper levels of hypnosis in a possibly endless search for his patient's real personality. Although I do not think I have a final opinion on this matter, in view of the earlier content it appears to me that the postulation of higher-order desires is neither deductively justifiable nor empirically falsifiable.

6 If one is a moral rationalist, I believe that one could rightly accuse X of being morally irrational, for instance, on the grounds of simultaneously exercising one's right to free action and denying the same right to those with whom he interacts, which, in view of the requirement of universalizability, generates a performative contradiction (Gewirth 1978; Pilon 1979) (for an elaboration of this line of thought, see the discussion in Section 6.3). I do not think, however, that one can justifiably accuse him of being prudentially irrational.

7 This section incorporates material from Wisniewski (2011a, 2012b).

8 Recipients are to be understood as those who stand opposite agents and who are affected by their actions.

9 For a comprehensive explication of this issue, see the discussion in the previous section.

10 This section incorporates material from Wisniewski (2011b).

11 From now on, for the sake of brevity, by legal polycentrism I shall mean legal and protective polycentrism. In any event, it seems difficult to imagine one functioning without the other.

12 For the sake of clarity, it might be worthwhile to distinguish the kind of selfishness described here from selfishness understood as grasping behavior, or lack of proper regard for the interests of others. In this usage someone who, for instance, grabs all the desserts at a party, leaving none for others, could be said to be selfish. If we consider the behavior in question in the moral sense, that is, in the sense of violating an unwritten, non-enforceable convention that everybody else implicitly agrees to follow, then it seems to me that we can classify it as immoral to the extent that it is logically indefensible. In other words, it might be said to run afoul of the Kantesque principle "act in accord with the generic rights of your recipients as well as of yourself" (Gewirth 1978, p. 135), because it presupposes that the grasper has more rights than the rest of those who implicitly agreed to be bound by a certain convention (e.g., the convention of leaving enough food for others at a party table), even though there is no logically cogent reason for affirming such a presupposition. Hence, it appears clear that this particular variety of self-interestedness is very unlike the more familiar profit-seeking drive, which need not regard satisfying the interests of others as its ultimate goal, but which regards it as the most efficient means of satisfying the profit seeker's own interests.

13 Whenever I deny the existence of a tradeoff between efficiency and equity, I certainly
do not mean that there cannot exist any situation in which someone increases the efficiency of one's actions in an inequitable manner, but that it is not the case that a social
order focused on increasing Pareto-superior efficiency necessarily sacrifices a concern
with matters of equity. Likewise, I take it that the familiar claim that there is a tradeoff between liberty and security is not meant to suggest that there cannot exist any
situation in which someone uses his personal liberty to buy insurance or take other
precautions, but that a social order focused on maximizing personal liberty necessarily
exposes itself to ever more dangers (I believe this claim to be false as well; I mention
it here exclusively for the sake of drawing an explanatory parallel).

14 Thus, it cannot be thought of as morally praiseworthy given the rather uncontroversial
premise that there is no moral worth in pursuing what can be reasonably established to
be impossible or incoherent.

Bibliography

Boettke, P. J. and Leeson, P. T. (2004), 'Liberalism, Socialism, and Robust Political Econ-
omy', *Journal of Markets & Morality*, 7 (1), 99–111.
Boorse, C. (1977), 'Health as a Theoretical Concept', *Philosophy of Science*, 44, 542–73.
Boorse, C. (1997), 'A Rebuttal on Health', in J. M. Humber and R. F. Almeder (eds.), *What
Is Disease?* (Totowa, NJ: Humana Press).
Bradley, K. and Rector, R. (2010), 'Confronting the Unsustainable Growth of Welfare
Entitlements: Principles of Reform and the Next Steps', *Backgrounder*, 2427, retrieved
August 12, 2011, from www.heritage.org/research/reports/2010/06/confronting-the-
unsustainable-growth-of-welfare-entitlements-principles-of-reform-and-the-next-steps.
Buchanan, J. M. (1982), 'Order Defined in the Process of its Emergence', *Literature of
Liberty*, 5, 7–58.
Byron, M. (ed.) (2004), *Satisficing and Maximizing: Moral Theorists on Practical Reason*
(Cambridge: Cambridge University Press).
Carens, J. H. (1981), *Equality, Moral Incentives, and the Market* (Chicago: University of
Chicago Press).
Chartier, G. (2014), *Radicalizing Rawls: Global Justice and the Foundations of Interna-
tional Law* (London: Palgrave Macmillan).
Cohen, G. A. (2009), *Why Not Socialism?* (Princeton, NJ: Princeton University Press).
Dworkin, R. (2000), *Sovereign Virtue: The Theory and Practice of Equality* (Cambridge,
MA: Harvard University Press).
Frankfurt, H. (1971), 'Freedom of the Will and the Concept of a Person', *Journal of Phi-
losophy*, 68, 5–20.
Freeman, S. (2012), 'Original Position', in E. N. Zalta (ed.), *The Stanford Encyclopedia of Phi-
losophy*, retrieved from http://plato.stanford.edu/archives/spr2012/entries/original-position/.
Friedman, D. (1989) [1973], *The Machinery of Freedom: Guide to a Radical Capitalism*
(2nd ed., La Salle, IL: Open Court).
Gewirth, A. (1978), *Reason and Morality* (Chicago: University of Chicago Press).
Griffin, J. (1986), *Well-Being: Its Meaning, Measurement, and Moral Importance* (Oxford:
Clarendon Press).
Gumplowicz, L. (1899), *The Outlines of Sociology* (Philadelphia: American Academy of
Political and Social Science).
Hayek, F. A. (1945), 'The Use of Knowledge in Society', *American Economic Review*, 35,
519–30.

Hayek, F. A. (1978a), *Law, Legislation and Liberty, Vol. 2: The Mirage of Social Justice* (Chicago: University of Chicago Press).

Hayek, F. A. (2002), 'Competition as a Discovery Procedure', *Quarterly Journal of Austrian Economics*, 5 (3), 9–23.

Herbener, J. (1996), 'Calculation and the Question of Arithmetic', *Review of Austrian Economics*, 9 (1), 151–62.

Herbener, J. (1997), 'The Pareto Rule and Welfare Economics', *Review of Austrian Economics*, 10 (1), 70–106.

Huemer, M. (2012), *The Problem of Political Authority* (London: Palgrave Macmillan).

Hurley, S. L. (2003), *Justice, Luck, and Knowledge* (Cambridge, MA: Harvard University Press).

Jouvenel, B. de (1949), *On Power* (New York: Viking Press).

Kingma, E. (2007), 'What Is It to Be Healthy?', *Analysis*, 67, 128–33.

Kirzner, I. (1984), 'Economic Planning and the Knowledge Problem', *Cato Journal*, 4 (2), 407–18.

Klein, P. G. (2008b), 'Opportunity Discovery, Entrepreneurial Action, and Economic Organization', *Strategic Entrepreneurship Journal*, 2, 175–90.

Leeson, P. T. and Subrick, J. R. (2006), 'Robust Political Economy', *Review of Austrian Economics*, 19 (2–3), 107–11.

Long, R. T. (2000), *Reason and Value: Aristotle versus Rand* (Poughkeepsie, NY: Objectivist Center).

Mises, L. (1996) [1949], *Human Action* (4th ed. revised, San Francisco: Fox and Wilkes).

Murray, C. (1994), *Losing Ground: American Social Policy, 1950–1980* (10th Anniversary ed., New York: Basic Books).

Narveson, J. (2004), 'Maxificing: Life on a Budget: Or, If You Would Maximize, Then Satisfice!', in M. Byron (ed.), *Satisficing and Maximizing: Moral Theorists on Practical Reason* (Cambridge: Cambridge University Press), 59–70.

Niskanen, W. A. (1996), 'Welfare and the Culture of Poverty', *Cato Journal*, 16 (1), 1–15.

Nock, A. J. (1935), *Our Enemy, the State* (New York: William Morrow & Company).

Oppenheimer, F. (1922) [1914], *The State* (New York: B.W. Huebsch).

Parfit, D. (1984), *Reasons and Persons* (Oxford: Oxford University Press).

Pilon, R. A. (1979), 'Ordering Rights Consistently: Or What We Do and Do Not Have Rights to Do', *Georgia Law Review*, 13, 1171–96.

Porter, M. E. and Kramer, M. R. (2006), 'Strategy and Society: The Link between Competitive Advantage and Corporate Social Responsibility', *Harvard Business Review*, 84 (12), 78–92.

Rawls, J. (1971), *A Theory of Justice* (Cambridge, MA: Belknap).

Reynolds, M. O. (1998), 'Impossibility of Socialist Economy, or, a Cat Cannot Swim the Atlantic Ocean', *The Quarterly Journal of Austrian Economics*, 1 (2), 29–43.

Robbins, L. (1935), *An Essay on the Nature and Significance of Economic Science* (2nd ed., London: Macmillan).

Rothbard, M. (1956), 'Toward a Reconstruction of Utility and Welfare Economics', in M. Sennholz (ed.), *On Freedom and Free Enterprise: Essays in Honor of Ludwig von Mises* (Princeton, NJ: Van Nostrand), 224–62.

Rothbard, M. (1998) [1982], *The Ethics of Liberty* (New York, NY: New York University Press).

Rothbard, M. (2004) [1962], *Man, Economy, and State: A Treatise on Economic Principles with Power and Market* (Scholar's ed., Auburn, AL: Ludwig von Mises Institute).

Salerno, J. T. (2008a), 'The Entrepreneur: Real and Imagined', *Quarterly Journal of Austrian Economics*, 11 (3), 188–207.

Scanlon, T. (1975), 'Preference and Urgency', *Journal of Philosophy*, 72, 655–69.

Simon, H. (1955), 'A Behavioral Model of Rational Choice', *Quarterly Journal of Economics*, 69, 99–118.

Slote, M. (2004), 'Two View of Satisficing', in M. Byron (ed.), *Satisficing and Maximizing: Moral Theorists on Practical Reason* (Cambridge: Cambridge University Press), 14–29.

Steele, D. R. (1992), *From Marx to Mises: Post-Capitalist Society and the Challenge of Economic Calculation* (La Salle, IL: Open Court).

Tilly, C. (1985), 'War Making and State Making as Organized Crime', in P. Evans, D. Rueschemeyer and T. Skocpol (eds.), *Bringing the State Back* (Cambridge: Cambridge University Press).

van Dun, F. (2003), 'Natural Law: A Logical Analysis', *Etica & Politica*, Vol. 2. https://www2.units.it/etica/2003_2/vandun.pdf.

Wisniewski, J. B. (2009), 'Well-Informedness and Rationality: A Philosophical Overview', *Quarterly Journal of Austrian Economics*, 12 (3), 43–56.

Wisniewski, J. B. (2011a), 'Well-Being and Objectivity', *Libertarian Papers*, 3 (7).

Wisniewski, J. B. (2011b), 'Robust Political Economy and the Question of Motivations', *Quarterly Journal of Austrian Economics*, 14 (1), 56–65.

Wisniewski, J. B. (2012b), 'A Note on Being Healthy', *Diametros*, 31, 133–5.

7 Conclusion

The aim of the present book was to investigate the putative theoretical desirability, both from the economic and the ethical point of view, as well as the practical inevitability of the presence of a monopoly of force in any given system of political economy. As described in Chapter 1, the primary methodological tool used for this purpose was praxeological analysis in the spirit of the Austrian School of Economics, coupled with the analysis of institutional robustness of the relevant economic and social frameworks. Chapter 2 presented a general theoretical critique of the neoclassical theory of public goods, thus undermining the contention that their effective production requires the existence of territorial monopolies of force, as well as pointing out various logical problems with the concept of public goods as such. Chapters 3 and 4 made the critique in question more specific and practically grounded by analyzing the ways in which the two most paradigmatic public goods in the neoclassical theory – namely, law and defense – could be effectively produced in a contractual, entrepreneurial order of legal polycentrism. Furthermore, they suggested that it is not just the case that territorial monopolies of force are inferior producers of these goods, but that their production of these goods can even deprive them of their goods-character. Chapter 5 tackled the claim that, although not necessary for the production of public goods, monopolies of force are nonetheless inevitable due to the combined influence of the iron law of oligarchy and the collective action problem. More specifically, it suggested that both of the aforementioned concepts appeal exclusively to the importance of incentive structures, while overlooking the fact that the shape of these structures is crucially conditioned by the configuration of the underlying preferences and ideologies, just as the shape of hard institutional frameworks is crucially conditioned by the configuration of the underlying customs, traditions, and social norms. Finally, Chapter 6 tried to pin down various ethical conceptions of public goods and argue that none of them can sustain the notion that a fully voluntary and contractual social order generates a tradeoff between efficiency and equity, which can be countered only by corrective interventions of a monopoly of force. It claimed that, on the contrary, the order in question promotes efficiency and equity alike, while, in contrast to some of its centralized, coercive counterparts, remaining careful not to make any utopian, universal moral guarantees.

Hence, the conclusion of the present book is that neither economic nor ethical considerations surrounding the notion of public goods establish the desirability or inevitability of the existence of territorial monopolies of force, thus lending support to the suggestion that the emergence of a worldwide contractual, competitive, entrepreneurial order of legal polycentrism would be a welcome alternative.

This conclusion has some interesting implications for a number of related disciplines and fields of research. Most importantly, it opens up new avenues for exploration in the area of institutional entrepreneurship. Following Baumol (1990), entrepreneurship is typically divided into productive, unproductive, and destructive. In the context of specifically institutional entrepreneurship, a parallel tripartite distinction has been suggested – that between abiding, evading, and altering variety of entrepreneurial activities (Henrekson and Sanandaji 2011). In view of this latter distinction, institutional entrepreneurship counts as productive if it strengthens institutions that promote market entrepreneurship or weakens (or reforms) those that hamper it, and counts as destructive if it strengthens or utilizes institutions that hamper market entrepreneurship or weakens those that promote it.

Because the institutions in question are typically implicitly assumed to be political in nature, an institutional entrepreneur is typically assumed to be a political entrepreneur of some kind. He is also typically assumed to combine the roles of a political and market entrepreneur insofar as he treats exercising an influence on political institutions as a means of furthering his business activities. In view of the critical arguments raised in the present book regarding the notion of public goods and the supposedly necessarily political character of their effective provision, the relationship between market entrepreneurs and their impact on political institutions can be cast in a new light.

Most significantly, it has to be noticed that, as far as the inherent mode of operation of all political institutions is concerned, the attitude of market entrepreneurs towards them is assumed to be evasive by default; otherwise, such institutions would be maintained on the basis of voluntary contributions or fees, not on the basis of coercive taxation. The coercive nature of all political institutions coupled with their non-competitive character makes it a legitimate question whether they can be truly conducive to, let alone necessary for, productive entrepreneurship. In light of the tenets of methodological individualism and subjectivist economics, their coercive character precludes their existence and operation from being Pareto-superior, because they run contrary to the demonstrated preferences of market entrepreneurs (who, by definition, are assumed to prefer to spend their tax money on other purposes), and their monopolistic, non-competitive character necessarily separates them from the allocative rationality of the market price system.

At the same time, it is clearly not the case that entrepreneurs are assumed to adopt a default evasive stance towards political institutions because they do not desire effective provision of law and order. After all, their competitive advantage lies in operating effectively in the business environment, which implies at least an elementary (and more likely a fairly advanced) understanding of the necessary preconditions of a robust commercial culture, an equally robust legal and protective framework being the most important of them. Nor can the majority of them be reasonably accused of trying to engage in free riding – the arguments adduced in

Chapter 3 of the present book suggest that every entrepreneur worthy of the name realizes that the business environment confronts him with what is essentially a repeated prisoner's dilemma situation, where in the long run free riding is a sub-optimal approach. In other words, it is reasonable to conclude that by assuming an inherently evasive attitude towards inherently coercive, monopolistic political institutions, market entrepreneurs do not act against law and order, but against their inefficient, morally objectionable, and emphatically non-entrepreneurial methods of implementation.

Thus, insofar as market entrepreneurs are assumed to adopt a default eva-sive stance towards political institutions, and insofar as productive institutional entrepreneurship of the altering variety is typically described as altering political institutions in the direction of their greater conduciveness to market entrepre-neurship, it seems logical to conclude that the ultimate culmination of productive institutional entrepreneurship in the political context would be to replace politi-cal institutions with market-based entrepreneurial institutions.[1] In other words, the tripartite distinction between abiding, evading, and altering varieties of insti-tutional entrepreneurship should be supplemented with the fourth category – creative institutional entrepreneurship, that is, the art of establishing competitive, contractual structures of law and order tied directly to the informal institutions prevailing in a given society.

Introducing and analyzing such a category would, I believe, be particularly helpful in shedding new light on what has been called "the paradox of embedded agency", the theoretical puzzle concerned with the following question: "if actors are embedded in an institutional field and subject to regulative, normative and cognitive processes that structure their cognitions, define their interests and pro-duce their identities . . ., how are they able to envision new practices and then sub-sequently get others to adopt them?" (Garud, Hardy and Maguire 2007, p. 961). In the context of opening new avenues for analyzing this puzzle, it might be argued that political institutional entrepreneurship undertaken by market entrepreneurs – be it of the abiding, evading, or altering variety – is truly productive only inso-far as it embodies elements of creative institutional entrepreneurship. Given that market entrepreneurship is inherently characterized by innovativeness, alertness to profit opportunities, and the ability to forecast the uncertain future, it should not be surprising that its power to create and modify institutions is capable of discov-ering the kind of mix of institutional stability and adaptability, or predictability and dynamism, that allows the society relying on it to enjoy robust rule-based order while remaining open to creative evolution. Thus the paradox of embedded agency loses much of its paradoxical nature.

Furthermore, the insights concerning the potential of entrepreneurial, competi-tive institutional creation may prove useful in shedding further light on the nature and importance of cultural entrepreneurship. Because, as was repeatedly pointed out in Chapter 5 of the present book, the efficiency of specific incentive struc-tures depends crucially on their grounding in prevalent social preferences, beliefs, and ideas, it becomes clear that a crucial and perhaps the hardest part of cre-ative institutional entrepreneurship is the preparation of fertile ground for cultural and ideological change. Moreover, because, according to the new institutionalist hierarchy of levels of social analysis (Williamson 1998, 2000), soft institutions – that is, the fundamental cultural-normative core of the hierarchy in question – emerge largely spontaneously and develop in an evolutionary manner spanning many generations, it appears clear that influencing them and speeding up their development in a desirable direction through entrepreneurial efforts is a singularly difficult and elusive task. However, the fact that there exists a considerable amount of evidence of substantial ideological and cultural change throughout history (North 1981, 1990), sometimes within surprisingly short time frames, indicates that the task under consideration is not insurmountable. This should direct the attention of entrepreneurship researchers to the question of which factors and what circumstances are particularly conducive to successful cultural institutional entrepreneurship – and if they find out that some features of the present-day socio-economic environment (e.g., the development of social media, cultural globalization, increasingly universal access to repositories of specialized knowledge, etc.) count prominently among them, it might strongly suggest that the ascendancy of competitive, contractual structures of law and order is closer than most expect.

Finally, the conclusion of the present book may have important implications for the field of business ethics. As noted by several authors (Marcoux 2009; Rasmussen and Den Uyl 2009), a fairly common approach to business ethics is to try to turn it into a form of political philosophy, with the ideal business firm treated as the "private workplace equivalent of [a] cradle-to-grave welfare state" (Marcoux 2009, p. 25), which is an approach that crowds out any serious philosophical concern with the practical ethical problems faced by entrepreneurs and other participants in commercial culture. However, if we accept the conclusion that, far from operating purely reactively within a given framework of formal and informal institutions aimed at enabling and facilitating social cooperation, market entrepreneurs are actually capable of actively creating such frameworks, it might be suggested that it is not just inappropriate to try to turn business ethics into a form of political philosophy, but that it is appropriate to eventually turn political philosophy into a form of business ethics. Such a suggestion might be treated as a qualitatively novel attempt at reconciling philosophical anarchism with the necessity and desirability of effective and just governance, as well as a reconsideration of concepts such as the social contract, the unanimity principle, and the stakeholder theory in the light of praxeological economics and the theory of institutional entrepreneurship. In other words, it might indicate that the scale and scope of ethical considerations that entrepreneurs are uniquely suited to undertake and address are much greater than most contemporary business ethicists, let alone lay commentators, could reasonably imagine. In particular, it might indicate that entrepreneurs are uniquely capable of dealing with so-called moral dilemmas, that is, situations in which the complexity of moral reality outruns the usefulness of all ethical master principles and theoretical systems, confronting a given person with the moral necessity of doing something morally wrong. Insofar as it might be argued that the only way to deal with such situations is to try to minimize their occurrence through keen forecasting skills and careful attention to specific circumstances of time and place (Wisniewski 2011c), it is not unreasonable to conclude that entrepreneurs, with their expertise in uncertainty bearing and utilizing tacit knowledge, should be thought of as particularly capable of taking on this challenge.

In sum, I believe that it would not be an exaggeration to suggest that the research avenues opened by the central conclusion of the present book – the economic and ethical viability of replacing monopolistic, coercive institutions of law and defense with their competitive, contractual, entrepreneurial counterparts – are as disciplinarily wide-ranging as they are far-reaching. Thus, their pursuit promises to be a fruitful, challenging, and potentially groundbreaking scholarly endeavor.

Note

1 Upon being confronted with this conclusion, the majority of present-day entrepreneurs would probably shy away from it, but this could be explained in a number of ways without questioning its validity. First, the competitive advantage of entrepreneurs is practical business acumen, not theoretical political economy; thus, they might need some time to familiarize themselves thoroughly with the relevant arguments and think them through before passing an appropriately informed judgment on their cogency. Second, their short-term prudential concerns might prevent them from being completely honest about their views on the matter. And third, just like the majority of people, they might turn out to be victims of the standard psychology of authority, which, as it is sometimes argued, is largely based on ultimately non-rational factors, as shown, for example, in the Milgram and Zimbardo experiments (Huemer 2012, ch. 6).

Bibliography

Baumol, W. J. (1990), 'Entrepreneurship: Productive, Unproductive, and Destructive', *Journal of Political Economy*, 98 (5), 893–921.

Garud, R., Hardy, C. and Maguire, S. (2007), 'Institutional Entrepreneurship as Embedded Agency: An Introduction to the Special Issue', *Organization Studies*, 28 (7), 957–69.

Henrekson, M. and Sanandaji, T. (2011), 'The Interaction of Entrepreneurship and Institutions', *Journal of Institutional Economics*, 7 (1), 47–75.

Huemer, M. (2012), *The Problem of Political Authority* (London: Palgrave Macmillan).

Marcoux, A. M. (2009), 'Retrieving Business Ethics from Political Philosophy', *The Journal of Private Enterprise*, 24 (2), 21–33.

North, D. (1981), *Structure and Change in Economic History* (New York: W.W. Norton).

North, D. (1990), *Institutions, Institutional Change and Economic Performance* (Cambridge, MA: Cambridge University Press).

Rasmussen, D. B. and Den Uyl, D. J. (2009), 'Making Room for Business Ethics: Rights as Metanorms for Market and Moral Values', *The Journal of Private Enterprise*, 24 (2), 1–19.

Williamson, O. E. (1998), 'Transaction Cost Economics: How It Works; Where It Is Headed', *De Economist*, 146 (1), 23–58.

Williamson, O. E. (2000), 'The New Institutional Economics: Taking Stock, Looking Ahead', *Journal of Economic Literature*, 38 (3), 595–613.

Wisniewski, J. B. (2011c), 'Do Moral Dilemmas Tell against the Consistency of a Given Moral System?', *Reason Papers*, 33, 44–59.

Index

For Product Safety Concerns and Information please contact our EU
representative GPSR@taylorandfrancis.com
Taylor & Francis Verlag GmbH, Kaufingerstraße 24, 80331 München, Germany

www.ingramcontent.com/pod-product-compliance
Ingram Content Group UK Ltd.
Pitfield, Milton Keynes, MK11 3LW, UK
UKHW020947180425
457613UK00019B/570